# Peace and Justice

# Peace and Justice

### Seeking Accountability after War

# Rachel Kerr and Eirin Mobekk

polity

Copyright © Rachel Kerr and Eirin Mobekk 2007

The right of Rachel Kerr and Eirin Mobekk to be identified as Authors of this Work has been asserted in accordance with the UK Copyright, Designs and Patents Act 1988.

First published in 2007 by Polity Press

Polity Press
65 Bridge Street
Cambridge CB2 1UR, UK

Polity Press
350 Main Street
Malden, MA 02148, USA

ISBN-13: 978-07456-3422-7
ISBN-13: 978-07456-3423-4 (pb)

A catalogue record for this book is available from the British Library.

Typeset in 10.5 on 12 pt Plantin
by Servis Filmsetting Ltd, Manchester
Printed and bound in India by Replika Press PVT Ltd, Kundli, India

The publisher has used its best endeavours to ensure that the URLs for external websites referred to in this book are correct and active at the time of going to press. However, the publisher has no responsibility for the websites and can make no guarantee that a site will remain live or that the content is or will remain appropriate.

Every effort has been made to trace all copyright holders, but if any have been inadvertently overlooked the publishers will be pleased to include any necessary credits in any subsequent reprint or edition.

For further information on Polity, visit our website: www.polity.co.uk

# Contents

# Acknowledgements

This book has been many years in the making. As with the issues discussed here, it has undergone several different phases and reflects the development of our own thinking on these matters over the past decade. Hence, there are many who have contributed to this book by offering their own reflections and encouraging us to consider additional questions and issues as they arose.

We first started discussing these issues together at a series of graduate conferences organized by King's College London Department of War Studies under the auspices of the Regional Security in a Global Context Programme, supported by the John D. and Catherine T. Macarthur Foundation. Our 'Peace and Justice road-show' went on to perform at a number of other conferences where we jointly and individually presented papers over the years. The feedback from fellow panelists and others at these conferences helped considerably in the development of our thinking. We are also grateful to the War Crimes Research Group at King's College London and the Africa seminar series for the opportunity to deliberate on the issues discussed in the book with others working in the field, who brought historical, sociological, legal and area studies perspectives to bear. We would like to thank especially Madoka Futamura, James Gow, Claire Gunter, Jessica Lincoln, Tony Millett and Ivan Zverzhanovski as well as students on the 'Prosecuting War Crimes' course and others who have contributed by providing feedback and being generally engaged with the work, in particular Funmi Olonisakin, Vesselin Popovski, Jason Ralph and Nathalie Wlodarczyk. Thanks should go also to the Geneva Centre for the Democratic Control of Armed Forces for encouraging discourse and arranging workshops where transitional justice issues were on the agenda, and which have been most useful in the process of writing this book. Any errors or omissions that remain are, of course, our own.

In addition, we would like warmly to thank the British Academy for their support, without which the fieldwork for this book could not have been undertaken. In this connection, the input of Jo Spear and David Held was invaluable. The interviews undertaken during this fieldwork were of critical importance to the research and we would accordingly like to thank all the individuals who gave up their time to speak to us, both those working in the field in the Democratic Republic of Congo, Sierra Leone, Kosovo, East Timor, Haiti and The Hague, and those working out, particularly at the United Nations Headquarters in New York and the International Centre for Transitional Justice. Without their willingness to share their experiences, expertise and insights, this book would have been substantially lacking in substance.

Finally, heartfelt thanks to all at Polity, and especially to Louise Knight and Emma Hutchinson for their enduring patience and tolerance of missed deadlines. And also to our friends and family, especially Rachel's beautiful daughter Catherine, whose impending arrival hastened the book's completion by imposing her own non-negotiable deadline!

RK & EM

# Abbreviations

| | |
|---|---|
| AFRC | Armed Forces Revolutionary Council |
| ATCA | Alien Tort Claims Act |
| BCS | Bosnian, Croatian, Serbian |
| CAVR | Commission of Reception, Truth and Reconciliation (Timor-Leste) |
| CDF | Civil Defence Force |
| CDR | Coalition for Defence of the Republic |
| CEC | Cambodian Extraordinary Chambers |
| CEDAW | Convention on the Elimination of Discrimination against Women |
| CEH | Historical Clarification Commission (Guatemala) |
| CNRT | National Council of Timorese Resistance |
| DJA | Department for Judicial Affairs |
| DRC | The Democratic Republic of Congo |
| EU | European Union |
| FAR | Rwandan Armed Forces |
| FMLN | Farabundo Marti National Liberation Front |
| FRY | Federal Republic of Yugoslavia |
| HRC | Human Rights Court |
| ICC | International Criminal Court |
| ICCPR | International Covenant on Civil and Political Rights |
| ICL | International Criminal Law |
| ICTs | International Criminal Tribunals |
| ICTR | International Criminal Tribunals for Rwanda |
| ICTY | International Criminal Tribunal for the former Yugoslavia |
| IER | Equity and Reconciliation Commission (Morocco) |

| | |
|---|---|
| IFOR | Implementation Force (Bosnia-Herzegovina) |
| IHL | International Humanitarian Law |
| IJPs | International Judges and Prosecutors |
| ILC | International Law Commission |
| INTERFET | International Force for Timor-Leste |
| JEM | Justice and Equality Movement |
| KFOR | Kosovo Force |
| KLA | Kosovo Liberation Army |
| KWEEC | Kosovo War and Ethnic Crimes Court |
| LMG | Like-Minded Group |
| LRA | Lord's Resistance Army |
| MONUC | UN Mission in Congo |
| MRND | National Republican Movement for Development |
| NATO | North Atlantic Treaty Organisation |
| NGOs | non-governmental organizations |
| NMOG I | Neutral Military Observer Group |
| NRC | National Reconciliation Commission, Ghana |
| OAU | Organization for African Unity |
| OTP | Office of the Prosecutor |
| P5 | 5 permanent members of the Security Council |
| RPA | Rwandan Patriotic Army |
| RPF | Rwandan Patriotic Front |
| RUF | Revolutionary United Front |
| SCSL | Special Court for Sierra Leone |
| SFOR | Stabilisation Force (Bosnia-Herzegovina) |
| SFRY | Socialist Federal Republic of Yugoslavia |
| SICT | Supreme Iraqi Criminal Tribunal |
| SLM/A | Sudan Liberation Movement/Army |
| SRSG | Special Representative of the Secretary-General |
| TACJPS | Technical Advisory Commission on Judiciary and Prosecution Service |
| TC | Truth Commission |
| TIJM | Traditional Informal Justice Mechanisms |
| TNI | Tentara Nasional Indonesia |
| TRC | Truth and Reconciliation Commission |
| UDHR | Universal Declaration of Human Rights |
| UN | United Nations |
| UNAMIR | United Nations Assistance Mission for Rwanda |
| UNDP | United Nations Development Programme |
| UNMIK | United Nations Mission in Kosovo |
| UNOMUR | United Nations Observer Mission for Uganda and Rwanda |

UNPROFOR    United Nations Protection Force in Bosnia
UNTAES      United Nations Transitional Authority in Eastern
            Slovenia
UNTAET      United Nations Transitional Administration in
            Timor-Leste
UNPOL       United Nations Civilian Police
WW1         World War One
WW2         World War Two

# Peace and Justice: An Introduction

In the two decades or so since the end of the Cold War, we have witnessed significant changes in the conduct of international relations and contemporary warfare. One important element of change was an increased tendency towards intervention in situations that would hitherto have been deemed to be beyond the purview of an outside entity, and a marked increase in the number and scope of peace operations, in some cases involving the rebuilding of state structures. Together with economic, military and political intervention came an emerging trend of 'international judicial intervention' to address serious and widespread abuses of international humanitarian law and human rights.[1] Beginning with the establishment of ad hoc international criminal tribunals (ICTs) for the former Yugoslavia and Rwanda (ICTY and ICTR), and culminating in the establishment of a permanent International Criminal Court (ICC), there appeared to be a new normative trend of using international judicial mechanisms to address past crimes in war-torn societies. Each new initiative was welcomed as potentially offering advantages over other approaches, from the 'shiny new hammer' of the ICTY to the 'magic-bullet' solution offered by universal jurisdiction and the ICC to combat impunity. Meanwhile, scholars and practitioners debated the role of amnesties, truth commissions and traditional informal justice mechanisms in fostering restorative rather than retributive justice in light of the increasing implementation of non-judicial mechanisms for accountability. In the late 1980s and early 1990s, this focused on countries in transition from dictatorship or tyranny to democratic rule, in Latin America (Argentina, Chile, Brazil, Uruguay) and Southern and Eastern Europe (Spain, Greece, Poland, East Germany, Hungary) and, in a different, but critical context, South Africa. More recently, it has been revived in relation to countries emerging from violent conflict, such as Sierra Leone, Liberia, the Democratic Republic of Congo, Timor-Leste, Sudan and Uganda.

In his 2004 report, 'The rule of law and transitional justice in conflict and post-conflict societies', the United Nations Secretary-General formally acknowledged that some form of transitional justice mechanism is crucial for societies emerging from violent conflict as the task of addressing past crimes is seen as essential to building sustainable peace.[2] Peace, justice and reconciliation go hand in hand, as mutually reinforcing objectives. The link between international peace and security and international criminal justice had already been made explicit with the establishment by the Security Council ten years earlier of the ICTY and then the ICTR – judicial institutions with a mandate to contribute to the restoration and maintenance of peace. Although concerns are still raised in relation to the potentially destabilizing impacts of transitional justice, and about sequencing of peace and justice processes, the debate now has largely shifted from *whether* to pursue some form of transitional justice, to *what form* it should take, what the degree of international involvement should be and who should be targeted.

In order to take this debate forward, we need to understand better what the relative merits and drawbacks are to the range of possible mechanisms. The debate needs to move on from a knee-jerk reaction to the perceived failures of the last attempt, so that, rather as generals ought to avoid fighting the last war, those planning for transitional justice ought to avoid the pitfalls of simply correcting the last effort. This could be seen through the 1990s, when frustration at the length and cost of trials at the international criminal tribunals and their remoteness from the affected population prompted a search for better alternatives. To correct the apparent shortcomings of the ICTs, 'mixed' or 'hybrid' courts have been established, involving domestic and international elements in, for example, Sierra Leone, Cambodia, Timor-Leste and Kosovo. But, although the lessons of what has gone before are extremely valuable, we need to be careful about taking these out of context and wary of a 'one-size-fits-all' solution that can be grafted onto any post-conflict situation. Advancing justice, peace and reconciliation in a fragile post-conflict setting requires careful planning and a solid understanding of what might be possible. It is important to consider issues of complementarity between a range of different approaches, and to be realistic in setting expectations. Moreover, whilst there may be a formal acknowledgement of the link between justice and peace as mutually reinforcing rather than mutually incompatible objectives,[3] reconciliation is still frequently described as incompatible with justice, and justice with peace, leading some to argue for a necessary, if unpalatable, trade-off between these three objectives.[4]

This book interrogates the relationship between peace, justice and reconciliation through a systematic examination of various ways of dealing with issues of justice and accountability in countries in transition from war to peace. Starting with the establishment of the ICTY and ICTR in 1993 and 1994 respectively, it surveys the development of international criminal justice with the establishment of the ICC, the Special Court for Sierra Leone and 'hybrid' courts, as well as looking at the role of purely domestic courts in the transitional justice process. Having surveyed a range of judicial approaches, the book moves on to consider the use of non-judicial mechanisms for accountability, including truth commissions and traditional informal practices. While there is no 'one-size-fits-all' solution to the difficult and complex question of how to deal with past abuses, lessons from past and current endeavours can help provide a framework through which we might be able better to assess the best possible solution for a given situation. A common thread is the importance of assessing, understanding and responding to local context and fostering local engagement with whatever process is decided upon, as well as understanding and acknowledging the ways in which different approaches might be complementary.

## Transitional/Post-Conflict Justice

The terms 'transitional justice' and 'post-conflict justice' are used here interchangeably to denote the range of judicial and non-judicial mechanisms aimed at dealing with a legacy of large-scale abuses of human rights and/or violations of international humanitarian law. These mechanisms are designed, to a greater or lesser extent, to address the need for accountability, to provide justice and to foster reconciliation in societies in transition from authoritarian to democratic rule or from war to peace. In the majority of cases discussed in this book, however, we are examining transitional justice in post-conflict settings. The aim of transitional or post-conflict justice in these cases is to contribute to sustainable peace and the rebuilding of a society based on the rule of law.

Proponents of transitional justice have suggested that there are a number of legal, moral, political, pragmatic, sociological and psychological imperatives for having some form of transitional justice process.[5] Broadly speaking, justice is thought to contribute to the restoration and maintenance of peace in the following ways: by establishing individual accountability, deterring future violations, establishing an historical record, promoting reconciliation and healing, giving victims a means of redress, removing perpetrators and supporting capacity-building and the rule of law. These potential advantages are discussed briefly below and will be referred to in relation to the different approaches considered in this volume.

## Accountability

The notion of accountability is linked to the desire among many to see an 'end to impunity' for those responsible for gross violations of human rights. It can operate in two ways. The first is often stressed by supporters of judicial approaches, who point to the role of criminal justice in locating responsibility with the individual. It was 'the great hope of tribunal advocates that the individualisation and de-collectivisation of guilt . . . would help bring about peace and reconciliation'.[6] This, it is argued, can be particularly helpful where blame might otherwise be placed on entire nations or ethnic groups, leading to never-ending cycles of violence. The concept of accountability is also important in the context of truth commissions, in a different way. It has been suggested that insisting on individual accountability might in fact be detrimental to the goals of peace and reconciliation, and some argue for an alternative conception of accountability based on establishing patterns of abuse and creating institutional government and security sector responsibility for such abuses, rather than targeting named individuals. These different perceptions of accountability have marked the discourse on transitional justice.

The goal of ending impunity is also thought to operate at an international level. For example, it has been argued that by 'embodying universal condemnation, lawfully imposed punishments would be a reaffirmation not only of the laws that prohibit the crimes that were committed but also of the idea of law'.[7] Establishing accountability for gross violations of human rights, whether at an individual or an institutional level, is supposed to contribute to establishing a norm of accountability, which is linked to the purported deterrent role of transitional justice. The case of the 'forgotten genocide' of the Armenians before the First World War is often invoked to illustrate this point. The leaders responsible for organizing the genocide were never brought to account, a lesson that Adolf Hitler is said to have taken on board wholeheartedly when contemplating the extermination of the Jews. He is alleged to have remarked: 'Who, after all, speaks today of the annihilation of the Armenians?'[8]

## Deterrence

One of the main aims for both judicial and non-judicial transitional justice mechanisms is to deter future conflict and war. Proponents of criminal trials focus on their role in deterring future crimes and in consolidating the new order, arguing that, 'by laying bare the truth about violations of the past and condemning them, prosecutions can deter potential lawbreakers and inoculate the public against future temptation to be complicit in state-sponsored violence'.[9] Supporters of non-judicial mechanisms also emphasize how they can deter renewed conflict by establishing the truth and ensuring account-ability. However, the potential of any transitional justice mechanism for deterring future violence, whether in the society immediately affected or elsewhere, is at best dubious and is extremely difficult to measure.

## Historical record

A claim that is made of both judicial and non-judicial transitional justice mechanisms is that they play an essential role in creating an impartial historical record of the pattern of abuses and violations of international humanitarian law that might have occurred. Criminal trials establish this record through the introduction of evidence and final judgement, but are restricted in so far as they focus on the guilt or innocence of an individual accused. Truth commissions and com-missions of inquiry focus on establishing patterns of behaviour of both state and non-state actors. Creating an historical record not only helps to identify the patterns of abuse and its actors, thus rein-forcing a sense of accountability; it also helps ensure against the setting in of a collective amnesia and reduces the possibility for revi-sionism. In relation to post-apartheid South Africa, Archbishop Tutu warned: 'We must deal effectively, penitently with our past or it will return to haunt our present and we won't have a future to speak of.'[10] The creation of an historical record is vital as a tool of remembrance, but it might also play a more active role as official acknowledgement of past abuses, and unearthing the truth about lost loved ones can contribute to the process of individual and national reconciliation.

## Reconciliation and healing

Reconciliation is almost always touted as a key objective of transitional justice processes but often it is unclear what is meant by it and how, exactly, different processes might foster reconciliation. It has been variously referred to as acknowledgement and repentance from the perpetrators and forgiveness from the victims,[11] as non-lethal coexistence,[12] as democratic decision-making and reintegration,[13] and as encompassing concepts of truth, mercy, peace and justice; concepts which in themselves are difficult to define.[14]

In this book, a distinction will be made between national reconciliation and individual reconciliation. National reconciliation is achieved when societal and political processes function and develop without reverting to previous patterns or the framework of the conflict. Individual reconciliation is the ability of each human being to conduct their lives in a *similar* manner as prior to the conflict without fear or hate. This distinction is crucial because it is possible to achieve national reconciliation without achieving individual reconciliation. National reconciliation may come at the expense of reconciliation at individual level, where individual needs are set aside for the good of society as a whole. Equally, however, reconciliation at individual level can be entirely independent of reconciliation at national or societal level.[15] As will be discussed, some forms of transitional justice promote one type of reconciliation more than the other.

In the discourse on non-judicial mechanisms the concept of healing is often also prominent. There is an assumption that, for example, truth commissions can lead to individual healing of victims of violence. However, the notion of healing is perhaps even more problematic than that of reconciliation. What is meant by healing in these contexts is unclear. It is undoubtedly an extremely personal experience and will vary extensively from person to person, and it can be questioned how much healing can come about irrespective of what form of transitional justice is being implemented.

## Redress for victims

Some argue that the primary purpose of criminal trials is not deterrence, but to provide redress for victims, eliminating the need to carry out individual acts of retribution. A distinction has been drawn between crimes against the state, which the state can forgive, and crimes against individuals, which it cannot, and many feel that there is an obligation to prosecute these types of crimes.[16] However, it should be noted that although prosecutions may seek redress for victims in so far as the individual perpetrator is punished, they may not in all circumstances be the right solution. Proponents of non-judicial mechanisms argue that redress need not only come in the form of criminal trials, but be sought more broadly. Redress can also in some cases result from recommendations made by a truth commission or other non-judicial process.

## Removal of perpetrators

A significant contribution that transitional justice can make, especially criminal trials, is to identify, stigmatize and even physically remove certain individuals from a region of conflict. Indictment and arrest of potential 'spoilers' can ensure that they do not partake in the peace processes or continue unduly to influence a fragile transitional society, nor can they continue to elicit fear in victims and their families. On the other hand, since it is not possible to remove all perpetrators, those who are targeted might be perceived as scapegoats or even martyrs. Even more damaging is that this strategy risks alienating the very people with whom peace is being negotiated, thus prolonging the conflict in the interests of justice but at the expense of peace. However, as has been demonstrated, relying on such persons as the guarantors of peace is a risky strategy in itself.[17]

## Capacity-building and the rule of law

A wider goal of transitional justice is to contribute to capacity-building and the rule of law. In many cases where transitional justice is pursued, there is also a wider peace-building effort in place aimed at reforming the political, economic, judicial and security sectors. It is hoped that transitional justice can help reinforce aspects of this, both conceptually by helping to establish and solidify the rule of law and practically by contributing to capacity-building in the domestic judicial system and to judicial and security sector reform.

Dealing with past abuses is seen as an urgent task because it highlights the fundamental character of the new order being established, whether in countries in transition to democratic rule or those emerging from violent conflict, or both. This does not have to be a judicial process, but some form of accountability is required in order to demonstrate a clean break with the old order by drawing a 'thick line' between past and present.[18] Redressing the wrongs committed through human rights violations 'is not only a legal obligation and a moral imperative. . . . It also makes good political sense in the transition from dictatorship to democracy.'[19]

## Risks and Dangers

Set against all the purported benefits of transitional justice are a number of risks and dangers that also need to be taken into account. Foremost is the potential for destabilization of a fragile peace process and the risk that pursuing justice might heighten tensions and reignite conflict between warring factions. Other dangers include the potential for retraumatization of the victims, and that transitional justice processes, if not carefully managed, risk becoming politicized, whether actual or perceived, especially if they are imposed by the victors over the vanquished.

### Destabilization

New governments navigating the transition from authoritarian to democratic rule or from violent conflict to peaceful reconstruction face considerable challenges. All transitional justice mechanisms can lead to *destabilization* by highlighting past abuses and identifying abusers who still may have some grip on power or the capability to disrupt a relatively fragile peace. For a new regime, demanding justice, whether judicial or non-judicial in form, could upset a relatively fragile grip on power. New regimes therefore face a 'Hobson's choice between their very survival and the principles upon which their existence was founded'.[20] A way out of this dilemma, it has been suggested, is that because there is a legal obligation to prosecute, they cannot forgo justice simply because it is politically expedient to do so, even if an amnesty is supported by the majority of the population.[21] A new government, whose legitimacy may remain tenuous, would have to carry out such a legal obligation even if it was destabilizing and unpopular. However, this legalistic view fails to take into account the pragmatic obstacles to justice and the political ramifications of such an approach. Moreover, there is no evidence to support the view that *ignoring* transitional justice will lead to greater stability.

For proponents of international criminal justice, the tribunals established in the 1990s heralded a welcome 'end to impunity'. For others, however, the pursuit of justice for yesterday's victims 'risks making today's living the dead of tomorrow. . . . The pursuit of criminals is one thing. Making peace is another.'[22] In a country that is in the process of negotiating an end to years, sometimes even decades, of conflict, the same people involved in securing the peace have often been involved in the worst abuses. The threat of international or domestic prosecution or non-judicial mechanisms for seeking accountability in these cases might prolong or even reignite conflict. On the other hand, a peace made by such people might not be worth the paper it is written on. Transitional justice needs, therefore, to tread a fine line, balancing the imperatives of short- and long-term peace with those of justice.

## Retraumatization

A further risk of transitional justice is that of *retraumatization*. It has been suggested that rather than rake over the past, it is better to draw a line under what has happened and forgive and forget. Seeking justice for past abuses involves to some extent reliving them, especially for victims and witnesses brought to testify before a court, or at a truth commission. Retraumatization has been particularly emphasized by supporters of restorative justice, arguing that court cases bring about revictimization. However, truth-telling in any context, even that of a truth commission, can lead to retraumatization. While some argue that the process of retelling horrific stories of abuses committed against oneself, one's family and neighbours can be cathartic, others suggest that reliving these experiences can be extremely traumatic, particularly in societies that do not have the resources or capabilities to deal with psychological trauma and provide individual support.

## Politicization

A third danger is that of *politicization*, which can occur in both judicial and non-judicial transitional justice mechanisms. This can be perceived or actual, but both are potentially damaging to the ability of transitional justice to deliver on the objectives set out above. With regard to criminal trials, because it is unrealistic to expect that all perpetrators will be prosecuted, some degree of selectivity will need to be exercised. The exercise of prosecutorial discretion is politically charged and subject to intense scrutiny, and even if exercised on the basis of legal, rather than political, criteria, it can be difficult to avoid perceptions of tokenism or scapegoating. It can also be difficult to draw the line between political and legal criteria, especially where the prosecutor is expected to determine who should be prosecuted with reference to apparent political considerations such as who bears the 'greatest responsibility' or what is in 'the interests of justice'. It might be suspected that selectivity is not applied on legal or moral grounds but that more crudely 'prudential' considerations are really at work.[23] Linked to this, a further criticism is that there is a danger of trials turning into 'victor's justice', where the victors sit in judgement over the victims, and where the conduct of only one side is subject to investigation. In order to guard against these dangers, transparency and consistency are important. International involvement can also, in some cases, lend greater legitimacy to the process.

## Context, Context and Context

The most important consideration is the context in which transitional justice is pursued. This book argues that a one-size-fits-all approach to transitional justice is deeply flawed, as is an approach that merely takes the lessons from the last experience and applies them wholesale to the next. Advancing justice, peace and reconciliation in a fragile post-conflict setting is a complex task, requiring careful planning and nuanced understanding of the particular historical, social, cultural and political context.

There are various enabling and constraining factors that influence and determine what transitional justice mechanisms are chosen and their subsequent success. Sensitivity to cultural norms and values is important, as is understanding the nature of the conflict, the extent and types of abuses and the needs of those involved, whether as victims, perpetrators or survivors, and the nature of the peace agreement, if there is one. There are also practical considerations such as the available infrastructure, financial constraints and political considerations, including whether there is sufficient political will to support transitional justice at both the domestic and international level. These variables all interact and affect the process of transitional justice.

### Cultural norms and values

It has now been recognized that there is a need to take into account local customs, norms and values and to devise strategies of transitional justice that accord with these, in collaboration with local people. It is important to understand the way in which the society views issues of justice. In particular, one needs to take into account the extent to which the existing justice system – whether it is based on a formal legal system or a traditional dispute resolution mechanism, or a combination of the two – reflects a predominantly retributive or restorative approach. If traditional dispute resolution mechanisms are widely used and accepted, this may be a reason to adopt it as a way of dealing with past abuses as well, whereas in a culture where norms of retributive justice and individual liability is strong, criminal trials might be more appropriate than more restorative forms of justice including truth commissions and measures aimed at reintegration.

## Nature of the conflict and extent and types of abuses

The context, history and background to the conflict and the actors involved are of crucial importance in determining not only what types of transitional justice processes are possible, but also how successful they will be. If, for example, the conflict was a proxy war, or a civil war involving multiple parties, or a civil war with external involvement, this will affect both choice and outcome of the transitional justice process. If state security forces committed the bulk of the abuses, but felt justified because of issues of national security, this will again affect the process of justice and therefore will need to be addressed in a different way.

As well as looking at the causes and course of the conflict, and who might be responsible for committing abuses, it is important to take into account the type and extent of abuses committed. Some have argued that certain crimes are beyond prosecution, that the evil is so 'radical' it mocks our efforts to punish it.[24] In these cases, a process that focuses on the bigger picture, rather than the individual perpetrator, might work best. In addition, one needs to consider that victims of different types of crime, and their families, have different needs. For example, when dealing with a past regime where disappearances were common, there is frequently a demand for the truth – to know what happened to the disappeared. In cases such as this, a truth commission or commission of inquiry plays a significant part in establishing these facts. Where political killings, rape and sexual assault have been rife, prosecutions have often been sought by victims and their families, although not necessarily implemented. The nature of the crimes will therefore influence the mechanisms sought to deal with it.

## Needs of victims, survivors and perpetrators

Understanding the nature of the conflict is crucial if we are to be able to draw sensible distinctions between victims and perpetrators, and between victims and survivors, and adequately address their needs.

There is an ongoing debate surrounding the use of the terms 'victim' and 'survivor'; some argue that 'victim' should not be used, because it belittles the fact that they have come through and survived. For the sake of simplicity, the term 'victim' will be used here. However, it is important to emphasize that it is recognized that not all are, or feel themselves to be, victims, even if horrific abuses have been committed against them personally or against members of their families; instead, they may choose to view themselves as survivors.

Moreover, the distinction between perpetrator and victim can frequently be blurred in post-conflict societies. Retributive justice necessitates that someone must either be a victim or perpetrator, but this is often not clear-cut. A significant number might be both victims and perpetrators, albeit at different levels. In some cases, people might not have been directly involved in the organization or commission of abuses, but still they are deemed to have blood on their hands by virtue of not having acted to prevent such abuses, or being part of the system that carried them out. In other cases, perpetrators who directly participated may have done so under duress.

Treating all as either perpetrators or victims also ignores the distinctions between different levels of responsibility. There is a distinction between, at one end of the scale, a government official or military officer actively participating by ordering assassins, disappearances or other gross violations of human rights, and, at the other end, a person passively accepting the situation, but not taking an active part. These distinctions are crucial. However, although the sometimes blurred categories of victim and perpetrator should be acknowledged, it should not be used as an argument for avoiding issues of justice. Rather, they should be designed to address particular needs.

### Peace agreement

The existence of a peace agreement and what it stipulates will directly affect the transitional justice process – it might even be a part of it. In some cases, peace agreements have included a provision relating to transitional justice, as in Sierra Leone, Liberia and the DRC. This simplifies the task somewhat. Where there is no such agreement, and where peace has yet to be negotiated, some argue that the interests of peace should come before those of justice. Implementing transitional justice in such a fragile environment carries risks of destabilization or even of prolonging the conflict, as discussed above. Set against this, however, is the argument that justice can play an integral part in the pursuit of peace by excluding potential spoilers from the process. It is a difficult balance to strike, especially for new regimes that may be more reluctant to pursue certain types of transitional justice mechanisms as a result.

## Finance and infrastructure

Financial capabilities, existing infrastructure and local capacity in the post-conflict setting have a direct impact on the available choice of different transitional justice mechanisms. In a post-conflict setting, infrastructure may have been destroyed, the economy devastated and the personnel missing. Where this is the case, the emphasis is not only on transitional justice, but on rebuilding local capacity in the justice sector as a whole, along with rebuilding the economy, government and security sector. Transitional justice can contribute to rebuilding local capacity, and/or can draw resources away from the domestic sector, depending on the extent to which it is tied into the local system. The vast cost of mounting trials may be prohibitive, and truth commissions are often promoted as a less costly and demanding option.

## Political will

Implementation of any or a combination of transitional justice processes is dependent upon political will. Whether or not the political will exists to deal with past abuses is contingent on the calculation that a new regime makes on the merits and drawbacks of transitional justice – in particular, the risk of destabilization. It will also be contingent on the degree of culpability the new regime might in itself have and the extent to which erstwhile opponents are relied upon to maintain peace and stability. They may be tempted to set aside questions of justice, at least for the initial period of transition. The international community may have a crucial role to play here in pushing forward transitional justice, although careful sequencing is required to ensure that the interests of peace and the interests of justice are mutually supportive, not contradictory.

## International involvement

A final element in determining the form that transitional justice will take is international involvement and the degree of commitment shown by the international community. International interest in pursuing transitional justice in a given setting will have enormous impact on the choices that the country in question has regarding what type of mechanisms can be applied. In particular, international involvement can make up for some of the shortfalls in the domestic system, especially in providing resources and expertise. In some, but not all, cases, United Nations peace operations have been specifically mandated to address transitional justice. International involvement is not always an unqualified advantage, however, as it has in several cases tended to ignore the needs of local people in favour of the interests of international peace and security writ large.

## The Book

The aim of this book is to investigate how the contextual factors set out above influence the success or failure of transitional justice in achieving the objectives set out for it. We begin in chapter 1 with the post-WW2 tribunals at Nuremberg and Tokyo, which paved the way for the development of international law and the evolution of international norms of human rights and criminal law and the creation of ad hoc international criminal tribunals in the 1990s, the focus of chapter 2. It will be argued that both the Nuremberg and Tokyo tribunals and the ad hoc tribunals have an ambiguous legacy. Whilst both sets of trials were undeniably important in terms of their *international* impact, in as much as they were instrumental in establishing norms of accountability and in pushing the boundaries of international criminal law and procedure, they had a less auspicious impact on *domestic* peace and reconciliation – especially the ad hoc tribunals. The apparent shortcomings of the ad hoc tribunals were addressed in two separate developments, both aimed at creating a better model of transitional justice. Chapter 3 discusses the establishment of the International Criminal Court and chapter 4 discusses the evolution of 'hybrid' or 'internationalized' courts, such as the Special Court for Sierra Leone, the Extraordinary Chambers in Cambodia, and the insertion of international judges and prosecutors (IJPs) into the domestic judicial system in Timor-Leste and Kosovo. Apart from the significant advances in international criminal law and procedure, lessons have been learned from all these experiences about the cost and timeliness of criminal trials, about the need for outreach and communication, and engaging the local population in the process, and the importance of transparency and fairness in the exercise of prosecutorial discretion.

Underlying the jurisdictional criteria for the ICC is the principle of *complementarity*. The Rome Statute of the ICC reinforces the role of domestic courts as the courts of first resort. However, domestic courts do not always have the capacity to undertake trials, especially in the immediate aftermath of conflict. Chapter 5 discusses the potential for domestic prosecutions, setting out the numerous difficult issues that need to be considered, underlining the potential advantages of such an approach and outlining how they have been used in recent years in tandem with other forms of transitional justice, including international trials. Domestic prosecutions offer significant advantages, including the fact that they take place within the context of where the abuses occurred, so have a much greater potential impact on the local population and judicial system. However, the potential for unfair and biased trials can be increased in this context and, even if the political will exists, they may be unable to mount such trials due to lack of capacity, resources and infrastructure. There have also been a number of domestic trials on the basis of universal jurisdiction, where there is little or no direct link between the accused, the crime and the country in which the trial takes place. This fairly recent phenomenon carries with it an additional set of dilemmas and has been lambasted as a form of 'judicial tyranny'. Universal jurisdiction is dealt with in the context of the ICC in this book (see chapter 3, box 3.2, for details of cases and suggestions for further reading).

The principle of complementarity should not be restricted to domestic and international criminal trials, but should also be applied to judicial and non-judicial forms of transitional justice. Although not mentioned in the Rome Statute, except obliquely with regard to the role of the prosecutor who must use his discretion in 'the interests of justice', it is important to consider the extent to which different forms of transitional justice might be complementary to one another. In order to do this, we need to understand properly the relative merits and drawbacks of non-judicial as well as judicial approaches. Chapter 6 examines truth commissions and their role in reconciliation, healing and reintegration of society as a restorative process of justice, using the many examples of truth commissions that have been established throughout the world in the last 25 years. In many cases, truth commissions have been established as the only recourse to justice and accountability; in others, they were established alongside formal judicial mechanisms of accountability. Often truth commissions have been chosen as the only recourse to justice as a way of limiting potential destabilization, but this has not always led to reconciliation. The former head of the South African Truth and Reconciliation Commission, Desmond Tutu, reflecting on the experience ten years after the end of the commission, acknowledged that 'we probably should have done what the legislation requires and prosecuted people'.[25]

Chapter 7 focuses on traditional informal justice mechanisms and how these have been used to address past violations of human rights. Traditional mechanisms of justice have been increasingly promoted as a manner in which to deal with past abuses. They come in a multitude of forms and can include both retributive and reconciliatory elements. Critically, they all reflect local culture, norms and values. But they are not always consistent with international human rights law or indeed with local formal law. Moreover, although they have often been touted as a solution, they have not been subjected to close scrutiny. Nevertheless, they have the potential to contribute significantly to processes of reconciliation and reintegration of post-conflict societies.

Although they are often seen as the antithesis to justice, amnesties also have a significant role to play in transitional justice. We do not consider amnesties as a separate category in this book, but rather include discussion of amnesty in so far as it relates to the different forms of transitional justice outlined above. Amnesty is here understood as when an individual or group of individuals are granted immunity from criminal prosecution for a crime committed in the past. Amnesties can be in the form of a general/blanket amnesty usually covering all crimes committed in a specific time period, or they can be conditional, where amnesty is granted only when certain conditions are met by the perpetrators, in which case individual responsibility is assessed but the perpetrator is exempt from punishment.[26] Amnesties can be declared where political leaders confirm that certain people cannot be prosecuted by a court of law, but they can also be by default – that is, when issues of justice and past abuses are simply ignored.

Although amnesties have frequently been granted in respect of crimes committed during a period of conflict, international lawyers argue that such amnesties are inconsistent with international human rights law.[27] Importantly, the UN Secretary-General stated: 'Amnesty cannot be granted in respect of international crimes, such as genocide, crimes against humanity or other serious violations of international humanitarian law'.[28] However, as discussed above, even where there is an obligation to punish, the decision whether or not to act on this will depend on a range of other factors. There may be situations in which amnesties are not diametrically opposed to other processes of transitional justice, where, for example, they apply to different levels of perpetrators or are conditional. Other possible mechanisms for transitional justice, which may be employed in combination with those set out above are vetting, reparations, memorialization and the exercise of universal jurisdiction by national courts.

These methods all aim to secure an 'end to impunity' and to facilitate the transition from conflict to sustainable peace. These are laudable goals, but also possibly unrealistic ones. Reconciliation takes a protracted period of time and vast goals such as ending impunity should be modified and be more realistically calibrated to what can be achieved within the constraints operating in a given setting. A combination of mechanisms spanning several years can begin this process of rebuilding, reconstructing and reconciling, but alone it cannot achieve that goal. This book argues for an approach based on the principle of *complementarity* that takes into account the specific context, whilst at the same time recognizing the mutually reinforcing capacities of justice and peace.

### A note on boxes

*Rather than break up the text with detailed descriptions and background to the cases discussed in this book, basic information is to be found in the boxes at the end of each chapter.*

# 1

# The Nuremberg Legacy

The developments referred to in the Introduction, and considered throughout this volume, shed new light on the law as well as the politics of accountability. New interpretations of the law have emerged through the jurisprudence of international and domestic courts, alongside differing perspectives on wider questions of justice versus peace and prosecution versus amnesty. This process did not begin with the establishment of ad hoc tribunals in the 1990s, however. The genesis of international criminal law and enforcement was the post-WW2 tribunals at Nuremberg and Tokyo. These tribunals were a crucial element in the development of international law and the politics of enforcement, and the legacy of Nuremberg was deliberately invoked in relation to the decision to establish the ICTY, in 1993.

This chapter discusses the Nuremberg and Tokyo trials and their legacy. It examines the impact of the trials, their contribution to the development of international law, and the post-1945 legal and normative framework for war crimes prosecutions, focusing on three overlapping bodies of law: international humanitarian law or laws of armed conflict, international criminal law and human rights law.

## Nuremberg and Tokyo

While the regulation of armed conflict has a long history, enforcement is a relatively modern phenomenon. The Nuremberg and Tokyo trials, conducted in the immediate aftermath of the Second World War, marked a watershed in international law. By holding individuals accountable for abuses, these trials demonstrated that accountability was not only desirable, but also feasible. In spite of flaws in law and procedure, which will be discussed below, the legacy of Nuremberg and Tokyo was the further development and codification of international humanitarian law and human rights law, providing the foundation for the establishment of ad hoc international criminal tribunals in the 1990s, and for subsequent developments in transitional justice discussed in this book.

Prior to that experience, international prosecution for war crimes was extremely rare. The earliest recorded trial in an international court for war crimes was that of Peter von Hagenbach, who was prosecuted for violations of the laws of God and humanity in 1494.[1] Von Hagenbach was installed as Governor of the town of Breisach by Charles the Bold, and proceeded to impose a reign of terror. He was tried under the aegis of the Holy Roman Empire, by 28 judges from different parts of the Empire, so in that sense, his trial was international. There are a couple of other noteworthy aspects: he was accused of violations of the laws of God and humanity the modern reading of which would be crimes against humanity, or war crimes, since they were committed during a military occupation; second, von Hagenbach pleaded a defence of superior orders.[2] This was denied and he was convicted and condemned to death.

There were no other significant attempts to hold individuals accountable under international law until the end of the First World War, but that ended in ignominy. McCoubrey viewed this as lucky, given that: 'The presupposition of guilt and the transparently vindictive motivation of these proceedings would so have tainted them with victor's vigilantism that their ultimate failure can only in retrospect be thought fortunate.'[3] The situation at the end of the Second World War was radically different. The Allies had achieved a total victory and were in occupation of Germany and Japan, and the German government had collapsed. In addition to creating a new regime in Germany, the Allies were also embarking on the creation of a 'new world order', based on the United Nations and the maintenance of international peace and security. The trial and punishment of German and Japanese war criminals comprised an important element of this. It has been described as the last act of the war and the first act of the peace. As the last act of the war, it was intended to publicize Nazi atrocities and provide vindication of the Allied victory in the name of justice. As the first act of the peace, it was seen as a manifestation of a new world order.[4] Robert Jackson, in his final report to President Truman in October 1950, said that the endeavour should not be measured in terms of the personal fate of the defendants.[5] It was argued that the primary purpose of the Nuremberg tribunal was 'to bring the weight of law and criminal sanctions to bear in support of the peaceful and humanitarian principles that the UN was to promote'.[6]

But the Nuremberg legacy is ambiguous. It has been noted that, 'for persons of liberal convictions and a strong commitment to legalistic politics [Nuremberg] was a genuine moral crisis'.[7] There were a number of grounds for criticism. First, all the judges appointed to the bench of the tribunal were from the Allied nations; none came from Germany. Second, only a handful of individuals were brought to trial. Third, the tribunal did not subject the conduct of the Allies to legal or moral scrutiny – for example, for the 'wanton destruction of cities'; the failure to investigate such acts as the aerial bombing of German cities is often cited as an example of 'moral tunnel vision'. The Soviet record does not bear scrutiny either and contains acts which, it could be argued, constitute crimes against peace: for example, the conclusion of the Nazi–Soviet Pact in August 1939, and the invasion of Finland by Soviet forces. In addition, individual Soviet soldiers involved in the massacre of civilians in the Katyn Forest in Poland could have been arraigned for war crimes. Finally, the reluctance to prosecute Admiral Doenitz for 'unrestricted U-boat warfare', because his defence of *tu quoque* rested on the assertion that the Allies were practising the same tactics, was taken as a supreme act of hypocrisy. The final criticisms concerned the procedure and applicable law. It was alleged that Nuremberg applied *ex post facto* law and thereby violated the fundamental principle *nullum crimen sine lege, nulla poena sine lege* (no crime without a law; no punishment without a law).

The most contentious of the charges was that of 'crimes against peace'. The charge was broken down into two counts of conspiracy and waging aggressive war. In relation to the first count of conspiracy, the tribunal cited the record of a meeting in the Reich Chancellery on 5 November 1937. The now famous Hossbach Memorandum, named after the adjutant who took the minutes, revealed Hitler's plans to achieve *Lebensraum* (lit. 'living space') for the German people by taking over first Czechoslovakia and Austria, then moving eastward by 1943–5 to take Poland, and Russia. At this point, Hitler envisaged war with Great Britain and France, Germany's 'hate inspired antagonists', but did not think that they would be roused to defend Czechoslovakia or Austria.[8] The legal basis for the second count, of waging aggressive war, was the Kellogg–Briand Pact for the Renunciation of War, 1928, and the League of Nations Charter. It is debatable whether or not these instruments were sufficient basis to deem the use of force illegal in 1939, and even more uncertain whether, even if it was illegal, it gave rise to individual, as opposed to state, responsibility. The judgement of the Court was: 'To initiate a war of aggression . . . is not only an international crime, it is the supreme international crime, differing only from other war crimes in that it contains within itself the accumulated evil of the whole.'

There was also criticism of the prosecution of a new category of 'crimes against humanity'. It has been argued that the crimes committed by the Nazis were of such a heinous character that they clearly violated basic principles of justice recognized by civilized nations.[9] The third category of 'war crimes', on the other hand, had a much firmer basis in international law, and had been codified in a number of international conventions and declarations, as well as recognized as norms of customary international law. The Judgement of the Tribunal stated that it was 'too well settled to admit of argument'; and further that the weight of evidence on this count was 'overwhelming in its volume and its details'. Taken together, these criticisms undermined the process. As Justice Robert Jackson noted in his opening statement: 'We must never forget that the record on which we judge these defendants is the record on which history will judge us tomorrow. To pass these defendants a poisoned chalice is to put it to our own lips as well.'[10]

The Tokyo tribunal has not been the subject of as great a volume of literature as the Nuremberg tribunal. It has, however, been subject to the same criticism – namely, that it was victor's justice. The most damning overall critique of the tribunal is mounted by Richard Minear, in his book *Victor's Justice*, which by the author's own admission adopts a polemical tone.[11] The concluding paragraph of this book sums up his arguments and is worth quoting in full:

> We come then to the end of our study of the Tokyo trial. We have examined lofty motives and base motives. We have found its foundation in international law to be shaky. We have seen that its process was seriously flawed. We have examined the verdict's inadequacy as history. 'Victor's Justice' is a harsh judgement, but a harsh judgement is called for. It is only slight mitigation that in punishing the Japanese leaders we deceived ourselves.[12]

It is not within the scope of this chapter to examine the merits or otherwise of Minear's conclusions. It is, however, instructive for this study to assess some of its shortcomings. Minear refers to motives 'lofty and low'. The lofty motives being the desire to construct a new world order, based on respect for international law and the UN; the low motive being the need to find justification for the Allied war effort, and only 'barely disguised revenge'.[13] The most conspicuous omission from the list of indictees was the Japanese Emperor. General Douglas MacArthur, appointed Supreme Commander of the Allied Powers in Japan in 1945, claimed the credit for this decision; he realized that any attempt to put the Emperor on trial would have tragic consequences for peace and stability in Japan. Yet, in the long term, this decision contributed to an ambiguous legacy for the Tokyo trial in Japanese politics and society.[14]

Notwithstanding its flaws, the legacy of Nuremberg and Tokyo is more than the sum of its parts: 'The defendants and their fates were not the reason why Nuremberg has remained a bench-mark in international law and the lodestar of thought and debate on the great moral and legal questions of war and peace.'[15] Nuremberg documented the atrocities committed by the Nazi regime 'with such authenticity and in such detail that there can be no responsible denial of these crimes in the future and no tradition of martyrdom of the Nazi leaders can arise among informed people'.[16] The key contribution of Nuremberg and Tokyo was that it demonstrated that international resolve can, on occasion, be sufficiently compelling to result in the prosecution and punishment of individuals.[17] It also firmly established that there are certain crimes of international concern which incur individual criminal responsibility.

## International Humanitarian Law post-1945

The Nuremberg Charter and Judgement was valuable in providing 'an authoritative body of law upon which to base the establishment and jurisdiction of the two ad hoc Criminal Tribunals of the former Yugoslavia and Rwanda'.[18] Madeleine Albright, the United States Ambassador to the UN, stated during the discussion on the adoption of Resolution 808 (which concerned the setting-up of an international tribunal) that, 'international humanitarian law today is impressively codified, well understood, agreed upon, and enforceable'.[19]

The UN General Assembly unanimously adopted Resolution 95(I) on 11 December 1946, affirming the 'principles of international law recognised by the Charter of the Nuremberg Tribunal and the Judgement of the Tribunal'.[20] The principle of individual responsibility in international law for war crimes and crimes against humanity was therefore verified. Furthermore, the defence of Acts of State was denied and the defence of Superior Orders was held not to free an individual from responsibility, although it could be considered in mitigation of punishment.

While the concept of individual criminal responsibility in international law for war crimes was 'too well settled to admit of argument', the concept of crimes against humanity was novel. That it violated legal principles in applying *ex-post facto* law is technically correct, even though the Charter restricted its application to crimes committed in connection with the other two charges.[21] There is no doubt about the validity of the rule now. The recognition of crimes against humanity led to the adoption of the 1948 United Nations Convention on the Prevention and Punishment of the Crime of Genocide, which is unique in providing for the trial of alleged perpetrators before an international tribunal.

In 1944, Raphael Lemkin defined genocide as: '[The] destruction of a nation or ethnic group . . . not only through mass killings, but also through a co-ordinated plan of different actions aiming at the destruction of the essential foundational life of a national group, with the aim of annihilating the groups themselves.'[22] The Genocide Convention itself is clearly predicated on the experience of the Holocaust, and there is some debate now as to whether it could and should be broadened to include persecution on political grounds, and not based solely on ethnicity or religion. However, the strength of the legal meaning of genocide is to be found in the requisite intent to destroy a group, as such, and not because of political belief. The same acts, if systematic and widespread, are now prosecutable under crimes against humanity, even if committed in an internal armed conflict.

The Nuremberg definition of war crimes was codified and further developed in the 1949 Geneva Conventions and the 1977 Protocols Additional thereto. Unlike the Hague Conventions, which largely dealt with the means and methods of warfare, the Geneva Conventions were designed to protect victims of war (the wounded, sick and shipwrecked, prisoners of war and civilians). The 1977 Protocols Additional to the 1949 Geneva Conventions were an attempt to bring the law into line with developments in the conduct of contemporary warfare, including irregular war and insurgency/counter-insurgency and civil wars. Historically, international law governed states and applied only to interstate conflicts. Civil wars were deemed to be within the purview of the state concerned, and conduct was to some extent covered by domestic law. In comparison with international armed conflict, the law applicable to non-international armed conflict remains fairly limited and is mostly concerned with the protection of victims. Regulation of irregular wars and non-international armed conflict gives rise to a number of challenges, namely that the distinction between combatants and non-combatants can become easily blurred where there is a range of actors, including local armed groups and private militias. The distinction between military and non-military targets can also become blurred as a result of the strategic significance of civilian targets. In many cases, as we shall see, civil wars are characterized by ethnically or racially motivated violence and ethnic cleansing, where attacks on civilian population are not the unfortunate and unintended consequence, but the strategic purpose of one or other or all sides. Many of the conflicts of the 1990s were also characterized by widespread abuses and involved the extensive recruitment of child soldiers, all of which presents significant challenges for enforcement.

## International Criminal Law (ICL)

In spite of the obligation to punish grave breaches of the Geneva Conventions and genocide, prosecution was rare in national jurisdictions, and immediate post-war efforts to create a permanent ICC soon foundered. The development and codification of ICL has not been a systematic or cohesive process. Its development is tied to efforts to establish a permanent ICC, which finally came to fruition in July 1998 with the adoption of the Rome Statute and its coming into force in July 2002 (see chapter 3).

In 1948, the General Assembly requested the International Law Commission (ILC) to study the desirability and feasibility of establishing an ICC.[23] After studying the ILC's report, the General Assembly set up a Committee on International Criminal Jurisdiction, comprising 17 member states, to prepare concrete proposals for the establishment of a court. A draft statute was submitted in 1951, and amended in 1953. The 1953 Statute provided for the establishment of a court with jurisdiction over individuals for international crimes. International crimes were generally considered to be those contained in the 1954 Draft Code of Offences against the Peace and Security of Mankind. However, work on the Draft Code and towards the establishment of a permanent ICC was stalled for some time by the referral to the General Assembly of the question of finding a definition of aggression for the purposes of the code. The 1974 Definition of Aggression confirms the political nature of the definition of aggression, for which the Security Council has primary responsibility. Bassiouni laments that the 1974 definition cast the die firmly in favour of 'the politicisation of aggression rather than of its juridicization'.[24]

Broadly defined, ICL is the body of international law that gives rise to individual criminal responsibility. There are significant overlaps therefore with international humanitarian law (IHL) on the one hand, and Human Rights Law, on the other. Compared with IHL however, it is relatively new and rudimentary. The objective and subjective elements of the crimes are gradually evolving through the jurisprudence of international courts, as we shall see. Based on the Rome Statute, the threshold seems to be 'atrocity' (genocide, crimes against humanity, war crimes). A second tier of offences might comprise slavery, forced labour, apartheid, forced disappearances, (acts of) terrorism, hostage-taking, hijacking and torture. A number of international conventions have been agreed upon which could form the basis of jurisdiction for an international court: namely, the 1961 Convention on Narcotic Drugs; the 1963 Tokyo Convention on Offences Committed on Board an Aircraft; the 1970 Hague Convention for the Suppression of Unlawful Seizure of Aircraft; the 1971 Montreal Convention for the Suppression of Unlawful Acts against the Safety of Civil Aviation; the 1973 UN International Convention on the Suppression and Punishment of the Crime of Apartheid; and the 1984 United Nations Convention against Torture and Other Cruel, Inhuman or Degrading Treatment or Punishment. These all require the state to prosecute and punish in the absence of a permanent ICC.[25]

With the end of the Cold War, and on the initiative of a coalition of 16 Caribbean and Latin American countries led by Trinidad and Tobago, the UN renewed efforts to create a permanent court. The impetus to put the issue back on the agenda of the UN was that it was viewed as an effective means of dealing with the problems associated with the prosecution or extradition of drug offenders. It was also motivated by the evidence of atrocities being committed in the former Yugoslavia.[26] The General Assembly again requested the ILC to consider the issue and a special working group was established in 1992, mandated by the General Assembly to produce a draft statute, which it did in 1994. The Rome Statute of the International Criminal Court was signed on 17 July 1998, and came into force four years later, in July 2002.[27]

## Human Rights Law

Parallel to the development of ICL, the latter half of the twentieth century witnessed the development and consolidation of an international human rights regime. Although human rights law developed on the basis of the same humanitarian impulse as ICL, it should be viewed as distinct. The clearest differentiation is that, while ICL imposes obligations on individuals, human rights law imposes obligations on states with respect to their treatment of individuals. There is, however, considerable overlap between human rights law and the laws of war, and both share the same philosophical and historic origins in natural law.[28] Human rights law is, of course, of particular relevance to all forms of transitional justice aimed at dealing with past abuses, whether or not they come under the rubric of IHL or ICL.

The underlying principle of human rights law is that there are certain rules applicable *jus gentium* – that is to say, inalienable rights common to all humanity – and it is the duty of the state to uphold those rights. Both propositions are contentious. Some would argue that human rights are not universal and inalienable, that in spite of the fact that many cultures have developed ideas about the intrinsic dignity of human beings, the notion of human beings as 'rights bearers' is derived from the European liberal tradition and cannot therefore be applied wholesale to other areas of the globe. The fact that 48 states voted for the adoption of the Universal Declaration of Human Rights (UDHR) in 1948 suggests that the fundamental rights set out there were broadly accepted. But the abstentions tell a different story and point to major areas of contention. Eight states abstained, namely South Africa, the Soviet Union and five other Soviet bloc countries, and Saudi Arabia. Saudia Arabia's objections were based on religious grounds and were thus a direct challenge to the wisdom of universalism; the Soviets abstained on political grounds (that not enough attention was given to economic and social rights); and South Africa objected on the basis that it violated sovereignty and the right of states to non-interference in domestic matters. The assertion of the rights of peoples over the individualistic bias of Western human rights standards was made in the 1990s with the promotion of 'Asian values' embodied in the 1993 Bangkok Declaration. These are seen by many, including human rights activists in the non-Western world, as excessively conservative, however, and not necessarily any more reflective of the views of ordinary people than a Western conception of human rights. While we can debate about the applicability of certain provisions, however, there are fundamental norms that should be universally applicable, such as the prevention and punishment of the crime of genocide and other crimes against humanity.

Meanwhile, South Africa's objections highlight the contest between norms of sovereignty and of universal human rights. It relates to more recent debates about the rights and duties of states vis-à-vis their own citizens, and even vis-à-vis the citizens of other states. In the nineteenth and early twentieth century, some argued that regimes that failed to uphold the requisite standards, such as the Ottoman Empire in the 1870s, forfeited their claim to sovereignty. Post-1945, the UN Charter embodies a commitment to international order, peace and security, as well as to upholding human rights and fundamental freedoms. The practice of the 1990s demonstrated that violations of human rights were now regarded as threats to international peace and security, warranting collective action under the auspices of the UN, and the argument has gained force in more recent debates about the legitimacy of 'unilateral' humanitarian intervention.[29]

So-called 'first generation rights', such as the right to life, liberty, security of person, equality before the law, the presumption of innocence and right to a fair trial, freedom of opinion and expression, and freedom from oppression, slavery, torture and other inhuman and degrading treatment, were set out in the UDHR, adopted by the UN General Assembly on 10 December 1948.[30] The Declaration also recognized certain second generation rights, such as the right to work and an adequate standard of living, education and property. Subsequent agreements reinforced and supplemented these rights, including the 1966 International Covenant on Civil and Political Rights (ICCPR), the 1979 Convention on the Elimination of Discrimination against Women (CEDAW), and the 1989 Convention on the Rights of the Child. Important in the context of this study, Article 14 of the ICCPR provides for basic standards for a fair trial, including equality before the law, the presumption of innocence, the right to defend oneself and to be tried without undue delay.

Although it saw a proliferation of treaties designed to uphold human rights and of non-governmental organizations dedicated to enforcing those rights, the period 1945–90 was inauspicious for the UN in terms of enforcement of human rights and international humanitarian law. According to Bailey, 'the UN seemed unable to act effectively, other than to utter pious words'.[31] On the fiftieth anniversary of the UDHR, Mary Robinson, the UN Human Rights Commissioner, lamented the 'failure of implementation on a scale that shames us all'.[32] While Articles 55 and 56 of the Charter impose legal obligations on member states to promote 'universal respect for, and observance of, human rights and fundamental freedoms for all' and to take joint action for the achievement of that goal, in effect the organization has been prohibited from taking enforcement action in respect of human rights. Article 2(7) states: 'Nothing contained in the present Charter shall authorize the UN to intervene in matters which are essentially within the domestic jurisdiction of any State.' The only exception to this rule is the application of enforcement measures under Chapter VII.

There are only two cases where Chapter VII was invoked in situations where human rights were being seriously threatened within the borders of a single state, and even then there was a nexus with international order. In Southern Rhodesia it was not made explicit what exactly the threat was – whether it was the denial of the right to self-determination or the spill-over effect;[33] and in 1977, when the Security Council finally imposed a mandatory arms embargo on South Africa, the basis for the invocation of Chapter VII was not the policy of apartheid per se, but the acquisition by South Africa of arms and related matériel.[34] In both these instances, the Security Council Resolutions had a nexus with a military threat to international peace and security. Without this nexus, the protection of human rights was outside the scope of the Security Council, at least in practice, until the 1990s.

Nevertheless, significant advances were made in the development of human rights law and in the codification and further development of international humanitarian law through the auspices of the UN. Crucially, the body of human rights law developed during the 1945–90 period made a serious contribution to piercing the armour of state sovereignty and demonstrating that the way a state treats its own citizens can be a matter for international concern.[35] It only remained to act on this principle.

## Conclusion

The creation of ad hoc ICTs for the former Yugoslavia and Rwanda, discussed in the next chapter, were predicated on the legacy of the Nuremberg and Tokyo tribunals. The explosion of interest in transitional justice and belief in normative standards of human rights can also be traced to the post-WW2 reordering of international law and international politics. Nuremberg and Tokyo were predicated on the principle of ending impunity, differentiating right from wrong in the conduct of international affairs, and establishing a link between peace and justice – at both an international and a domestic level. In spite of significant flaws, and a somewhat ambiguous legacy as far as the latter is concerned, the post-WW2 trials were of monumental significance in setting a precedent and in pushing forward international law. In 1993, Madeleine Albright could affirm that, 'international humanitarian law today is impressively codified, well understood, agreed upon, and enforceable'.[36]

However, it was not until the end of the Cold War that this precedent was followed up – first with the establishment of ad hoc tribunals
and then with a range of other mechanisms aimed at securing peace
through justice. There existed extensive and well-developed rules of
international humanitarian law, which were being flouted on a daily
basis and those responsible were liable to be held criminally responsible. The 'missing link' was the absence of an international institution competent to carry out the trials. The reasons why these
violations were acted upon in 1993, where they had continued with
impunity elsewhere, will be examined in the following chapter.

# 2

# Ad hoc International Criminal Tribunals: The ICTY and ICTR

Almost 50 years after the close of proceedings at Nuremberg, its legacy was a crucial element in the decision to establish international criminal tribunals for the former Yugoslavia and Rwanda, in 1993 and 1994 respectively. The creation of the first ICT since Nuremberg and Tokyo, the International Criminal Tribunal for the Former Yugoslavia (ICTY), was the result of the convergence of a set of political, legal and diplomatic factors: the development of international humanitarian law and the Nuremberg legacy; developments in international relations following the end of the Cold War allowing for more concerted action on humanitarian issues and focus on 'softer' elements of security; and events in the former Yugoslavia and Rwanda, especially the nature and extent of atrocities and the failure of the international community to take effective action to curb the violence. The establishment of the ICTY and ICTR appeared to signal the advent of a developing norm of 'international judicial intervention',[1] based on the understanding that justice was a non-negotiable element of sustainable peace-building. It was a crucial step on the road to the establishment of a permanent International Criminal Court (ICC) – see chapter 3 – with the adoption of the Rome Statute in July 1998, and the experience of the tribunals holds important lessons for the ICC.

Yet, aside from this major contribution, their record has been mixed, and forceful criticisms have been voiced about the costly and time-consuming process and its relative lack of impact on peace and reconciliation in the Balkans and Rwanda, respectively.[2] In part, this is due to the fact that expectations were set too high in the first place and there was a tendency to underestimate the scale of the undertaking. As time went on, 'tribunal fatigue' set in, leading to the demand for completion strategies from the ICTs and a search for alternative less costly and time-consuming measures, such as the hybrid systems of domestic and international justice being implemented in Cambodia, East Timor, Kosovo and Sierra Leone.[3]

Both tribunals are now over a decade old, so this is a good time to examine their records. This chapter provides a history and background to the establishment of the ICTY and ICTR and discusses some of the main obstacles they have faced in bringing justice to the former Yugoslavia and Rwanda. It considers political and legal issues surrounding the establishment of the tribunals, their organization and structure, the process of launching investigations, issues of jurisdiction and procedure, state cooperation and obtaining custody of accused. It will be argued that the record of the ICTs demonstrates that the pursuit of international criminal justice is not only a complex, lengthy and difficult process, but is also inextricably tied up in political considerations. Moving on to discuss the tribunals' role in bringing peace through justice, it will be argued that expectations about the tribunals role in international peace and security, as a deterrent to future atrocities and as a mechanism for reconciliation, need to be carefully assessed in light of what the tribunals *can* do, rather than what some have argued they *should* do.

## International Judicial Intervention

The decision to establish the ICTY was taken by the UN Security Council in Resolution 808, adopted on 22 February 1993. The tribunal was established and the Statute adopted on 25 May 1993 (Resolution 827). The ICTY was the first such undertaking since Nuremberg and Tokyo. It was the first international *criminal* tribunal, the first to enforce the body of modern international humanitarian law and to create an international system of justice based on an amalgamation of common and civil law procedures, and including a victims and witnesses programme, a legal aid scheme and training and provision for defence counsel. It was also the first international tribunal to have to grapple with issues of state cooperation, including obtaining custody of accused, and to have to decide what, with whom and where to begin investigations. As such, it offers a number of important lessons. Moreover, the mode of establishment under Chapter VII of the UN Charter as a measure for international peace and security was truly innovative and had a number of implications for its mandate and operation.

The decision to invoke Chapter VII for this purpose was essentially political. Although no similar undertaking had been made before 1993, the establishment of a tribunal did not require any change to the legal framework. The important shift that occurred was in the interpretation of the powers and responsibilities of the Security Council. This shift was part of a process that saw the reinterpretation of the meaning of 'threat to international peace and security' paving the way for the invocation of Chapter VII in situations that, prior to the early 1990s, would have been considered outside the remit of the Security Council, such as the protection of human rights within the borders of a single state.[4] The watershed in the determination of a threat to international peace and security directly opened the way for the establishment of a tribunal, since it meant that violations of international humanitarian law could formally be determined a threat to international peace and security. Coupled with this was the decision to employ a wholly new tool in relation to the former Yugoslavia – international criminal justice. This was an explicit recognition of a perceived link between peace and justice as mutually reinforcing objectives.[5]

The creation of the ICTY was the culmination of a series of incremental measures taken by the UN Security Council starting in July 1992, when the Council reaffirmed that all parties were under an obligation to respect international humanitarian law. On 4 August 1992, the Security Council expressed its deep concern at reports of 'widespread violations of international humanitarian law and in particular reports of the imprisonment and abuse of civilians in these camps'. Later that month, following the transmission on 6 August 1992 of ITN footage from the Omarska camp in the Prijedor region of north-western Bosnia, Resolution 771 demanded the immediate cessation of all breaches of international humanitarian law, including those involved in the practice of 'ethnic cleansing', and unimpeded access for relevant international humanitarian organizations to camps, prisons and detention centres. The Resolution also called upon states and international humanitarian organizations to collate 'substantiated information' relating to violations to be made available to the Security Council. Finally, on 6 October 1992, the Council requested the Secretary-General to establish a Commission of Experts to examine evidence of international humanitarian law violations, including information collected by states and international organizations.[6] Meanwhile, the German Foreign Minister, Klaus Kinkel, proposed the establishment of a tribunal at the London Conference on Former Yugoslavia on 26 August 1992 and in December 1992, Lawrence

Eagleburger made what has become known as his 'naming names speech' in which he announced that the US had identified ten suspected war criminals who should be prosecuted, including Slobodan Milošević, and the Bosnian Serb political and military leaders, Radovan Karadžić and Ratko Mladić.

The decision to establish the ICTY was essentially political. However, although it was set up to serve a political goal – the restoration and maintenance of international peace and security – it was in itself a judicial institution. Some, like David Scheffer, former US Ambassador at Large for War Crimes Issues, welcomed the establishment of the tribunal as a form of 'international judicial intervention' that could prove to be the 'shiny new hammer' in the 'civilized world's box of foreign policy tools'.[7] Others were less optimistic, raising a number of pragmatic, political and legal objections.[8] Some argued that it was no more than a 'fig leaf' to cover up the lack of more concerted action to put a stop to the atrocities that were being committed in the Yugoslav war.[9] Others raised concerns that it was unrealistic to expect it to work, that it was inherently selective because it could not address all crimes and that, far from contributing to peace, it was an obstruction to the peace process.[10] These criticisms will be addressed below.

The ICTY's first major contribution was to provide a precedent for the establishment of a second ad hoc tribunal for Rwanda in November 1994. The ICTR is often treated as the poor relation to the ICTY and certainly attracts significantly less international and scholarly attention than its older sibling, but its record is equally important. As with the ICTY, it was condemned as being just a means by which the international community was seen to be 'doing something' in the wake of abject failure. Unlike the ICTY, however, the ICTR was established at the request of the new government of Rwanda, although it later raised objections as to its precise form and location. The Rwandan government's request for a tribunal was based on a number of interlocking factors, including the sheer scale of the genocide that had occurred; in order to avoid suspicion of vengeful justice; to promote national reconciliation and construction of a new society through equitable justice; and for the pragmatic reason that it would be easier to obtain custody of those at higher levels who had sought refuge outside Rwanda.

When the establishment of the tribunal was put to the vote, however, the Rwandan government came out against it. This was not because it had changed its mind as to the desirability of an international tribunal, but rather because it was unhappy with its form. The government had hoped for more control, and argued that its temporal jurisdiction was too restrictive (covering 1994 only), its composition and structure 'inappropriate and ineffective', that it would waste resources on crimes short of genocide and that it allowed for the participation in choosing judges of those who were alleged to have taken an active part in the war (namely, French judges). In addition, the government argued that holding trials and imprisoning those found guilty outside Rwanda, together with disparity in sentencing between the ICTR and national courts, would lead to inequality of justice. The relationship between the ICTR and the Rwandan government has been a difficult one, which has hindered the tribunal's ability to dispense justice, as well as its ability to contribute to peace and reconciliation, as discussed below.

The political, practical, legal and logistical challenges[11] faced by both the ICTY and the ICTR can be grouped under three headings: first, the process of setting up the court and launching investigations; second, ensuring that standards for fair trial are not only met, but exceeded – that justice is not only done, but is seen to be done; and third, and linked to all of these, the need to obtain state cooperation.

## Establishing a Court and Launching Investigations

For the ICTY, Resolution 827 established the bare bones. The task following the adoption of this Resolution was to put the meat on the bones. This was by no means a simple or straightforward task, particularly in light of difficulties with funding and political wrangling over the appointment of a Chief Prosecutor.[12] Largely because of this, the first organ to be established was the Chambers, which was staffed even before there were cases to be tried. In their first session, from 17 to 30 November 1993, the judges wrote the first set of Rules of Procedure and Evidence, as well as regulations for the appointment of a defence counsel and rules of detention. After this, there was not a great deal else for them to do until the confirmation of the first indictment in November 1994 and the commencement of the first trial, that of Duško Tadić in May 1995.

The ICTY also faced a number of issues in the early period of operation to do with staffing, organization, amalgamation of different procedures and backgrounds, and launching investigations. The ICTR faced additional logistical obstacles. Both the tribunal in Arusha and the investigation unit in Kigali had to be set up and function in towns with limited infrastructure.[13] They also had more difficulty attracting high-calibre staff compared to its sister tribunal in the more salubrious setting of The Hague. The ICTR suffered in many regards from being the poor relation of the ICTY. It also shared the Chief Prosecutor with the ICTY until as late as September 2003 – Carla Del Ponte – when a replacement Prosecutor was appointed for the ICTR.[14]

Launching war crimes investigations threw up a number of practical, technical, logistical and philosophical questions. Where to start, given the sheer scale of crimes committed? How to gain access to the crime scene, especially while the war was ongoing? How to gain access to evidence, including collections of documents? How to carry out forensic investigations? How to identify potential witnesses? How to identify suspects and obtain custody of accused? Resolving these questions was made more difficult by problems relating to the guarantee of witness protection and to linguistic and cultural issues with victims and witnesses, which proved to be even more of a worry with regard to the ICTR. In addition, the investigation and prosecution teams were faced with trying to amalgamate different legal systems and expertise, which raised questions about the precise form of the indictment and witness statements. In the absence of precedent, it was not clear what the precise requirements were for putting forward a prima facie case. This was compounded by inherent difficulties in trying to enforce international humanitarian law as criminal law, in particular with regard to the necessity of proving a number of subjective elements for jurisdiction, as well as the objective elements of the crime.

Most important was the decision about where to focus investigations. Because it was impossible to prosecute everyone, there had to be a degree of selectivity. There were two possible approaches: either investigate crimes and identify perpetrators then move up the chain of command, or pick targets and build cases. Unlike the ICTR, which focused from the outset on the leaders of the genocide, the ICTY's early indictments were largely targeted at 'small-fry'. This was because early investigations were made considerably more difficult by the fact that an armed conflict was ongoing, making access to evidence, victims and witnesses almost impossible, but, at the same time, the Prosecutor was facing considerable pressure, both from the judges who had been appointed and from the tribunal's international sponsors, to begin to be seen to be acting concretely.[15]

The ICTY's Office of the Prosecutor (OTP) took the UN Commission of Experts Report as their starting point and concentrated primarily on four areas: Vukovar, Prijedor, the Lasva River

Valley and Celebici. This has been characterized as a 'pyramid approach', whereby the indictment and prosecution of a large number of lower-level perpetrators would lead to the few at the top. The first indictment was confirmed on 4 November 1994,[16] and a further 19 Bosnian Serbs were indicted on 13 February 1995 for atrocities allegedly committed during summer 1992 at the Omarska Camp in north-western Bosnia.[17] With the handover of Tadić from Germany in April 1995, the Dutch daily newspaper *De Telegraaf* felt able to declare that 'The paper tiger is roaring'.[18] By 1999, when the second Chief Prosecutor, Louise Arbour, departed, the ITCY was a fully functioning international court. The indictment later in 1995 of higher-level accused, including Radovan Karadžić and Ratko Mladić, the former political and military leaders of the Bosnian Serbs, as well as the detention and transfer of a number of accused from summer 1997 onwards and the indictment of Slobodan Milošević in May 1999, were important landmarks.

A notable element was the shift from issuing public indictments and Rule 61 hearings (whereby the evidence would be heard in open court in the absence of the accused, leading to an international arrest warrant being issued) to sealed indictments. Arbour also shifted towards more targeted investigations at higher levels. This was demonstrated most dramatically during the Kosovo crisis. The indictment of Milošević in the middle of NATO's bombing campaign at the end of May 1999 was seen by some as a political act, but Arbour maintained that it was a result of the evidence being made available. It certainly raised questions about how far the Prosecutor could allow him- or herself to be led by the evidence when it was provided or withheld on political grounds, but it is difficult to see how else, in an international context, they might operate. Nevertheless, it did not help the perception of the ICTY among the Serbian population; nor did the decision not to investigate alleged war crimes committed by NATO during its bombing campaign.[19]

Unlike the ICTY, the Rwanda tribunal focused, from the start, on higher-level perpetrators, leaving others to national courts and the *gacaca* system.[20] Although this has satisfied some, who feel that *international* justice should be reserved for those bearing the 'greatest responsibility', it created a rather uncomfortable situation with regard to Rwandan domestic courts, which were mandated to try lower-level accused. Whilst those in international custody were well treated and faced the prospect of life imprisonment, at worst, those in domestic prisons were held in appalling conditions and faced the death sentence should they be convicted. The list of indictees includes the former prime minister, four other ministers, prefects, bourgmestres and others holding leadership positions in 1994, including the leadership of the *Interahamwe*. But all of the accused so far have been Hutu, with the exception of one Belgian-Italian, Georges Ruggui, which has led to allegations of 'victor's justice'.[21] Even limited attempts to investigate both sides have been stymied by the government of Rwanda.

## Jurisdiction and Procedure

Another significant challenge for the ICTs was the fact that they were operating in a wholly novel context. Both were *international* courts, working within a novel and innovative system of law, comprising elements from adversarial and inquisitorial criminal procedure traditions. They also had to operate on relatively small budgets, and with limited staff. And it was a steep learning curve, with no margin of error. At the most fundamental level, if the tribunals were to fulfil their mandates, it was crucial to ensure that the conduct of trials not only met international standards for a fair trial, but even exceeded them. With regard to the ICTY, former President Cassese stated in 1997:

> [T]he Tribunal relies on the widespread publication of its judicial acts and commentaries thereon for the fulfilment of its mandate. In accordance with the well-known maxim, 'Justice must not only be done, but must be seen to be done', it is not enough for the International Tribunal simply to administer international criminal justice impartially and with due regard for the rights of the accused. It must also carry out this activity under the scrutiny of the international community.[22]

The method of establishment and the external mandate of the tribunals had a number of core implications for jurisdiction and procedure. First, there was a need to exert 'reasonable judicial flexibility', in order to strike the correct balance between competing imperatives of politics, justice and equality.[23] But legal and political imperatives were not always coincidental. There was a set of balancing acts that had to be successfully juggled by the tribunals: the fair, impartial and expeditious administration of justice set against the sheer volume of material and complexity of cases; and the rights of the accused versus the rights of victims and witnesses, and the international interest in prosecution. Second, in the context of an international tribunal there were additional tensions created by the welding together of a number of different legal traditions, most obviously civil law and common law procedures and principles. Third, for the ICTY, the speed with which the Statute was drafted and adopted – the flurry of activity to turn what Cassese termed a 'nebulous idea' into a living reality – meant that there was no room for debate on the technicalities, save for a number of interpretative statements made by members of the Security Council. As one of the judges at the ICTY stated, the tribunal was 'navigating uncharted waters'.[24] Finally, the drafters of the Statute were keen to avert one of the major criticisms of the Nuremberg and Tokyo tribunals being levelled at the ICTY – that the prosecution of individuals for acts which were illegal only after the fact violated the principle *nullum crimen sine lege, nulla poena sine lege* (no act is criminal unless it is laid down in law and no act can be punished unless punishment is prescribed by law; see chapter 1).

This helps explain why the ICTY Statute was very conservative.[25] As an ad hoc tribunal, it had a limited and specific mandate, and its competence was restricted accordingly in terms of subject matter and temporal and territorial jurisdiction. The ICTR Statute was less restrictive in scope. Unlike at the ICTY, crimes against humanity did not require a nexus with armed conflict, and the Statute specifically included jurisdiction for violations of the laws and customs of war committed in non-international armed conflict. At the ICTY, the question of whether or not the conflict was international, crucial for the application of the 'grave breaches' provision of the Geneva Conventions, was left open, to be determined on a case-by-case basis. This was politically significant because the question of the character of the conflicts raised issues of statehood, sovereignty and recognition, which could only be resolved with reference to political as well as legal criteria, such as the timing of events and the motives of the recognizing states.

The Statute of the ICTY was compiled by common law experts who made some concessions to civil law, and it contains inherent tensions. The Prosecutor is independent, as in adversarial systems, but the judges take a more active role than they would normally, and there is no jury. The hybrid system, comprising elements from adversarial and inquisitorial traditions, also had implications for procedure – in particular, rules of evidence. Whilst a common law system has stringent rules, civil law judges have a much wider remit in terms of admissibility. In the Tadić case, the admission of hearsay evidence was challenged, but the Trial Chamber found it could admit such evidence as long as it was 'relevant and found to have probative value'.

Both tribunals have also been harshly criticized about the length of trials, which in some cases has come close to abrogating the right of the accused to be tried 'without undue delay'. In the tribunals' defence, both had to deal with cases that were legally and factually very complex, involving large volumes of documents, most of which needed translating into at least one of the three official languages (BCS, English and French at the ICTY and Kinyarwanda, English and French at the ICTR), and hundreds of witnesses, whose statements and testimony required translation into all three languages. As well as the complexity of the cases, part of the reason trials took so long was that there were not enough judges or courtrooms to deal with the volume of work. However, there have been attempts to find a way of speeding things up. In 2000, a UN Group of Experts made a number of recommendations, including that there should be a pool of *ad litem* judges established who could serve as needed. In November 2000, the Security Council duly established such a pool for the ICTY and in August 2002 for the ICTR. Other measures were implemented in both tribunals in order to ensure speedier trials, including amending the Rules of Procedure and Evidence to ensure that more could be dealt with at the pre-trial stage, and on the basis of written submissions only. Some motions could even be dealt with by a single judge, rather than requiring the full chamber to sit.[26] Also, a fourth courtroom was built in Arusha and a third in The Hague.

Equality of arms has been another bone of contention. Although the tribunals eventually succeeded in establishing a unique legal aid system, and provided some degree of training and resources for defence counsel, the resources available to the defence have not been as extensive as for the Prosecutor. The ICTR in particular has been tainted by allegations of corruption, with defence counsel splitting fees with clients.

## State Cooperation and Judicial Assistance

A major practical difficulty facing the tribunals was their lack of authority over the area in which they have jurisdiction, meaning that they are reliant on the state apparatus for access to evidence and witnesses and for obtaining custody of accused. According to Cassese, the ICTY is 'like a giant who has no arms and no legs. To walk and work he needs artificial limbs. These artificial limbs are the state authorities. Without their help the Tribunal cannot operate.'[27] In Bosnia, the situation was alleviated to some extent by the presence of an international force, but that force was not tasked with providing assistance to the ICTY as its primary role, nor was it able, even it were willing, to carry out all the tasks that would be expected of a police force operating in a domestic environment.

There are several ways in which the ICTs are reliant on state cooperation: political and diplomatic support, financial support, assistance in obtaining evidence and locating and interviewing witnesses, security and logistical support to investigations, obtaining custody of accused, and provision of detention facilities in which convicted persons serve sentences. The military in particular were faced with additional new tasks. Calls for the UN Protection Force in Bosnia (UNPROFOR) to assist tribunal investigators met with initial resistance as it was felt that non-military tasks compromised the impartiality of the peacekeeping force. It was said that the UN was 'torn between its black robes and its blue helmets'. [28] Ultimately, the degree of cooperation depended on an individual state's or even an officer's interpretation of mandate. Cooperation increased with the military after the deployment of first the Implementation Force (IFOR) and then the Stabilisaton Force (SFOR). Again, there was no consistent pattern of cooperation and, initially, IFOR was more concerned with urgent tasks to do with the immediate implementation of the peace agreement such as the withdrawal of forces and disarmament. The first arrest was carried out by the UN Transitional Authority in Eastern Slovenia (UNTAES) in June 1997. The fact that this was not followed by widespread unrest emboldened SFOR troops to carry out their first detention operation in Bosnia on 10 July 1997.

Although the establishment of the ICTs under Chapter VII created binding obligations on all states, reiterated in Articles 28 and 29 of the Statutes of the ICTR and ICTY respectively, in practice, the model of 'voluntary compliance' best describes the mechanism for cooperation and the role of the Prosecutor is crucial in oiling this mechanism and ensuring its effective operation. This worked better with some states than with others. Carla Del Ponte, who took over as Prosecutor following Arbour's departure in 1999, pursued a markedly different approach to that of her predecessors, which ruffled some feathers within and outside the Office. It would be an understatement to say that she has not been popular in the former Yugoslavia, particularly among Serbs, who talk of her and the Office as 'the new Gestapo'.[29]

Although 'voluntary compliance' works with the willing, there is a need to innovate new means of effecting 'involuntary compliance' where cooperation is not forthcoming. For many years, Serbia and Montenegro (formerly the Federal Republic of Yugoslavia, FRY) consistently refused to cooperate, while Croatia cooperated on some things, and stalled on others. In Bosnia, the attitudes of the authorities of the different entities reflected their attitudes towards the tribunal.

On the surface, Belgrade initially adopted a conciliatory tone, and some progress was made shortly after the Dayton Agreement was signed; in January 1996,[30] President Cassese obtained the agreement of the Belgrade authorities for the Prosecutor to open a field office there. In addition, the Belgrade authorities suggested that they might be willing to arrest and transfer non-nationals to the tribunal, although they maintained that transfer of nationals was precluded by extradition laws.[31] The failure to arrest Karadžić and Mladić either when they visited Belgrade to attend Djordje Djukić's funeral on 21 May 1996, or on 28 May when they attended talks with Milošević, provided hard evidence of their attitude towards the tribunal. Then, in 1998 and 1999, the Belgrade government put an effective halt to investigations being carried out in Kosovo. Following the Račak massacre in January 1999, the President of the Security Council issued a statement 'deplor[ing] the decision by the Federal Republic of Yugoslavia to refuse access to the Prosecutor of the International Tribunal and call[ing] upon the Federal Republic of Yugoslavia to co-operate fully with the International Tribunal'.[32] But no further concrete action was taken, which prompted the President of the tribunal to question whether it was 'worse to condemn behaviour and then tolerate it than *not* to condemn it at all'.

During and after the Kosovo campaign and the indictment of Milošević along with senior members of his government, there was no relationship between Serbia and Montenegro and the tribunal. The Yugoslav Justice Minister, Petar Jojić, called Del Ponte a 'prostitute for the US', in a 25-page open letter, which was 'laced with obscenities'. He said that the tribunal was using tricks to obtain custody of accused, and that Del Ponte was 'running [a] dungeon which, like the worst whore, you have sold out to the Americans and to which you bring innocent Serbs by force, by kidnapping and murder'.[33] After he lost the election, in October 2000, there were high hopes that Milošević would be delivered to The Hague, but Vojislav Koštunica, who succeeded Milošević, pledged that he would not pursue Milošević or his family.

Milošević's eventual transfer to The Hague on 28 June 2001 was a watershed, not only in the attitude of Belgrade towards the tribunal, but also that of the Bosnian Serb entity and the Croatian government. Both made highly visible demonstrations of cooperation: in Croatia, two members of the Cabinet resigned in protest at the decision to hand over two Croatian army officers indicted by the tribunal; and the Bosnian Serb administration pledged that it would make every effort to detain and transfer accused, including making an amendment to the constitution in order to allow for it.[34]

Croatia has also been more than fully cooperative. In early 1996, the President of the tribunal issued a press release stating that although the Croatian authorities in Zagreb had allowed the OTP to set up a field office in Zagreb, and to carry out investigations unhindered, the Croatian government had not at that point passed implementing legislation to give effect to the Statute of the tribunal, nor had it executed arrest warrants.[35] In 1996, one accused was arrested and another surrendered voluntarily through the mediation of the Croat authorities; and in October 1997, ten Bosnian Croats surrendered to the custody of the tribunal. In spite of these developments, the Croatian government was almost as intransigent as Serbia and Montenegro in its dealings with the ICTY. The difference was that it professed a desire to cooperate and blamed any lack of cooperation on legal obstacles; whereas Serbia and Montenegro and the government of Republika Srpska refused point blank on political as well as legal grounds.

The situation improved following the death of Franjo Tudjman – the new Croatian state's first President – in December 2000. The new President, Stipe Mesić, had already given evidence before the tribunal in 1998. In February 2000, Mesić said in an interview with the Serbian opposition TV station, Studio B, that he was ready to testify against Milošević.[36] The Prime Minister, Ivica Račan, pledged cooperation. In November 2000, Del Ponte acknowledged that there had been an improvement in relations 'when compared with the previous policy of obstruction and delay adopted by the former government'; but that 'where Croatia perceives cooperation to be against its political or narrow security interests, a real difficulty still exists'. Indeed, for Zagreb, it largely boiled down to the fate of one man, Croatian Army General Ante Gotovina, widely seen as a national hero for his part in the August 1995 campaign to retake the Krajina from the Serbs, 'Operation Storm', and indicted for war crimes and crimes against humanity by the ICTY.[37]

The relationship between the ICTR and the government of Rwanda has been no less troublesome. It was further damaged by then Prosecutor Carla Del Ponte's determination to pursue 'special investigations' into the conduct of Rwandan Patriotic Front (RPF) forces in 1994.[38] The Rwandan government repeatedly called for her resignation and she was eventually removed in September 2003, when a single Prosecutor was appointed for each tribunal. The official reason given for this was pragmatic, but it fuelled suspicion that the Security Council had succumbed to pressure from the Rwandan government and that this signalled the end of the 'special investigations'.[39] The verdict on how Del Ponte's successor, Hassan B. Jallow, has handled the issue remains to be seen, but given that 31 December 2004 was the cut-off for investigations at both tribunals, it seems likely that there will be no cases concerning former RPF personnel.

## Justice, Peace and Reconciliation

The ICTY and the ICTR have both now embarked on 'completion strategies' aimed at finishing all investigations by the end of 2007, all trials by the end of 2008 and all appeals by 2010. More than ten years after their establishment, and as they near completion of their mandates, how should we judge their achievements?

Both tribunals were created as measures for the restoration and maintenance of international peace and security. Resolution 808 (22 February 1993) emphasized the purpose of the ICTY: 'to put an end to such crimes and to take effective measures to bring to justice the persons who are responsible for them. *Convinced* that in the particular circumstances of the former Yugoslavia the establishment of an international tribunal would enable to be achieved and would contribute to the restoration and maintenance of peace.' The mandate was threefold: deterrence, justice and peace. The mandate of the ICTR specifically includes a fourth element: its purported contribution to 'a process of national reconciliation'.

The ICTY's 'five core achievements' are also helpful in setting out the goals the tribunal set for itself (and what it considers it has achieved): spearheading the shift from impunity to accountability; establishing the facts; bringing justice to thousands of victims and giving them a voice; accomplishments in international law; and strengthening the Rule of Law.[40] Although some headway has been made in all these areas for both tribunals, there are significant failings as well.

### Delivering justice

Easiest to measure is the tribunals' record in delivering justice. By June 2006, the ICTR had handed down 22 judgments involving

28 accused.[41] As mentioned above, the judgments delivered so far have involved one prime minister, four ministers, one prefect, six bourgmestres and several others holding leadership positions during the genocide of 1994. Of these, 25 were convicted and 3 acquitted. Eleven trials were in progress as of June 2006, involving a total of 27 accused. They include eight ministers, one parliamentarian, three prefects, three bourgmestres, eight military officers, and others holding leadership positions; 18 remain at large.[42]

At the ICTY, a total of 161 have been charged. By June 2006, proceedings had been completed against 55 people, with 47 convictions and 8 acquittals. Indictments were withdrawn against 37 accused (3 of whom died in the Detention Unit whilst on trial). At the time of writing, 45 remain in custody at the Detention Unit in The Hague and 17 are on provisional release. Trials are ongoing against 24 accused and a further 13 are at the appeal stage. There are 22 at the pre-trial stage and 9 cases have so far been transferred to national courts. Meanwhile, 6 accused remain at large, including Karadžić and Mladić.

Both the ICTY and the ICTY have provided some measure of justice to victims. Not only have they enabled victims and witnesses to come forward and have their stories heard; also, a number of landmark judgments have been handed down. In January 2001, Biljana Plavšić, former Republika Srpska President, voluntarily surrendered to the ICTY. The case did not come to trial; instead, she entered into a plea agreement with the Office of the Prosecutor. In return for her guilty plea to one count of persecution, the Prosecutor dropped charges for genocide and recommended a sentence of less than life imprisonment. Plavšić was sentenced to 11 years' imprisonment in February 2003. This was controversial: while some welcomed her expressions of remorse and the fact that it put on record the accountability of the highest echelons of the Bosnian Serb wartime leadership, others argued that the practice of plea-bargaining was inappropriate because it did not allow for sufficient retribution and that dropping such serious charges undermined the overall record.[43] The trial of another senior Bosnian Serb leader, Momćilo Krajišnik, began on 4 February 2004. He was accused of participation in the same 'joint criminal enterprise' as Plavšić, which resulted in 'the partial destruction of the Bosnian Muslim and Bosnian Croatian national, ethnical racial or religious groups, in the territories within Bosnia and Herzegovina'.

Another significant judgment concerned Radislav Krstić, former Chief of Staff/Deputy Commander, VRS Drina Corps. Krstić's was the first conviction for genocide in connection with the massacre at Srebrenica in 1995.[44] This ruling was an important landmark for the ICTY, setting a precedent for other cases. However, while the ruling that genocide had in fact occurred at Srebrenica was welcomed, the Appeals Chamber judgment attracted some criticism on the grounds that the conviction for 'aiding and abetting' might be stretching the legal definition of genocide too far.[45] Other landmark cases concerned the bombardment of Sarajevo (Stanislav Galić), the trial of a prominent Bosnian Croat, Dario Kordić, and the trial of three Bosnia Muslim commanders for crimes committed against Bosnian Serbs at the Celebici camp. The absence of a judgment in the Milošević case might be seen as a drawback, but by others as a blessing in disguise. Either way, the judgment might have provided grist to the mill of his supporters as evidence of either his innocence (if he were acquitted) or the fact that the ICTY was so politicized that it was a foregone conclusion (if he were convicted).[46]

## Contribution to international criminal law

Both tribunals have made substantial inroads into substantive law issues, in particular with regard to the definition of genocide, the application of 'grave breaches' provisions, elucidation and expansion of the laws applicable to non-international armed conflict, the definition of crimes against humanity and the nature of command responsibility.[47] The ICTR has created a rich body of jurisprudence, especially on genocide. It was the first trial of genocide held at an international tribunal (*Akayesu*), the first to establish rape as act of genocide (also *Akayesu*) and the first time that a head of government was convicted for the crime of genocide (Jean Kambanda, Prime Minister of Rwanda). The *Kambanda* case also established that heads of state were not immune from prosecution. His guilty plea was also the first time that an accused person acknowledged his guilt for the crime of genocide before an ICT. The judgment in the 'Media case' at the ICTR was the first since the conviction of Julius Streicher at Nuremberg in which the role of the media has been examined in the context of international criminal justice.[48] In spite of the *Akayesu* case, critics argue that the ICTR should have focused more on crimes of rape and sexual violence, since they were so endemic during the conflict. By May 2005, rape and sexual assault had featured in respect of only 5 out of 25 accused in completed cases. However, of the 25 on trial at the time of writing, 19 have been charged with rape and sexual assault.[49]

The tribunals have also made significant innovations in international criminal law and practice that will be important for subsequent attempts to enforce international humanitarian law, including in the areas of protective measures for witnesses, the confidentiality and disclosure of information relevant for the national security of states, guilty pleas of accused and duress as a defence.[50] However, one of the ICTR's main goals, and something that was expected of the ICTY, was to aid in the development of the domestic legal system and help reinforce a culture based on the rule of law. In both cases, the tribunals have failed in this regard. It is only relatively recently that they have even begun to address this issue, pressured by completion strategies which envisage handing over cases to domestic courts.

## Restoring and maintaining peace

Providing justice and contributing to the development of the law is not enough; it is a means to an end, not an end in itself. As discussed in the Introduction to this volume, the nexus between peace and justice is to be found in the contribution that justice can make to the process of establishing sustainable peace. In the case of the ICTY and ICTR, international criminal justice was intended to make a direct contribution to the restoration of international peace and security, as already discussed. In both cases, the nature and extent of atrocities meant that lasting peace and reconciliation were deemed impossible without some form of accountability for the ordering and commission of such crimes.

Criminal trials can play an important role by providing a form of individual accountability, acting as a deterrent and ensuring that victims' needs for retribution and punishment are met. They can also help contribute to the establishment of a society based on respect for the rule of law and help move the peace process forward by removing or excluding perpetrators and fostering reconciliation. They can also provide a much-needed impartial record of the conflict based on concrete evidence admitted in court, although this is limited in so far as it relates to an individual accused, rather than explicitly seeking to establish a pattern of events and naming those most responsible. Set against these potential benefits must be warnings as to the ways in which such a process might in fact undermine efforts to achieve peace. The judicial process is slow and cumbersome and there are dangers that it might be destabilizing to a fragile peace, especially in the short term. There is also the risk that proceedings are perceived as thinly disguised mechanisms for exacting revenge – a possibility that is to some extent obviated in an international court, although, as we have seen, both the ICTY and ICTR have attracted allegations of bias and victor's justice.

## Deterrence

In the short term, given that the ICTY was established while the conflict was ongoing, it was hoped that it would act as a deterrent, preventing further atrocities. Clearly, it failed in this regard, as the tribunal was established in May 1993 and the worst single atrocity of the war occurred in July 1995, at Srebrenica, after both Radovan Karadžić and Ratko Mladić had been indicted. Equally, although there has been no resumption of violence in Rwanda, it did not prevent widespread commission of atrocities in neighbouring DRC, or in other parts of Africa, including Uganda, Sierra Leone, Liberia and Sudan.

## Historical record

Both tribunals have made some headway with the establishment of a record. Landmark judgments concerning key individuals and cases have helped to provide an impartial and comprehensive account of the genocide in Rwanda and during the Yugoslav War. For the ICTY, in particular, the ability to move from indicting relatively low-level criminals to prosecuting those at the apex of political and military leadership was a positive development. At the ICTR, the establishment of an historical record is important to show that the genocide was not the product of primitive tribal hatreds, but was orchestrated by a military and political elite that sought to maintain its power through extermination of an entire section of the population.

## Reconciliation

However, while it is acknowledged that the ICTR has played a crucial role in shedding light on the atrocities and raising awareness of the plight of victims at an international level, the nature of the conflict and ongoing instability in Rwanda have hindered progress in efforts at national reconciliation.[51] Given that the genocide tore apart the social fabric and infrastructure of Rwanda, it may be unrealistic to hope that a tribunal alone can put it back together. Similarly, in the former Yugoslavia, societies remain divided along ethnic lines, and in spite of some progress on the political level, reconciliation with the past and between victims and perpetrators seems to be still some way off. Moreover, as one commentator has noted already, 'it is difficult to imagine circumstances in which *national* reconciliation could be created by an *international* institution'.[52] In both cases, reconciliation may not only be an unrealistic goal, but one which is extremely difficult to measure.

A recent study of attitudes towards the ICTY in the region pointed to 'a gap between the international community's aspirations for justice and how its application was perceived by those most affected in the region'.[53] A number of factors conspired to widen this gap, including the remoteness of the proceedings from the population, the lack of involvement of local actors and the relatively high cost and complexity of extremely lengthy trials; and, for the ICTY, the initial strategy of building cases against lower-level accused, the refusal of the Prosecutor to pursue investigations of alleged war crimes committed by NATO forces during the Kosovo campaign and the failure, to date, to obtain custody of Karadžić and Mladić. Meanwhile, James Meernik's study of the contribution of the ICTY to 'societal peace' in Bosnia found little evidence to suggest that the ICTY had an impact on cooperation amongst groups within society. In fact, in some instances, it had precisely the opposite effect, with groups reacting with more hostility towards each other after an arrest or indictment.[54] A significant problem is that it was perceived as biased on ethnic grounds. Mostly, it is perceived to be anti-Serb, even though the most cursory glance through the list of indictments would confirm that it has targeted all parties to the conflict.

A shift in attitudes was apparent with the release of the report of the Srebrenica Commission in late 2004, which was accompanied by a formal apology from the RS government: 'The report makes it clear that enormous crimes were committed in the area of Srebrenica in July 1995. . . . The Bosnian Serb Government shares the pain of the families of the Srebrenica victims, is truly sorry and apologizes for the tragedy.'[55] This apology echoed the statement made in June of that year by Dragan Čavić (now President of Republika Srpska), in which he acknowledged that the 'nine July days of the Srebrenica tragedy are a black page in the history of the Serb people'. In early 2005, substantive progress was also made on cooperation with ICTY as a number of former high-ranking officials were transferred to The Hague to face trial. Meanwhile, the inauguration in March 2005 of the War Crimes Chamber in Sarajevo meant that cases could be transferred from ICTY and take place in Bosnia instead.

## Removing perpetrators

There is another way of judging success or failure suggested by a more pragmatic approach. As a tool of politics, the role that judicial mechanisms can play in excluding 'spoilers' from peace processes is useful in and of itself. The exclusion of suspected war criminals such as Karadžić and Mladić from the negotiations leading to the Dayton Agreement and from participation in public life (at least overtly) was beneficial to the process. Even if they are not ultimately brought to justice, their indictment has already served a useful purpose. Aside from Karadžić and Mladić, in the immediate post-Dayton period, suspected war criminals remained at the heart of a network of criminal activity that was thwarting progress on issues as diverse as refugee return, education, healthcare reform and pensions. A November 2000 report lamented 'the continued presence in positions of some prominence of so many people suspected of grave crimes [which] remains a major obstacle to peace building'.[56] Removing some of these individuals through indictment and transfer to The Hague was therefore an important contribution to restoring peace. Removing Milošević was also a key contribution. During the NATO bombing campaign against Serbia in 1999, unprecedented levels of support were provided to the Prosecutor of the ICTY, resulting eventually, along with other factors, in Milošević's indictment in May 1999, his fall from power in October 2000, and his transfer to The Hague to face trial in June 2001.

In the case of Rwanda: 'Notwithstanding the various conflicts between the ICTR and the Rwandese government . . . this policy of accountability, aimed at discrediting the Hutu extremists, has also restrained the extent of anti-Hutu vengeance killings . . . the shadow of the ICTR proceedings . . . have exercised a moderating influence in the post-conflict peace-building process.'[57] Removing and putting on trial the leaders of the genocide has also ensured that they cannot continue to destabilize the country and 'aggravate the moral suffering of survivors'.[58]

## Political leverage

In very concrete terms, war crimes issues – in particular, cooperation with the ICTY – have been pushed to the fore because of pressure exerted by the EU on the governments of Bosnia and Herzegovina, Croatia and Serbia and Montenegro. Dealing with the war crimes legacy is critical not only for its own sake, but also because it is instrumental to these states' membership of Euro-Atlantic institutions, which bring their own set of economic and political benefits. In one sense, both sets of goals are complementary, in as much as each contributes to peace and security in the long term, but there are risks associated with this kind of instrumental approach to justice, especially where a judicial tool is already suspected of politicization, as in the case of the ICTY. [59]

In a statement to the UN Security Council on 9 October 2003, the High Representative of the International Community in Bosnia and Herzegovina, Lord Paddy Ashdown, pointed to a number of issues that indicated that Bosnia might be moving out of the polarized politics of the immediate post-conflict period. However, he said that in order for such progress to be sustainable, Bosnia must move forward on war crimes issues: '[P]eace cannot be described as fully entrenched until the perpetrators of these unspeakable crimes are finally brought to justice.'[60] Dealing with the legacy of war crimes was widely seen as symbolic of Bosnia's having moved forward from the immediate post-Dayton phase, creating a catalyst for progress on other issues and the building of a society based on the rule of law and respect for human rights. In that sense, dealing with the war crimes legacy was not an end in itself, but a means to an end. Getting rid of troublemakers helps, as does establishing a norm of accountability for past crimes, but long-term peace requires a change in the political make-up and outlook.

### Engaging the local population

The impact of these and other developments was somewhat lessened because of perceptions of the ICTY and ICTR among their respective constituencies. A key failing of both tribunals was the lack of a coherent and effective strategy for communication and outreach.[61] This heightened the sense of remoteness – geographical and cultural – from Rwanda and former Yugoslavia, which was manifested in Rwanda in conflicting conceptions of justice and anger at ICTR mismanagement and the slow pace of trials.[62]

An outreach programme was eventually established, but at a fairly late stage and its efforts to engage the Rwandan population have been largely ineffective. In September 2000, an Information Centre was established in Kigali with a library and information material, including video archives of the trials and films and internet access to the court materials. The Centre also organizes press briefings, training sessions and workshops outside Kigali.[63] Optimistically named

*Umusanzu mu Bwiyunge* (Contribution to Reconciliation), the Centre has, however, failed to live up to expectations. It remains out of reach to the majority of Rwandans living in rural areas, attractive only to a 'tiny part of the urban elite'.[64] A survey of 2,091 Rwandans in 2002 found that 87 per cent either were 'not well informed' or 'not informed at all' about the tribunal.[65] This would seem to indicate that it has failed to achieve its aim to provide 'better understanding of and confidence in' the tribunal's work, but this task was made all the more difficult in the face of negative images compounded by the government's criticisms and allegations by survivor groups that it was indifferent to the needs of victims.[66] As one observer has acknowledged: '[W]hether societies come to value tribunals as an equitable and effective way to confront their violent paths may ultimately depend more on the approval of a nation's leaders than in anything an outreach programme can do.'[67]

It should also not be forgotten that it was only in 2000 that Serbia and Montenegro and Croatia got rid of their nationalist governments, and even then not entirely. Combating an extremely effective propaganda machine intent on distributing malicious rumours and fostering negative perceptions of the ICTY may have been more than any tribunal outreach programme could be expected to achieve. After 2000, even when cooperation was forthcoming, it was motivated more by the promise of economic gain, acceptance into the EU and the desire to remove troublesome individuals.[68]

While more work needs to be done assessing their impact, clearly the lack of a concerted outreach strategy has hampered both tribunals' ability to affect the process of national reconciliation among their respective constituencies. The lesson taken on board comprehensively by the Special Court for Sierra Leone and by the ICC was the need for better communication and outreach involving engagement with local civil society groups and non-governmental organizations as well as dissemination of information about the process.[69]

## Conclusion

The ad hoc tribunals were judged by some to have been a missed opportunity. Harshly criticized for their cost and beset by allegations of excessive bureaucracy and inefficiency, the tribunals appeared not to have delivered on their mandates. This is rather a harsh judgement that fails to take into account the significant contributions they have made to international peace and security and international criminal justice. In the words of one victim:

> Were it not for the Tribunal, we would probably be very, very far from the truth and justice. Were it not for the Tribunal, we would perhaps still be discussing whether Srebrenica happened or not, whether the eight thousand people who were killed ever existed at all. All that would be in question were it not for the Tribunal. Keraterm, Manjaca, Trnopolje, all those camps, the crimes in Visegrad, the crimes in Foca, in many other places, in Celebitci, would be in question.[70]

Internationally, the ICTs have made significant contributions to the establishment of a norm of impunity and to consolidating and further developing international criminal law and procedure. As well as being instrumental in the developing normative trend of accountability, in practical terms they were instrumental in the establishment of the permanent ICC and the Special Court for Sierra Leone, both of which, in spite of their own drawbacks, offer improved models of international criminal justice. In conceptual terms, the shortcomings of international criminal justice in addressing the needs of post-conflict societies led to renewed interest in alternative forms of accountability, modelled on the truth commissions established in South Africa and Latin America. The example of the ad hoc tribunals demonstrated that the relationship between justice and peace is complex. We can point to pragmatic ways in which the ICTY in particular has made a contribution to peace, not least in removing perpetrators and creating space for change at the political level, but as for justice leading to reconciliation, this is, at least for now, at best negligible.

However, it should be acknowledged that the scale of the undertaking was mammoth, and, as discussed in chapter 4, a small budget is not always the best measure of an effective institution. The ICTY and the ICTR had very little on which to build; in many regards, they were making things up 'on the hoof', as former President of the ICTY, Gabrielle Kirk Macdonald once acknowledged. They also had to operate in a sometimes hostile international climate and with little or no cooperation from the states most directly affected. Moreover, expecting a tribunal to foster national reconciliation in the face of the tremendous political obstacles in the former Yugoslavia may have been setting expectations rather high. In Rwanda, the attitude of the government has been a significant obstacle to the tribunal's impact, as has its remoteness from the people of Rwanda. When seen in that light, it is remarkable that they made any progress at all, let alone achieved what they did.

## Box 2.1: The Yugoslav War

The dissolution of the Socialist Federal Republic of Yugoslavia (SFRY) in 1991–2 was the proximate cause of a succession of conflicts that made up the Yugoslav War. The war fundamentally altered the demographic make-up of what was the SFRY, leading to widespread displacement and the loss of many thousands of lives. In Bosnia alone, the war claimed over a quarter of a million lives – 7–8,000 of those in a matter of days in Srebrenica in July 1995, and more than 11,000 people were killed in Kosovo at the end of the decade.

A defining element of the war was the practice of 'ethnic cleansing'. This practice involved mass forced population transfers, detention centres where tens of thousands were being killed and tortured, organized massacres, physical destruction of whole towns including major historical, cultural and religious monuments, and the systematic and repeated rape of women. The aim was to clear areas of non-Serb population through mass killing, terror and deportation. In larger towns, the Serbs would lay siege, launching indiscriminate shelling and sniper fire into an area in order to terrorize the civilian population. In smaller, more vulnerable towns and villages, small armed bands, often paramilitary groups (such as Arkan's Tigers, and the White Eagles under the command of Vojislav Seselj) would carry out atrocities to induce capitulation and flight. Such tactics were also employed by Bosnian Croat forces against Bosnian Muslims in the Lašva River Valley area of central Bosnia in 1992–4, and in Operation Storm, launched in August 1995. There were also sporadic atrocities carried out by Bosnian Muslims against Bosnian Serbs, including at detention camps such as the one at Celebici.

The most tragic single occurrence of the war was the attack on Srebrenica in July 1995, in which it is estimated that between 7,000 and 8,000 Bosnian Muslim men and boys were killed. In a matter of days, from 10 to 19 July, approximately 25,000 Bosnian Muslims, most of them women, children and elderly people, were loaded onto overcrowded buses by Bosnian Serb forces and transported into Muslim-held territory. The massacre occurred under the noses of Dutch peacekeepers sent to defend the 'safe area' and more than two years after the Security Council had moved to establish the ICTY, in May 1993. It therefore sets in stark relief not only the brutal strategy of ethnic cleansing, but also the failings of the international community in Bosnia.

The dissolution of Yugoslavia presented the international community with a range of complex political, ethical, legal and military dilemmas with which it struggled to come to terms over the course of the 1990s. Protracted debates carried on through the first half of the 1990s about the use of force, the nature of the war, the relative importance of maintaining impartiality and/or neutrality, and the thorny issues of whether or not it was morally acceptable to cement ethnic cleansing by acknowledging the resulting demographic make-up in any peace agreement. Along with challenges presented by crises in Africa, the crisis in the former Yugoslavia was a crucial test case for the 'new world order'. The war in Bosnia, in particular, cut short the period of optimism that resulted from the end of the Cold War and concerted military action in the Gulf in 1991. The muddled response exposed the limitations of a united European front on defence and security matters and of the United Nations, which could do little without US power to enforce such an order. The international community generally, and either Britain or the United States specifically, are blamed for their inconsistency, lack of will, downright obstructionism and lack of understanding, which led to their failure to prevent or put a stop to the fighting in Bosnia until 1995.

NATO intervention in Kosovo at the end of the decade was very different. The lessons learnt by the West from the experience in Bosnia, namely that air power worked as a coercive tool against the Serbs and that quick, early and decisive action was required, were key factors in deciding when and how to use force to put a halt to the Serb campaign in Kosovo. For the ICTY, Kosovo provided an opportunity to act as a 'real time' enforcement body. The indictment of Milošević and the decision not to pursue investigations into allegations of NATO war crimes were both highly contentious and confirmed the extent to which issues of international criminal justice were now at the forefront of debates about international peace and security and the use of force.

## Box 2.2: Rwanda

From April to June 1994, it is estimated that between 800,000 and 1 million Rwandans were killed in one of the worst genocides in modern times. Some 2 million people fled to other countries and another 2 million were internally displaced. The victims of the genocide were mostly Tutsi, the minority ethnic group in Rwanda, but many moderate Hutus were also killed. In spite of warnings – including that of the Canadian commander of the UN force in the country, General Romeo Dallaire – that a massacre might be about to take place, very little was done by the international community to prevent it or to put a stop to it once it had commenced.

In the 1890s Rwanda and Burundi were both part of German East Africa, but Germany lost the colony to Belgium (the colonial power in neighbouring Congo) during WW1; in 1923, Belgium was mandated by the League of Nations to govern the region. After WW2, the region was put under UN trusteeship, and Belgian authorities governed through local Tutsi rulers. However, in 1959, they switched support to a new generation of educated Hutu intellectuals, who succeeded in overthrowing the Tutsi monarchy. The uprising, in which as many as 20,000 Tutsi were killed and many more fled into exile in neighbouring countries, resulted in the establishment of the Republic of Rwanda, under Hutu rule. In 1962, Rwanda and Burundi became separate independent countries, although their fates remained interlinked. In Rwanda, an army of Tutsi exiles began an uprising in 1963; this was put down by the government, leading to reprisals against the minority Tutsi population. A period of relative calm was interrupted in 1973, when General Juvénal Habyarimana came to power at the head of a military coup. Habyarimana instituted a new constitution in 1978, which confirmed him in power for five more years; he was re-elected in 1983 and again in 1988.

In 1990, the relative calm was shattered when a second Tutsi uprising was launched by the Rwandan Patriotic Front (RPF), operating from bases in Uganda. A ceasefire agreement was eventually reached in July 1992, which provided for the arrival of a 50-member Neutral Military Observer Group (NMOG I), under the auspices of the Organization for African Unity (OAU). Negotiations continued between the RPF and the Rwandan government, supported by the OAU and facilitated by Tanzania, but they were thwarted by the resumption of fighting in northern Rwanda in February 1993 around the border with Uganda. Rwanda and Uganda requested the deployment of a peacekeeping force along their common border to prevent the use of the area by the RPF. The UN Observer Mission for Uganda and Rwanda (UNOMUR) was established by the Security Council in June 1993.

In August 1993, talks in Arusha, brokered by Tanzania and the OAU, resulted in a peace agreement, which provided for the establishment of transitional administration to rule until a democratically elected government could be established, repatriation of refugees and integration of the armed forces of the two sides. The UN Assistance Mission for Rwanda (UNAMIR) was established by Security Council Resolution 872 in October 1993 to monitor the agreement. However, the parties failed to resolve issues arising from the Arusha Accords and, consequently, the transitional government was never inaugurated, with Habyarimana continuing to govern.

From 1990 onwards, radical Hutu parties, a wing of the National Republican Movement for Development (MRND) and the Coalition for Defence of the Republic (CDR), organized militias who carried out a number of raids against the Tutsi population and against Hutus who supported negotiations with the RPF. They also began spreading hate propaganda via the radio station Radio *Milles Collines*, which would later be a key instrument in the genocide, and the monthly journal *Kangura*. The militias, the *Interhamwe* and the *Impuzamugambi*, were made up of the youth wings of the MRND and the CDR. In 1993 and 1994, these militia were given arms and military training by the Rwandan Armed Forces (FAR).

The trigger for genocide was the shooting down on 6 April 1994 of a plane carrying the presidents of Rwanda and Burundi near Kigali airport. It is not confirmed who was behind this attack, but some blamed Hutu extremists opposed to the Arusha Accords. What is clear is that it set off a tidal wave of killings. Even before news of the attack had been announced, lists of names of moderate Hutus were distributed. Tutsis, not always identifiable by physical characteristics, were pinpointed using their identity cards, which were checked at the roadblocks set up by FAR and Hutu militia on 7 April. Meanwhile, militia leaders allocated one man to every ten households and went from house to house to search for and kill Tutsis. Many sought sanctuary in churches, but to no avail, as these became the scene of some of the worst massacres. The violence was finally ended when RPF forces captured Kigali and the Hutu government fled to exile in Zaire, followed by a tide of refugees. The RPF established an interim government of national unity in Kigali, led by President Paul Kagame.

Throughout the crisis, the international community's response was, at best, too little, too late. Some UN personnel tried to shelter civilians in their camps, but in general the peacekeeping forces were not mandated to intervene and were fearful of the consequences should they do so. International action was therefore limited to the rescue of nationals. In fact, the most forceful action taken by the United Nations was the establishment, on 9 November 1994, of the

ICTR. In March 1999, the Secretary-General, with the approval of the Security Council, commissioned an independent inquiry. The final report was scathing; it concluded that lack of political will and errors of judgement had contributed to the international community's failure in Rwanda.

# 3

# The International Criminal Court

The establishment of a permanent International Criminal Court (ICC) with the adoption of the Rome Statute in July 1998 and its coming into force four years later, in July 2002, was heralded as a triumph for international criminal justice. More than 60 years after the idea was first mooted, it had finally come into being.[1] And yet, in 1990 the establishment of a permanent ICC seemed a long way off, if not impossible. The establishment of the ad hoc tribunals was an important catalyst: despite their flaws, the Nuremberg legacy and the ad hoc tribunals for the former Yugoslavia and Rwanda, discussed in previous chapters, were instrumental in creating the conceptual and pragmatic stepping stones to the ICC. Once this happened, progress was startlingly quick. As David Forsythe pointed out in 2000, 'What started out in 1993 as mostly a public relations ploy, namely to create an ad hoc tribunal to appear to be doing something about human rights violations in Bosnia without major risk, by 1998 had become an important global movement for international criminal justice.'[2]

What are we to make of this development? Does a permanent ICC have inherent advantages over ad hoc international courts or over domestic or hybrid courts? Is it the 'shiny new hammer' in the international community's box of foreign policy tools that David Scheffer was looking for in 1994 when he wrote about the ICTY?[3] This chapter provides an overview of the ICC, the debates surrounding its establishment and its progress so far. A key concern is the relationship between peace and justice at the Court, or, more precisely, between the exercise of international criminal justice and the restoration and maintenance of peace and security at the international and at the local or domestic level. As we shall see, the ICC demonstrates that the two are not mutually exclusive, but nor are they necessarily mutually reinforcing. What is required for it to function effectively is the proper balance between the two.

## Establishing the Court: The Rome Statute

Although the establishment of the ICC was a remarkable development, the idea was not new. It was taken up by the United Nations International Law Commission following the Second World War and the Nuremberg and Tokyo tribunals. The ILC began work almost immediately and produced a draft statute in 1954, but further progress was stymied. It was only after the end of the Cold War and the establishment of ad hoc tribunals that it took on a new sense of urgency, resulting in the extremely rapid establishment of the ICC.

The idea was revived by Trinidad and Tobago in 1989, when they called for the establishment of an international court to address drug-trafficking. The proposal was sent back to the ILC, which was originally requested to establish a court to try drug-trafficking offences but, after the establishment of the ad hoc tribunals, its mandate was expanded. In 1994 the ILC produced a revised draft statute which formed the basis for discussions from 1995 onwards, first in an ad hoc committee and subsequently in a more formal preparatory committee (PrepCom).[4] On 15 June 1998, a UN Diplomatic Conference of Plenipotentiaries on the Establishment of an International Criminal Court met in Rome, culminating on 17 July 1998 with the adoption, by 120 votes to 7 (with 21 abstentions) of the Rome Statute of the ICC. The Court finally came into existence with the 60th ratification in July 2002.

After 19 weeks of negotiations at the ad hoc committee and PrepCom, there followed 5 weeks of intensive negotiations at Rome.[5] Crucially, the issue of complementarity was decided on prior to the conference in Rome, about which more below. Nevertheless, the most controversial elements of the Statute remained to be settled, namely those relating to the scope of the Court's jurisdiction and the ways in which it could exercise and establish jurisdiction. The draft statute that emerged from the PrepCom was riddled with 1,400 square brackets, indicating points of disagreement. The most heated discussions centred on three key issues: the applicable law, the role of the Prosecutor and the relationship with the Security Council.

There were three major groupings in the negotiations. The first was the so-called Like-Minded Group (LMG), led by Canada and Australia. Although there were shades of difference of opinion among states in this group, they broadly favoured a strong court with automatic jurisdiction, an independent prosecutor with the power to initiate proceedings on their own volition (*proprio motu*) and an expansive definition of war crimes, especially with regard to internal armed conflicts. The second group, made up of the permanent members of the Security Council (the P5) – until the UK and France joined the LMG in Rome – stood in opposition to this. Crucially, they were opposed to automatic jurisdiction and an independent prosecutor. Instead, they wanted to put the Court firmly under the control of the Security Council, making international criminal justice subsidiary to international peace and security, with the power to refer cases and to prevent cases being brought. They were also firmly opposed to including the crime of aggression in the subject matter jurisdiction of the Court. The third grouping, which included those states formerly part of the non-aligned movement (India, Egypt, Mexico) were deeply suspicious of the Security Council and opposed to subjecting the Court to its will. These states, along with most Arab states, Russia and China, were also opposed to giving the Court wide jurisdiction over non-international armed conflicts.[6]

In addition, the influence of what has been called a 'transnational advocacy movement', comprising civil society groups and non-governmental organizations (NGOs), especially the influence of such groups on the LMG, is a feature that has been the focus of much attention. Around 250 NGOs were represented at the conference and were active both in lobbying delegations and in providing expert advice on a wide range of issues.[7] As will be clear, the positions of the various groups reflected historical experience and current political and security concerns.

The conference reached its denouement with the presentation, by the Bureau of the Committee of the Whole of the Conference, of a draft statute passed to delegates in the early hours of 17 July and adopted later that day. Philippe Kirsch and John Holmes, who were involved in the negotiations (Kirsch was later appointed the first President of the ICC) attributed this 'historic achievement' to the degree of broad support for a court, whatever its form, from the so-called LMG, which otherwise differed on specific points, to the commitment of individual delegates and to the strong, vocal and committed support of civil society and NGOs.[8] The final package presented by the Bureau was sufficiently accommodating to the diverse viewpoints that nothing was deemed important enough to scupper the entire undertaking. The result, it has been argued, was an 'uncomfortable amalgam of near irreconcilable positions'.[9]

## Jurisdiction and Admissibility

The Rome Statute is an international treaty, and is therefore binding only on those states which formally express their consent to be bound by its provisions. It entered into force on 1 July 2002, once 60 countries had become State Parties; by 1 January 2007, there were 104 State Parties. Following the adoption of the Rome Statute, the UN convened the Preparatory Commission for the International Criminal Court. The PrepCom has already reached consensus on the Rules of Procedure and Evidence and the Elements of Crimes. Together with the Rome Statute and the Regulations of the Court, they comprise the Court's basic legal texts, setting out its structure, jurisdiction and functions. The core provisions of the Rome Statute relating to jurisdiction, admissibility and applicable law are contained in Articles 5–21.

In many ways, the Rome Statute of the ICC is a very conservative document, but in other important ways, it marked a radical departure. The ICC was essentially a compromise between those who wanted to see an independent international criminal court and those who were intent on safeguarding sovereign rights, especially the right to exercise jurisdiction over their own people and territory. This compromise is reflected in the negotiations leading to the establishment of the ICC, discussed above, and in its core provisions.

Perhaps most fundamental to a court is the basis on which it asserts jurisdiction. In a domestic setting, it is relatively clear-cut, in that the courts act in accordance with national law, made by a legislature, and exercise jurisdiction over a designated set of crimes, whether in a civil or criminal court setting. Of course, there are wide variations in the way such laws are enacted and in the way in which national courts exercise jurisdiction, but in each case, the question of what comes under the jurisdiction of the Court can be settled fairly easily. An exception might be found in cases where universal jurisdiction has been asserted (see box 3.2), but for the most part, national courts exercise jurisdiction in respect of the national law and in respect of crimes committed by or against the citizens of that country. An international court is a different matter. Although there is a body of international criminal law, there is no single legislative body (as discussed in the Introduction, international law is a mixture of treaty and custom) and the idea of having an international court to enforce the law is relatively novel.

## Applicable Law

The ICC has been criticized in some quarters for its overly conservative interpretation of the applicable law, especially in maintaining a distinction between international and non-international armed conflict, which made its contribution to substantive law somewhat retrograde.[10] Although the Statute provides a useful function in codifying existing law, the opportunity to further develop international humanitarian law was missed. Notwithstanding, the prevailing view was that the adoption of the Rome Statute was a significant achievement even if the precise details of the substantive law and enforcement mechanisms of the Court leave something to be desired. Moreover, even with a somewhat conservative jurisdiction, the ad hoc tribunals have been successful in pushing the boundaries of international law and defining existing law, especially with regard to genocide and crimes of rape and sexual violence. A key contribution of the ICC, as an international body, might be to continue this work.

The ICC has jurisdiction for the crime of genocide, crimes against humanity, war crimes and the crime of aggression, although the latter is subject to agreement on the definition of the crime among the State Parties. The Statute reproduces the definition of genocide given in the 1948 Genocide Convention and the Statutes of the ICTY and ICTR. The definition of crimes against humanity, however, moves beyond that of the ad hoc tribunals in that it does not specify a nexus with armed conflict of any kind (unlike the ICTY), there is no requirement to prove a discriminatory motive and crimes of apartheid and forced disappearance are now explicitly recognized as crimes against humanity. More contentious was the content and definition of war crimes, in particular provisions relating to individual criminal responsibility, command responsibility and defences. This reflects the concerns of states which, while they could be reasonably confident that their own forces were not going to set out to commit genocide and crimes against humanity, the definition and understanding of the boundaries of war crimes is more fluid and more often misunderstood, especially in a climate of increased scrutiny. In particular, the lack of consensus over the use of certain types of weapons, such as cluster munitions, made it more difficult to reach agreement on specifics. Because of this, Article 124 of the Statute allows for State Parties to opt out of jurisdiction for war crimes for a period of seven years after the coming into force of the Statute. Of course, much of this will be debated in the first cases to come before the the ICC, which will face similar challenges to those of the ad hoc tribunals in mounting trials for genocide, crimes against humanity and war crimes (and even more in respect of the crime of aggression, should a definition be agreed).

## The 'Essential Paradox' of Complementarity

Admissibility was one of the most contentious issues in the negotiations at Rome. Unlike the ad hoc tribunals, which exercise jurisdiction on the basis of the principle of universality for international crimes, the ICC exerts jurisdiction on the basis of nationality or territoriality, except in cases referred by the Security Council. The Court may only exercise jurisdiction if:

- the accused is a national of a State Party or a state otherwise accepting the jurisdiction of the Court;
- the crime took place on the territory of a State Party or a state otherwise accepting the jurisdiction of the Court; or
- the United Nations Security Council has referred the situation to the Prosecutor, irrespective of the nationality of the accused or the location of the crime.

It is also important to note that the Court's jurisdiction is not retrospective; it has jurisdiction only from the point at which the Statute entered into force (i.e. 1 July 2002), or, if a state joins after 1 July 2002, the ICC only has jurisdiction after the Statute entered into force for that state.

Even where the ICC has jurisdiction, it will not necessarily act. Unlike the ad hoc tribunals, which have primacy, the ICC can only act where domestic courts are 'unable' or 'unwilling'. For example, a case would be admissible if national proceedings were undertaken for the purpose of shielding the person from criminal responsibility, or if the ICC deemed that domestic courts were not equipped to deal with such cases. The ICC therefore plays a residual role, whereas national courts are the forum of first resort. In this context, its purpose is to reinvigorate domestic courts; according to the Chief Prosecutor, Luis Moreno Ocampo, 'the absence of trials before the Court, as a consequence of the regular functioning of national institutions, would be a major success'.[11] However, this provision has also raised serious concerns that the ICC will be meddling in domestic jurisdiction and involving itself in making determinations about the worthiness of a state's judicial system. Moreover, the ambiguity surrounding the meaning of 'unable' or 'unwilling' might mean that the Court will assert jurisdiction against the wishes of State Parties. There is also a further concern that provisions on admissibility allow for the Court to investigate a national of a non-State Party if the alleged crime took place on the territory of a State Party. This is a fundamental objection raised by the US, and they have taken great pains to install safeguards of their own in order to ensure that US nationals are not brought before the ICC. The US has asserted that jurisdiction over non-parties on the basis of territoriality or Security Council referral is contrary to international law, but this position is rejected by most international lawyers.

Another issue relating to the principle of complementarity is that of state cooperation. The 'essential paradox of complementarity' is that the Court is reliant on state cooperation, which is fine where a State Party has referred a situation to the Court (as with the DRC and Uganda); but where it has initiated investigations on the basis that the state concerned is unwilling or unable, cooperation is unlikely to be forthcoming.[12] This is not the 'ideal' of universal jurisdiction twinned with a 'vertical' cooperation regime, as practised by the ad hoc tribunals, but a more qualified approach, based on complementarity and a horizontal cooperation regime, which will have significant implications for the Court's operation, making it all the more difficult.

## The Role of the Prosecutor

There are three ways in which the ICC can admit cases: on the basis of a referral from a State Party, or by the Security Council, or the Prosecutor may initiate a case on his own initiative (*propio motu*). The most contentious of these in discussions at Rome and following the adoption of the Statute concern the role of the Prosecutor and the relationship with the Security Council.

In some ways, the Prosecutor of the ICC has considerable freedom, but in others is more constrained than the Prosecutor of the ICTY, ICTR or even the Special Court for Sierra Leone (see chapter 4). When the Prosecutor is given information about situations from State Parties or the Security Council, he evaluates the available details and determines whether there is reasonable basis to proceed with an investigation. He may also begin an investigation on his own initiative on the basis of information submitted by a variety of sources, but should he decide to proceed with a prosecution, he has to seek authorization from a Pre-Trial Chamber.

A crucial element in determining success for the Court will be the appointment of an astute Prosecutor with 'political smarts'.[13] The experience of ICTY demonstrated the crucial role of the Prosecutor, especially in balancing the judicial and political aspects of the tribunal's mandate. What is required is a strong, independent Prosecutor, able to play a political and diplomatic role, without jeopardizing the judicial independence and integrity of the post.[14] In particular, he or she will have to resolve difficult questions regarding how to determine whether prosecution is 'in the interests of justice'. For example, if an amnesty is deemed necessary in order to secure an end to a particular conflict, what is the position with regard to ICC jurisdiction? While some international lawyers will argue that there is no room for amnesties because there is a legal obligation to punish international crimes of genocide, crimes against humanity and war crimes, others take a more flexible approach, arguing that, notwithstanding the legal obligation to prosecute 'grave breaches' of the 1949 Geneva Conventions and Genocide, the Statute is sufficiently ambiguous to allow for due account to be taken of non-judicial mechanisms for truth-telling and accountability.[15] However, as discussed below, the trade-off between justice and peace is not as clear-cut as it may seem. In some cases, setting aside prosecutions merely stores up trouble for the future.[16]

The conduct of the Prosecutor will also be crucial in establishing the integrity of the ICC as a whole; the stance taken by the ICTY Prosecutor over allegations of misconduct by NATO in the Kosovo campaign might have helped to demystify the process of determining what to pursue and what not to pursue and to generate a level of comfort sufficient to see many of these states supporting an independent Prosecutor at Rome.[17] Others are less sanguine, however. US Senator Jesse Helms suggested that the investigation into NATO conduct during Operation Allied Force was suspended because any attempt to indict NATO commanders would have sounded the 'death knell' for the ICC; he railed against what he called the 'brave new world of global justice which proposes a system in which independent prosecutors and judges, answerable to no state or institution, have somehow unfettered power to sit in judgment on the foreign policy decisions of Western democracies'.[18]

## The Relationship with the Security Council

The relationship of the Security Council to the ICC is set out in the Statute. Article 13(b) provides for referrals by the Security Council to the Court of situations in which one or more crimes within its jurisdiction appear to have been committed. Conversely, Article 16 provides that investigations can be suspended for a period of twelve months (renewable) on the basis of a Security Council Resolution to that effect. In both cases, the Security Council would need to be acting under Chapter VII of the UN Charter, requiring a connection with international peace and security. As such, these provisions uphold the nexus of international peace and security and international criminal justice inherent in the establishment of the ad hoc tribunals.

The relationship between the Security Council and the ICC is crucial in establishing what Frank Berman calls a 'perfect symbiosis' of the interests of international justice and international peace and security.[19] Yet, it remains to be seen how all of this will play out in practice. To date, there has been one referral by the Security Council (Sudan) and discussion of another situation in which the interests of justice and those of peace might seem to be in conflict (Uganda) (see box 3.1).

## The United States and the ICC

The ICC faces a political and legal minefield as it comes into operation.[20] A major obstacle is the opposition of the US to the ICC. In spite of being heavily involved in the negotiations leading up to, and at, Rome, the United States eventually voted against the adoption of the Rome Statute, along with six others (Libya, Israel, Iraq, China, Syria and Sudan). Although they continue to be involved through the PrepCom, the US is not a State Party and is therefore not bound by the Statute. However, there are circumstances in which US citizens might be brought before the Court – the cause of much consternation in the US.

Opposition to the ICC in the US takes two forms. The first, perhaps most forcefully expressed by the likes of Jesse Helms and John Bolton, formerly Senior Vice-President of the American Enterprise Institute and then interim US Representative to the United Nations, reflects a deep-seated suspicion of international institutions, underpinned by a deeply rooted belief in American 'exceptionalism'.[21] Bolton famously remarked that the day he put his signature to the letter nullifying America's signature to the Rome Statute was the 'happiest moment' of his government career. More reasoned and nuanced arguments are made by other critics of the ICC, such as Ruth Wedgwood and David Scheffer, which reflect not simply opposition to international justice per se, as expressed by Bolton, but opposition to the form it finally took at Rome. While the legal objections to the Court put forward by the US government are regarded as largely unconvincing, the political implications of these objections are potentially disastrous.

So far, US opposition to the ICC has been manifested in the 'unsigning' of the Rome Treaty, threats to veto UN peacekeeping operations unless exemptions for US personnel were granted, the authorization of the use of 'all means necessary' to release US citizens should they ever be detained in The Hague and the withholding of US military assistance to ICC supporters who refused to sign bilateral agreements promising never to hand over US citizens. In this context, the fact that the US abstained when the Security Council adopted Resolution 1393 referring the situation in Darfur to the ICC, rather than use their veto, came as something of a surprise. It should not have been; the Sudan resolution was, in fact, an example of the Security Council and the ICC working in exactly the way that the US had wanted. It was this, rather than any potential embarrassment at having failed to take action in spite of then Secretary of State Colin Powell's assertion that genocide had been committed in Sudan that determined the US position on Sudan and the ICC. Richard Prosper, US Ambassador at Large for War Crimes Issues, stated, 'We've always envisioned that the Security Council has the authority to grant jurisdiction over particular matters.'[22]

## International Criminal Justice and International Peace and Security

What are we to make of the ICC as a model of transitional justice? At the international level, the establishment of a permanent ICC was highly significant. It was welcomed as a critical weapon in the 'fight against impunity'. As such, it reinforced the great strides made by the ad hoc tribunals in demonstrating a norm of accountability and encouraging respect for and confidence in the international rule of law. As discussed above, the mechanisms for jurisdiction and admissibility make it a court of last resort, to step in where domestic courts are unable or unwilling, or where the Security Council deems it to be in the interests of international peace and security. As such, success might be measured by the absence of cases, rather than volume. As with other international courts, it should be seen as exceptional. Seen in this way, it might represent a 'perfect symbiosis' of international criminal justice and international peace and security. [23]

There are, however, a number of potential drawbacks. One is the extent to which an institution such as the ICC, based in The Hague, can overcome the problems of remoteness experienced by the ad hoc tribunals. The ICC will also probably be less effective than, for example, hybrid or internationalized courts in terms of the concrete contribution it is able to make to capacity-building in the domestic legal system. Moreover, in all three cases under investigation by the ICC to date, there is a potential conflict with peace processes and/or other mechanisms for transitional justice. In the case of Sudan and Uganda, the Prosecutor has stated explicitly that the ICC is but one of a range of measures and that it will work with civil society organizations and alternative processes of accountability, but it is early days yet, and, as discussed below, it remains to be seen whether and how the ICC can indeed be complementary to these efforts.

## Engaging the Local Population and Meeting Victims' Needs

At a local level, as with the ad hoc tribunals, it is hoped that criminal trials will help foster peace by establishing an historical record, satisfying victims' needs for retribution and punishment and establishing individual, rather than group, responsibility, as well the potential concrete impact of excluding 'spoilers' and removing perpetrators. However, as discussed in the previous chapter, the impact of international trials at the domestic level is contingent on a well-developed communications and outreach strategy. The ICC recognized this at an early stage, and has drawn on the lessons of the two ad hoc tribunals, and the Special Court for Sierra Leone. It remains to be seen whether this will be sufficient to counter its relative remoteness from the populations affected. The geographical distance is already an obstacle, as all of the cases under investigation are in sub-Saharan Africa, while the Court has its seat in The Hague.

As regards its commitment to meet the needs of victims, the ICC is unique in establishing a trust fund for victims of the crimes before the Court. The Victims' Trust Fund aims to provide victims, including child soldiers, victims of rape, sexual assault and other abuses, and those who have had their property and livelihood destroyed, with help and compensation to enable them to rebuild lives shattered by war. The purpose of the fund is to channel money to victims. Sometimes this will be money that the Court orders an offender to pay as compensation. Under Article 75(2) of the Rome Statute, the Court may order a convicted person to pay money for compensation, restitution or rehabilitation. In addition, it disburses voluntary contributions from governments, international organizations or individuals.[24] This programme has come under criticism and is insufficiently funded, but it at least offers more than was the case for victims in the former Yugoslavia, Rwanda or Sierra Leone.

## Peace and Justice?

As indicated above, the ICC provides a model that could potentially be a 'perfect symbiosis' of international criminal justice and international peace and security. However, the success of this model depends on the way in which it is interpreted and implemented. Two situations currently before the court illustrate the dilemma very well, namely Uganda and Sudan.

On the surface, Sudan looks like a textbook example of the ICC working as a tool of international peace and security. The situation in Darfur was referred to the ICC by the Security Council in April 2005, acting under Chapter VII. On the surface, this looks like the ICC operating to all intents and purposes like an ad hoc tribunal, but with the added advantage of having a permanent structure behind it, and greater perceived legitimacy owing to its mode of establishment by treaty. However, the Court faces a significant obstacle in Sudanese opposition and refusal to cooperate. As with the ad hoc tribunals, a Security Council referral, although it creates binding obligations to cooperate, does not in itself ensure cooperation.

The peace versus justice dilemma was set in stark relief by the situation in northern Uganda in a different way. On the one hand, the government of Uganda sought international judicial intervention and referred the situation to the ICC. At the same time, the government, under a great deal of pressure from civil society groups and NGOs, enacted an amnesty law, and renewed efforts to secure a ceasefire finally bore fruit. Although all these developments are promising, there is the potential for them to be contradictory. In particular, the apparent conflict between the amnesty law and the ICC investigation and the potentially detrimental impact of the ICC's indictment of the five most senior commanders of the Lord's Resistance Army (LRA) to the ceasefire agreement has led some to suggest that the ICC was actually hindering the restoration and maintenance of peace in northern Uganda.[25]

Yet, there is no inherent contradiction between the three initiatives. Indeed, President Museveni has indicated to the Prosecutor his intention to amend this amnesty so as to exclude the leadership of the LRA, ensuring that those bearing the greatest responsibility for the crimes against humanity committed in northern Uganda are brought to justice. Relying on these same people to abide by a ceasefire appears to be somewhat foolish in light of the past 20 years, so getting them out of the way might in fact be a concrete contribution to the peace process. In fact, predictions of an escalation in violence following the indictments have been unfounded.[26]

It has also been suggested that the Acholi people have their own approach to justice, which will be violated by the ICC's intervention. This point has been made forcefully by civil society groups on the ground and it is now widely accepted as a truism that local understandings of justice are based on reintegration into society and a remarkable capacity for forgiveness. However, while there is undoubtedly some basis for believing in this seductive notion of justice, it should be treated with caution.[27] Having spoken with some of those in displacement camps, Tim Allen concluded that people did not reject international justice, but rather were concerned about how it would be applied and about potential security implications.[28] The two approaches are not necessarily mutually exclusive, although it is often assumed that they are. Even the Prosecutor of the ICC has explicitly welcomed alternative approaches to the problem of accountability. Following meetings in The Hague with leaders of the Lango, Acholi, Teso and Madi communities, he asserted: '[W]e are working together as part of a common effort to achieve justice and reconciliation, the rebuilding of communities and an end to violence in Northern Uganda.'[29] In relation to Darfur, also, the Prosecutor indicted his willingness to work alongside alternative systems of accountability:

> Additional efforts will be required to bring to justice other offenders and to promote the rule of law and reconciliation. This has particular significance in the context of Darfur where tribal and traditional systems exist for the promotion of dispute resolution. My Office will cooperate with and support such efforts, the combination of which will mark a comprehensive response to the need for justice.[30]

But these should not be invoked in order to abrogate the responsibility of the Sudanese government to cooperate with the ICC.

It is a difficult balance to strike and boils down to the interpretation of the Prosecutor's mandate to act 'in the interests of justice'. All indications so far point to a high level of discretion exercised by the Prosecutor and a nuanced understanding of what is meant by 'in the interests of justice'. In a September 2002 policy paper, the Prosecutor indicated a flexible approach, saying that the OTP will 'take into consideration the need to respect the diversity of legal systems, traditions and cultures'.[31] Given the ICC's mandate to investigate only 'the most serious crimes of concern to the international community as a whole', it is envisaged that in some cases it may be appropriate for the Court to agree a division of labour with a state, where only those who bear the greatest responsibility go before the ICC. So, although the ICC might be 'institutionally antagonistic' to amnesties, in practice it will not interfere except in relation to those indicted.[32]

## Conclusion

In spite of criticisms levelled at the ICC from some quarters, and its inherent limitations as an instrument of post-conflict justice, especially in promoting reconciliation at the national level, it has got off to a promising start. As the cases of Uganda, Sudan and, to some extent, the DRC have shown, the ICC does not necessarily represent a one-size-fits-all approach to transitional justice. The Prosecutor has demonstrated a willingness not only to take into account whether domestic *courts* are able and willing to undertake prosecution, but also to determine whether prosecution by the ICC would be in the interests of justice, a willingness to consider alternative non-judicial mechanisms for dealing with past abuses. If the ICC is able to be complementary to other systems of accountability at a local level, it may be able to play a greater role in the restoration and maintenance of *international* peace and security.

Understanding the relationship between the ICC as a body mandated to dispense international criminal justice and the Security Council as the body mandated to maintain international peace and security is crucial to understanding its potential contribution. As well as the more concrete contribution to peace it might make, and to reinforcing international norms of accountability for international crimes, the involvement of the ICC has been important in raising the profile of the three situations it is currently investigating and ensuring they remain on the international agenda. While this is not strictly a contribution to justice, it could be a significant contribution to peace if international attention is accompanied by action. Moreover, rather than subjecting international criminal justice to the whim of a political body, as some have argued, the relationship between the Security Council and the ICC safeguards the primary role of the Security Council in matters of international peace and security. Whether or not it reaches a 'perfect symbiosis' of international criminal justice and international peace and security remains to be seen.

---

### Box 3.1: Situations and cases

Four situations have been referred to the Prosecutor. Three State Parties (Uganda, Democratic Republic of the Congo and Central African Republic) have referred situations occurring on their territories to the Court, and the Security Council, acting under Chapter VII of the United Nations Charter, has referred a situation on the territory of a non-State Party (Sudan). The Prosecutor began investigations in three of the four situations: Democratic Republic of the Congo, Uganda and Sudan. These are discussed below.[33]

#### *Uganda*

The situation in northern Uganda has been called the 'biggest forgotten, neglected humanitarian emergency in the world today'.[34] The conflict has been ongoing for almost two decades and is being waged between a rebel group, the LRA and government forces. The LRA claims to fight for the freedom of the Acholi people in northern Uganda, yet the majority of the victims of the conflict were civilians. The LRA used terror tactics to great effect and the government has responded with aggressive counter-insurgency strategies. Almost 50 per cent of the civilian population of northern Uganda now live in camps for internally displaced persons and there has been a pattern of serious human rights abuses against civilians, including summary executions, torture and mutilation, recruitment of child soldiers, child sexual abuse, rape, forcible displacement, and looting and destruction of civilian property.

Uganda is a signatory to the Rome Statute. Its ratification of the Statute in June 2002 meant that it was among the first 60 states to come under the jurisdiction of the Court. In December 2003 Ugandan President Yoweri Museveni referred the situation concerning the LRA to the Prosecutor of the ICC – the first such state referral.[35] The Prosecutor responded saying that he would interpret the referral as concerning all crimes under the Statute committed in northern Uganda, not just those committed by the LRA, and that the investigation would be impartial. The investigation formally opened on 28 July 2004.[36] Although the conflict itself has been ongoing ever since Museveni took power in 1986, the ICC only has jurisdiction for alleged crimes committed since 1 July 2002.

Many of the alleged perpetrators are themselves victims, having been abducted and brutalized by the LRA leadership. The LRA is drawn largely from abducted villagers, particularly children aged between 11 and 15, who made up over 85 per cent of the LRA's forces. As part of initiation into the rebel movement, abducted children are forced into committing inhuman acts, including ritual killing and mutilations, beating and killing civilians and other abductees, and abducting other children. In order to evade capture, thousands of children have become 'night-dwellers', walking vast distances to the relative safety of centres run by NGOs to spend the night, only to return again at dawn. Many younger girls were reported to be assigned as servants to commanders, engaging in domestic work, while older female captives were forced into marriage with senior soldiers or were given as a reward for obedient boy soldiers, and subjected to rape, unwanted pregnancies and the risk of sexually transmitted diseases. The reintegration of these individuals into Ugandan society is key to the future stability of northern Uganda.

In a bid to encourage members of the LRA to return to normal life, the Ugandan authorities enacted an amnesty law. There have also been various efforts to secure a ceasefire with the rebels. Meanwhile, on 8 July 2005, the ICC issued the first arrest warrants against five senior commanders of the LRA: Joseph Kony, Vincent Otti, Raska Lukwiya, Okot Odhiambo and Dominic Ongwen.[37] Originally issued under seal, these were released publicly in October 2005. The apparent conflict between the amnesty law, efforts to secure a ceasefire and the ICC investigation has been the cause of much debate, with some arguing that the ICC was hindering the restoration and maintenance of peace in northern Uganda.[38] However, the three initiatives are not necessarily incompatible. President Museveni has indicated to the Prosecutor his intention to amend this amnesty so as to exclude the leadership of the LRA, ensuring that those bearing the greatest responsibility for the crimes against humanity committed in northern Uganda are brought to justice. Meanwhile, the Prosecutor of the ICC has asserted, following meetings in The Hague with leaders of the Lango, Acholi, Teso and Madi communities, that 'we are working together as part of a common effort to achieve justice and reconciliation, the rebuilding of communities and an end to violence in Northern Uganda'.[39]

## Democratic Republic of Congo (DRC)

Dubbed 'Africa's Great War', or 'Africa's First World War', the 1996–2003 war in the DRC involved at least eight African states in what was arguably the most complex war in Africa in modern times. In seven years of war, an estimated 3.8 million people have died and 3.4 million have been displaced. When added to the legacy of the years of decline under President Mobutu Sese Seko, it has further retarded economic and political development and deprived the DRC of its vast mineral resources, and had a significant impact on the strategic landscape in central Africa. Since 2002, there have been reports of thousands of deaths by mass murder and summary execution; these reports also allege a pattern of widespread abuse, rape, torture and forced displacement.[40] The war finally came to an end in July 2003 with the establishment of a new power-sharing government in Kinshasa after months of tortuous negotiations and arm-twisting by Pretoria.

The DRC signed the Rome Statute on 8 September 2000, when the conflict was still ongoing, and ratified it on 11 April 2002. In April 2004, the President of the DRC referred the situation of crimes within the jurisdiction of the Court allegedly committed in the territory of the DRC since the entry into force of the Rome Statute on 1 July 2002, and asked the Prosecutor to investigate. This seems to have averted a situation in which the Prosecutor would invoke his powers to initiate an investigation *propio motu*. The Prosecutor had already indicated in July 2003 that he was closely following the situation in the DRC, and in September 2003 he informed the Assembly of State Parties that he would be prepared to seek authorization from a Pre-Trial Chamber to start an investigation, but that a referral and active support from the DRC would facilitate his work.[41]

The ICC officially opened a formal investigation on 23 June 2004. Two field offices were established to aid the investigations, one in Kinshasa and one in Bunia. The investigations are restricted to the Ituri region of the DRC and have not as yet begun to deal with alleged crimes perpetrated elsewhere in the country. Together with criticism of its relatively limited jurisdiction, which necessarily commenced in July 2002, this has undermined its legitimacy among certain sections of the population. It was expected that the ICC should deal with a much broader geographical range, particularly because vast atrocities have been documented elsewhere, in for example the Kivu region. This has led to accusations voiced by some

Congolese that President Kabila and his government had an agreement with the ICC so that they, all of whom had been parties to the conflict, would not be investigated.[42] This is a shame, but it reflects a wider problem, which is that there is only limited understanding of the mandate of the ICC and what it can do – in spite of two seminars that were held by the ICC in the DRC in December 2004 and April 2005 to promote an increased understanding of the structure, mandate and objectives of the Court.

Another bone of contention was that local NGOs felt that the ICC had not cooperated or consulted with them sufficiently. In June 2005 there was a distinct feeling in the local NGO community that they could have contributed much more to the ongoing process, but that they had been somewhat sidelined.[43] Also in the DRC the ICC has faced the problem that it is too far removed from the local setting to have a direct and immediate impact upon the local population, especially in remote areas, particularly since as yet there are no established communication and outreach mechanisms.

## Sudan

The Darfur region in the western part of the Sudan is a geographically large area comprising approximately 250,000 square kilometres with an estimated population of 6 million. Since 1994 the region has been divided administratively into the three states of North, South and West Darfur. Since 2002, there has been fighting between rebel forces – the Sudan Liberation Movement/Army (SLM/A) and the Justice and Equality Movement (JEM) – and Sudanese government and militia forces (the Janjaweed). While only loosely connected, the two rebel groups cited similar reasons for the rebellion, including socioeconomic and political marginalization of Darfur and its people. The vast majority of the members of the two rebel movements came from three tribes: the Fur, the Massalit and the Zaghawa. Faced with increasingly serious attacks and lacking in military capabilities on the ground in Darfur, the government called upon local tribes to assist in the fighting against the rebels, exploiting existing tensions between different tribes. This new force became known as the 'Janjaweed', a traditional Darfurian term denoting an armed bandit or outlaw on a horse or camel.

Efforts aimed at finding a political solution to the conflict began as early as August 2003. Several rounds of talks took place, resulting eventually, on 8 April 2004, in a ceasefire agreement between the government and the SLM/A and JEM. Subsequent peace talks took place in Addis Ababa, Ethiopia, and in Abuja, Nigeria, under the mediation of the African Union. On 9 November in Abuja, the government, the SLM/A and the JEM signed two protocols, one on the improvement of the humanitarian situation and the second on the enhancement of the security situation in Darfur. At the time of writing, the parties have still not been able to find a comprehensive solution to the conflict. Continued fighting and violations of the ceasefire between the rebels and the government and its militias are still being reported; in March 2007, UN investigators accused Sudan's government of 'orchestrating and participating' in crimes in Darfur that include murder, mass rape and kidnap.[44] Regardless of the fighting between the rebels on the one hand, and the government and Janjaweed on the other, the most significant element of the conflict has been the attacks on civilians, which have led to the destruction and burning of entire villages, and the displacement of large parts of the civilian population.[45]

The international community and the UN have been roundly criticized for their lack of concrete action to put an end to the fighting in Darfur. Although most of the responsibility has been delegated to the African Union, the Security Council has put forward two initiatives aimed at the restoration of international peace and security in Darfur. In a sequence of actions reminiscent of the early response to the war in the former Yugoslavia, in September 2004 the Security Council, acting under Chapter VII of the UN Charter, adopted resolution 1564 requesting, inter alia, that the Secretary-General 'rapidly establish an international commission of inquiry in order immediately to investigate reports of violations of international humanitarian law and human rights law in Darfur by all parties, to determine also whether or not acts of genocide have occurred, and to identify the perpetrators of such violations with a view to ensuring that those responsible are held accountable'. Then, on 31 March 2005, again acting under Chapter VII, the Security Council adopted Resolution 1393 by a vote of 11, with none against and 4 abstentions (including the US) referring the situation in Darfur to the ICC. The basis of the argument was that the situation in Darfur, and specifically violations of international humanitarian law, constituted a threat to international peace and security. Seen as complementary to other efforts to bring peace, 'The referral of the situation in Darfur to the ICC has brought an international, independent and impartial justice component to the collective international and regional efforts to end the violence in Darfur.' Despite the US abstention, the ICC and Security Council were working in the way they had envisaged.

In terms of contribution to peace and reconciliation, Resolution 1593 emphasized the need to promote healing and reconciliation and encouraged the creation of institutions, involving all sectors of Sudanese society, such as truth and/or reconciliation commissions, in order to complement judicial processes and thereby reinforce the efforts to restore long-lasting peace. Prosecutor Luis Moreno-Ocampo stated:

> Additional efforts will be required to bring to justice other offenders and to promote the rule of law and reconciliation. This has particular significance in the context of Darfur where tribal and traditional systems exist for the promotion of dispute resolution. My Office will cooperate with and support such efforts, the combination of which will mark a comprehensive response to the need for justice.[46]

Formal investigations were opened by the Prosecutor in June 2005 and are continuing. By August 2006, no indictments had been handed down publicly. The ICC faces a significant obstacle in trying to investigate alleged crimes in Darfur – the ongoing fighting and the lack of cooperation from the Sudanese government. Although Resolution 1393 explicitly calls on Sudan and the rest of the international community to cooperate, affording the ICC the binding enforcement powers enjoyed by the ad hoc tribunals, no additional action has been taken to enforce it.

## Box 3.2: Universal jurisdiction

As well as punishment in domestic courts where the crimes took place, there have also been a number of instances of prosecutions in foreign domestic courts on the basis of universal jurisdiction.[47] In fact, since the mid-1990s, more cases have been brought on the basis of universal jurisdiction than in the whole history of modern international law.[48] Unlike the ICC, whose jurisdiction is based on principles of nationality or territoriality (except where cases are referred by the Security Council), the exercise of universal jurisdiction in its broadest sense requires no such link with the perpetrator, victim or location of the alleged offence.

The exercise of jurisdiction by domestic criminal courts for war crimes is nothing new; investigation and prosecution of alleged Nazi war criminals were undertaken in France, Germany, UK, Canada, New Zealand and Australia in the 1980s and 1990s.[49] Nor is the exercise of universal jurisdiction unusual for such crimes; the *Eichmann* and *Demanjuk* cases were based on this principle. What is new, and relatively rare, is the exercise of this principle in cases where there is no clear objective link between the state exercising jurisdiction and the state where the crimes took place, the perpetrators or the victims. The boldest example were cases brought in Belgian courts against Rwandan citizens for alleged crimes committed against other Rwandans in the 1994 genocide.

The exercise of universal jurisdiction is highly contentious and has been harshly criticized. One case that attracted a great deal of attention was the arrest of General Pinochet in London in October 1998 on the basis of a Spanish arrest warrant. In the end, the then UK Home Secretary, Jack Straw, decided to send Pinochet back to Chile, and not to Spain, to stand trial, on grounds of ill-health, but the ruling remains highly significant in legal and political terms.[50] The impact of the Pinochet arrest was tangible among would-be war criminals, especially taken together with the arrest of General Talić while attending a meeting in Vienna in August 1999, on the basis of a warrant issued by the ICTY.[51] According to Richard Goldstone, first Chief Prosecutor at the ICTY, Issat Ibrahim al-Duri, second in command to Saddam Hussein, also in Vienna at the time, made a hasty exit when Peter Pilz, a member of Vienna's city council, lodged a criminal complaint citing the mass murder of Kurds in 1988 and the murder and torture of other Iraqi citizens.[52] According to press reports, these developments also prompted the former President of Indonesia, Suharto, to forgo medical treatment in Germany.[53]

Belgian courts initiated the investigation of Ariel Sharon, indicating that he could even be tried in absentia when he left office for his alleged part in the massacres that took place in the Palestinian refugee camps of Sabra and Shatila in Lebanon in 1982, following the Israeli invasion. Forceful objections from both the US and Israeli governments forced them to retract and the law was amended in 2003 so that Belgium could only hear cases involving a Belgian national or resident as a victim or perpetrator.

The cases of Pinochet and Sharon were the most celebrated, but in addition to the Rwandan genocide cases, charges have also been brought in Belgium against the DRC's former Minister for Foreign Affairs Yerodia Ndombasi, and against a number of individuals in The Netherlands, Austria, Germany and Denmark for violations of international humanitarian law committed in the former Yugoslavia and in Spain. In addition, charges were brought concerning alleged crimes in Honduras, Guatemala and against former members of the Argentine Junta – in 2000, the Spanish Judge Garzon issued an indictment against Manuel Cavallo, a former Argentinean government official alleged to have committed serious human rights violations.[54] Meanwhile, on 3 February 2000, a Senegalese court indicted former Chadian President Hissène Habré on torture charges and placed him under house arrest.

In a separate but related development, groups of immigrants in the US have brought cases under the Alien Tort Claims Act (ATCA). The first of these concerned a group of Bosnian women who brought a case against Radovan Karadžić and were awarded a large settlement by a jury in Manhattan.[55] But very little has been paid out as a result of these cases.

While advocates of universal jurisdiction see it as the new 'magic bullet' in the fight against impunity,[56] at the other end of the spectrum people like Henry Kissinger view it as a form of 'judicial tyranny'.[57] Moreover, there is a danger of heavily politicized proceedings and a lack of real effect on the societies where the crimes occurred.[58] It has been suggested elsewhere that the unilateral exercise of universal jurisdiction in cases where there is no link to the offence or the offender, and in some instances, conducted in absentia, risks weakening the very principles the exercise of such a principle purports to uphold.[59] On this basis, it might be better viewed as an 'aberrant intermezzo' that filled the gap between the exercise of international criminal justice on an ad hoc basis at the ICTY and ICTR and the creation of a permanent international criminal court.[60]

# 4

# 'Internationalized' Courts

The establishment of first the ICTY and then the ICTR seemed to indicate a preference for international criminal justice over domestic courts or other non-judicial mechanisms for accountability, a trend that appeared to have reached its apex with the establishment of a permanent International Criminal Court (ICC) in 1998. However, by the beginning of the twenty-first century, as discussed in chapter 2, some degree of 'tribunal fatigue' was apparent, not helped by the apparent shortcomings of ad hoc tribunals. This prompted renewed interest in alternative forms of accountability, including truth and reconciliation processes and traditional justice.[1] For those still committed to the cause of international justice, however, an alternative was found in the form of 'internationalized' courts. In several cases where the ICC lacked jurisdiction, rather than establish an ad hoc international tribunal along the lines of the ICTY/R, the international community and the governments concerned opted for a form of 'hybrid' court, mixing international and domestic law, procedure and personnel.

This new model of international criminal justice was welcomed as having significant advantages over ad hoc international tribunals and even the ICC.[2] It had the potential to deliver a more effective and streamlined form of international criminal justice, while the involvement of local actors and their location in the country in which the crimes were committed was thought to bode well for their contribution to the process of peace and reconciliation and might also be expected to leave behind a legacy in practical and symbolic terms, by fostering respect for the rule of law, showing that justice can be done fairly, and training and equipping local lawyers. International involvement, meanwhile, was thought to lend legitimacy to the enterprise, as well as money and expertise. As such, they seemed to offer all of the advantages and none of the pitfalls of international courts. But, as they have come into operation, it has become clear that they might not be the universal solution.

This chapter examines recent efforts to establish 'hybrid' systems of justice in Sierra Leone, Kosovo, Timor-Leste and Cambodia. Recognizing that there are significant differences in the mode of organization, the level and form of international involvement and, crucially, the context in which they operate, the chapter will discuss some of the major cross-cutting aspects. The first section examines the organization and functioning of these four experiments in internationalized justice, focusing on issues of jurisdiction and procedure, financial and logistical challenges, state cooperation and judicial assistance, the relationship with domestic courts and other non-judicial mechanisms for accountability and strategies for communication and outreach. The second section examines the contribution each has made to peace and justice, focusing on the extent to which they have provided justice, promoted reconciliation and contributed to capacity-building and the rule of law. It will be argued that, while they represent a significant step forwards in many regards, the experience of these internationalized courts suggests that they may not be the panacea some thought they were.

## A New Breed of Tribunal?

'Hybrid', 'mixed' or 'internationalized' courts occupy a middle ground between the purely international model adopted for the ICTY, ICTR and ICC and the purely domestic courts. In Timor-Leste and Sierra Leone, they are also mixed in the sense that they operate alongside some form of truth and reconciliation process.

However, although general points of comparison can be made, in every situation where a form of 'internationalized' court has been established it has taken a somewhat different form. At one end of the scale are *international* courts with elements of *domesticization*, such as the Special Court for Sierra Leone (SCSL),[3] which was established on the basis of an agreement between the government of Sierra Leone and the United Nations. At the other end of the scale are *domestic* courts with elements of *internationalization*; in Kosovo, rather than establishing a sitting court, international judges and prosecutors (IJPs) become involved in the domestic system on a case-by-case basis,[4] whereas in Timor-Leste, a specially constituted internationalized court permanently composed of a mix of domestic and international judges was established within the local justice system (the Serious Crimes Unit and the Special Panel for Serious Crimes).[5] Meanwhile, in Cambodia the process of establishing Extraordinary Chambers (CEC) to try former members of the Khmer Rouge for crimes committed during their rule from 1975 to 1979 was stymied for a long time by debates about the extent of *internationalization* versus *domesticization*.[6]

## Jurisdiction and procedure

The SCSL was the first 'hybrid' court to be established and is more international than domestic in character. Its jurisdiction is based on a mixture of international and domestic law. Its jurisdictional scope is explicitly limited to those who bear 'the greatest responsibility' for serious violations of international humanitarian law and Sierra Leonean law committed in the territory of Sierra Leone since 30 November 1996. 'Serious crimes' include crimes against humanity, violations of Article 3 common to the Geneva Conventions and of Additional Protocol II and 'other serious violations of international humanitarian law' of special relevance to the war in Sierra Leone, namely, targeting civilians, recruitment of child soldiers and attacks on humanitarian assistance and peacekeeping personnel. It has jurisdiction for a limited set of crimes under Sierra Leone law, for example abusing girls of 'under 13' and 'between 13 and 14 years of age', abduction of a girl for 'immoral purposes' and arson. Controversially, the personal jurisdiction of the Court extends to persons between 15 and 18 years of age, which reflects an attempt to tailor the jurisdiction of the Court to suit the particular circumstances of Sierra Leone, where child soldiers, as well as themselves being victims, were also perpetrators of serious crimes.[7] The Special Court's mandate was also limited temporally to three years initially.

Like the ad hoc tribunals, the Court comprises three separate organs: the chambers, Registry and Office of the Prosecutor. Two trial chamber judges and three appeal chamber judges are appointed by the UN (i.e. the majority) and the rest by the government of Sierra Leone. The Chief Prosecutor is also a UN appointment, as is the Registrar, but other professional and support staff are recruited locally and internationally. The Special Court is fully independent of both the government of Sierra Leone and the UN, funded by voluntary contributions and managed by a committee made up of representatives from funding states, namely Canada, The Netherlands, Nigeria, Lesotho, Sierra Leone, the UK, the United States and the

UN Secretariat. In a conscious effort to avoid some of the pitfalls of the ad hoc tribunals, the Special Court appointed a Principal Defender to oversee the quality and professional standards of defence counsel and ensured that the defence team was provided with adequate resources.

Unlike the Special Court, 'Regulation 64 Panels' in Kosovo did not apply international law, except in so far as it was part of the domestic law of the province.[8] The rationale for inserting IJPs into domestic trials in certain cases was not in order to facilitate war crimes trials per se, but to prevent ethnic bias and ensure due process in particularly sensitive cases. IJPs were therefore assigned on a case-by-case basis and not restricted to special categories of war crimes, crimes against humanity or genocide. Michael Hartmann, one of the first IJPs to be assigned in Kosovo, argued that this was a double-edged sword. On the one hand, it gave a large degree of freedom and enabled IJPs to be assigned to cases in politically contentious cases that did not necessarily involve the commission of international crimes. However, selectivity is, at least in principle, open to political abuse and Hartmann is harshly critical of the power of discretion having been put in the hands of a political authority, the Special Representative of the Secretary-General (SRSG).[9] Of course, whether or not this is a problem depends on how discretion is exercised, but it does introduce an element of selectivity on political rather than judicial grounds.

The law applied by the UN Transitional Administration in Timor-Leste (UNTAET) was that applicable in the country prior to 25 October 1999 (the Indonesian Penal Code). Only the Special Panel for Serious Crimes of the Dili District Court had jurisdiction for 'serious crimes', including war crimes, genocide and crimes against humanity. This panel was made up of two international judges and one Timorese judge.

The jurisdiction, procedure and organization of the CEC were much more contentious. Negotiations between the Cambodian government and the UN resumed in 2003 (see box 4.4) and resulted in an agreement on 13 May 2003. Although the UN managed to retain the super-majority formula agreed in earlier negotiations as well as a streamlined trial chamber and appeals chamber, it did not secure any of its other proposed modifications. The fact that the negotiations were conducted in an atmosphere of suspicion and mistrust and that the final agreement contained a get-out clause for the UN, in that it could withdraw support if the Cambodian government changed the structure or organization of the chambers, did not bode well.[10] Amnesty International and Human Rights Watch roundly condemned the 2003 agreement.[11] Human Rights Watch cited, in particular, the fact that international judges constituted a minority in the chambers, which is a problem given the control that the Cambodian government has over the judiciary, the absence of any guarantees of prosecutorial and judicial independence and the lack of an independent prosecutor – which in itself means that the Cambodian prosecution service suffered similar problems to those that afflict the judiciary, namely 'crude political interference, low levels of professionalism and pervasive corruption'. It has also been suggested that the 'super-majority' formula (all decisions require a majority plus one international judge) is likely to impede trials, creating more problems than it solves.[12]

Also criticized was the lack of clarity concerning the CEC's subject matter jurisdiction, especially where it refers to Cambodian law, which is 'confused, inconsistent and internally contradictory',[13] the failure to establish a viable witness protection programme or specify how court personnel will be protected, and the fact that it did not resolve outstanding questions concerning previous pardons, such as that granted to Ieng Sary.[14] There was also considerable debate over the scope of the court's investigations and prosecutions – the UN indicated that 20–30 persons would be likely to stand trial. For some, this was a problem because it is inherently selective and focuses only on 'senior leaders and those most responsible', allowing many perpetrators to escape justice. The absence of any provision of reparations was also criticized.[15] Another controversial issue was whether to include the crime of genocide in the jurisdiction of the chambers. The Group of Experts report recommended inclusion because the people of Cambodia were subjected to 'almost all of the acts enumerated in the Convention'. Ben Kiernan also points out that, at least with regard to Cambodia's majority Khmer Buddhist community and ethnic minorities such as the Vietnamese, Chinese and Cham Muslims, an effort was made to eradicate substantial parts of an 'ethnic group', not just a political or social group, which is outside the strict terms of the Convention.[16]

All these courts face challenges that combine elements of domestic law and procedure and international standards. International involvement and sponsorship mean that it is imperative that they live up to international due process and human rights standards in order for justice not only to be done, but to be seen to be done. One of the main purported advantages of the internationalized courts is that international standards will infiltrate the domestic system, as will be discussed below. However, there is also the danger that trying to amalgamate domestic and international law and procedure will lead to confusion and impede trials, especially when put together with the significant financial and logistical challenges faced by these courts in mounting prosecutions.

## Financial and logistical challenges

The ad hoc tribunals have shown up the enormous cost of international justice. Annual budgets for the ICTR and ICTY are in excess of $100 million.[17] Although this figure is relatively small when set against other areas of UN spending, the high cost has recurred time and again as one of the key criticisms of ad hoc tribunals. Internationalized courts, on the other hand, were supposed to offer a more cost-effective solution, but this approach has considerable drawbacks. High expectations that these courts would contribute to the process of national reconciliation and rebuilding the rule of law were not matched with corresponding levels of economic and political support. The example of the SCSL demonstrates that the assumption that a more cost-effective model is necessarily more desirable might be misplaced. As the former Registrar of the Court remarked, it was not lean and mean, it was anorexic![18]

The budget for the Special Court was set at $56 million for three years of operation. This is tiny compared with that of the ad hoc tribunals. The budget for the CEC was also set at around $56 million for three years. Unlike the ad hoc tribunals, which are funded out of the UN regular budget, augmented by voluntary contributions, the Special Court and UN portion of the budget for the CEC is reliant on voluntary contributions. This is problematic in as much as it leads to considerable uncertainty and to a short-term approach to fundamental issues such as appointment of judges, staffing and premises. In relation to the CEC, the UN Secretary-General recognized that: 'A financial mechanism based on voluntary contributions would not provide the assured and continuous sources of funding that would be needed to make it possible to appoint judges. . . . Nor would it provide a secure basis for the conduct of investigations, prosecutions and trials.'[19] However, he could not obtain agreement in the General Assembly for a model of assessed contributions; voluntary contributions were therefore better than nothing at all.

The task of investigating and prosecuting international crimes is complex and difficult, as the ad hoc tribunals have shown. Moreover, unlike Timor-Leste, Kosovo and Sierra Leone, the CEC is dealing with crimes committed 30 years ago, which creates additional difficulties as regards the collection of forensic evidence and witness testimony. Having to do it within the constraints of a limited budget and timeframe only exacerbates the problem.

## State cooperation and judicial assistance

A significant drawback of internationalized courts is that they lack the Chapter VII mandate of the ad hoc tribunals, and cannot therefore demand state cooperation. It should be noted that even with this mandate, the ad hoc tribunals have faced enormous difficulties. Part of the problem was solved, at least in theory, by the fact that the courts, by their very nature, are established on the basis of cooperation with the state in which most of the crimes were committed, so cooperation can reasonably be expected (even if it is not always forthcoming). The real obstacle comes where cooperation is required of other states. For the SCSL, the difficulty in obtaining custody of Charles Taylor, who was granted asylum in Nigeria, presented a significant obstacle to its being able to fulfil its mandate to prosecute those who bear 'the greatest responsibility'.[20]

In Timor-Leste, although the transitional administration managed to put in place mechanisms for accountability, many of the perpetrators of the worst abuses will go unpunished unless the Indonesian government decides to cooperate. So far, its attitude has been one of obstruction and, most appallingly, many of the senior level military officers of the Tentara Nasional Indonesia (TNI) in command in Timor-Leste during the referendum period were promoted when they returned to Indonesia.[21] Although Indonesia and UNTAET signed a Memorandum of Understanding to facilitate cooperation with the Serious Crimes Unit and Special Panel for Serious Crimes, it has not been forthcoming. Meanwhile, considerable pressure was exerted on the post-transition government by Indonesia to discontinue prosecution of Indonesian personnel, resulting in a remarkable statement by President Gusmao in 2003, following the indictment of 48 individuals, including General Wiranto, and the former Timorese Police Chief. Gusmao said that he considered it 'not to be in the national interest to realise a judicial process of this nature in Timor-Leste'.[22]

## Relationship to domestic courts

The relationship with domestic courts depends to some extent on the degree of internationalization or domesticization. Panels comprising international judges operated within the existing legal system in

Kosovo and Timor-Leste, whereas the Special Court for Sierra Leone stood completely apart from the domestic legal system. In spite of early calls for a tribunal along the lines of the SCSL, or even the ad hoc tribunals, the CEC resembled much more closely the Timor-Lesteese model.

One of the main advantages of internationalized courts is purported to be the contribution they can make to rebuilding the domestic legal system and respect for the rule of law. The SCSL in particular has taken great pains to think carefully about the legacy it will leave behind, even though it stands apart from the domestic legal system. Robin Vincent, the former Registrar at the SCSL, described the legacy as being threefold: bricks and mortar (the courtroom building itself), people and organizational structure. Sierra Leonean staff are employed by the Court, in-house training is provided for investigators and trial attorneys in the Office of the Prosecutor and prison staff rotate through the Detention Unit. In addition, there are training programmes and meetings between Sierra Leonean judges and Special Court judges, and visits by Special Court judges to observe domestic trials. Other aspects of the Special Court's legacy programme include disseminating norms and values relating to the rule of law. Judicial reform is not explicitly a part of the Court's mandate, and it cannot address all the issues alone, but the Court's legacy programme is designed to contribute to the process through training programmes aimed at police, military, lay magistrates and prison officers and activities aimed at fostering community rehabilitation and self-reliance, for example empowering local courts and community-based initiatives such as reconciliation panels, involving Paramount Chiefs, religious leaders, the military, police and civil society leaders.

It is not clear to what extent these programmes have changed or informed Sierra Leonean attitudes and knowledge of international human rights norms and standards, or how far they might have succeeded in shifting expectations of the judicial system, especially with regard to fairness of proceedings, treatment of detainees and respect for the rights of the accused. A further question-mark hangs over the extent to which it might have contributed to the rehabilitation and protection of witnesses and victims, especially of sexual and gender-based crimes and wider problems, such as combating child-trafficking and promoting children's rights. Some have argued that grafting an international tribunal onto a weak domestic criminal justice system which cannot guarantee respect for fundamental human rights is unlikely to succeed in its task of bringing justice in accordance with international standards.[23] In both Kosovo and Timor-Leste, there was a need to rebuild the judicial system almost from scratch.[24] Whether this could reasonably be done in tandem with complex war crimes prosecutions is open to question. In Sierra Leone, the task of mounting trials rightly took precedence over other subsidiary tasks, whereas in Kosovo, IJPs dealt with a broad range of crimes, not just those committed during the war. It seems to boil down to a choice of whether to focus on the narrow judicial mandate or to focus on other tasks with the risk of losing the momentum of criminal trials.

## Communication and outreach

The other main advantage of internationalized courts was that because they operated in the country most affected by the crimes in question, they would have more of an impact on the local population than the relatively remote ad hoc tribunals. Of all the internationalized courts, the SCSL has made the most concerted effort to ensure that its work is communicated to its main constituency – the people of Sierra Leone. Very early on, the Court implemented an outreach programme, which is far more extensive and ambitious than anything that has previously been undertaken. At a basic level, it was designed to inform people about the Court and to enable them to follow developments in the investigations and trials. It began in August 2002, when the Registrar Robin Vincent and the Prosecutor David Crane travelled through the country to give presentations and answer questions relating to the work of the Court in so-called 'Town Hall Meetings'. It now involves the Office of the Prosecutor, the chambers and the Registry, including the Office of Press and Public Affairs and the Public Defender's Office. As well as distributing booklets describing the Court, the outreach programme relies on oral and visual communications – important in a largely illiterate society – such as radio and television panel discussions and screening of trials, televised weekly summaries of court proceedings, poster campaigns and theatre.

While it is largely deemed a success when compared to the efforts of the ad hoc tribunals, the outreach programme has also faced significant obstacles. Some are due to lack of funding and logistic difficulties, others to external factors over which the Court has little control. The Press and Public Affairs Office and the Outreach Programme have to content with embedded preconceptions and bias, fuelled by negative coverage in the Sierra Leone press. Although the Court is very effective at getting information out, it is much more difficult for it to affect deeply held attitudes and beliefs.[25]

## Justice, Peace and Reconciliation

As discussed in the Introduction, it is claimed that some form of post-conflict justice will contribute to peace by ensuring accountability, an end to impunity, acting as a deterrent, providing an historical record, promoting reconciliation and healing, providing a means of redress for victims, removing perpetrators and contributing to capacity-building and rule of law. To what extent have these internationalized courts managed to achieve this? Have they been able to provide justice, build capacity and respect for the rule of law and contribute to peace and reconciliation?

### Providing justice

In both Kosovo and Timor-Leste, internationalized domestic courts have been largely unsuccessful in adequately addressing post-conflict justice. In Kosovo, by June 2004, IJPs were involved in 92 cases,[26] but serious challenges remained, particularly in relation to capacity-building and integration of more Serbs into the judiciary.[27] There were only 16 Serbian judges, and 278 Albanian and 2 Serbian prosecutors, against 78 Albanian.[28] The March 2004 riots demonstrated the distance the province still has to travel, with inter-ethnic animosity barely disguised and latent aggression prone to break out at any time.

A key criticism of the Kosovo model is that the decision as to which cases merit international involvement was taken at the political level by the SRSG, which limits judicial and prosecutorial discretion.[29] However, Nicholas Booth and Jean-Christian Cady, representing the UN Mission in Kosovo's (UNMIK) perspective (Booth was Deputy Special Representative of the Secretary-General for Police and Justice, and Cady his Senior Adviser), argue that this criticism is misconceived.[30] Implementation of the model was also hampered by inadequate staffing, problems with the selection, recruitment and hiring practices for IJP, and terms and conditions of employment.[31]

Meanwhile, the Special Panels in Timor-Leste have made only a limited contribution. The obstacles in its way are significant. Chief among them was the lack of cooperation from Indonesia, but there were also practical constraints derived from a lack of funding, personnel and political will.[32] Sylvia de Bertodano argues that Timor-Leste has, in this regard, been 'seriously let down by the UN'.[33] The first case was heard in January 2001, using a combination of international and Indonesian law, and heard by both international and local judges from Timor-Leste. The major issue for the Court was 'providing competent legal representation to the accused'.[34] After the first trial, one observer stated that 'the Dili District court so far fails to meet even minimal standards for a fair trial'.[35]

The persistent problems in the Special Panels were reinforced by those facing the general judicial system. The Special Panels were working in an environment entirely without an infrastructure for conducting such cases. In addition, the local judges and prosecutors were fast-tracked to be able to deal with the cases. There was pressure to begin to prosecute even before any form of judicial reform had been implemented, but the courts lacked sufficient funding and personnel. The UN wanted accountability for crimes against humanity, but did not provide the required funds for setting up mechanisms to ensure that the work conducted would not run the risk of falling into disrepute. There was not the requisite expertise or capacity in Timor-Leste to continue with prosecutions after international withdrawal or without further donor support. Nevertheless, the fact that they were conducted with international involvement, albeit at a local level, gave the Panels more credibility, authority and legitimacy than would have been the case had they consisted solely of local judges, and, at the same time, the use of local judges made them more relevant to the Timorese. The Special Panels were particularly important in a context where the Indonesian Human Rights Court had failed, an international tribunal was not set up and the Commission of Truth, Reception and Reconciliation had a limited mandate.[36]

Sierra Leone, by contrast, has received more attention and more support, yet a key criticism remains that it was hampered by its mandate to provide justice on a 'shoestring' budget.[37] It is also grappling with a problem not of its own making; namely, that the highest-level perpetrators from the rebel side have either died (RUF leader Foday Sankoh and former RUF commander Sam 'Mosquito' Bockarie), are missing (AFRC leader Johnny Paul Koroma) or are out of the Court's reach (Charles Taylor was granted asylum by the Nigerian government in August 2003). According to the Security Council Mission to Sierra Leone in June 2004: 'Many believe that lasting reconciliation requires that former President Charles Taylor of Liberia stand trial.'[38] The Court therefore finds itself in the curious position of having the most prominent indictee as the man who is widely seen as a national hero: former leader of the Civil Defence Force (CDF) Chief Hinga Norman, who led the resistance against the Revolutionary United Front (RUF) and was a member of Kabbah's government.[39]

The extent to which the CEC can provide justice to the victims of the Khmer Rouge remains to be seen, but the omens are not good. The establishment of a tribunal in Cambodia is still extremely politically sensitive. Negotiations between the government of Cambodia and the UN boiled down to a conflict between a vision of an international criminal justice process and politically controlled judicial process. The Cambodian government was worried that if it were unable to control the process, it might exacerbate tensions and be detrimental to the process of peace and reconciliation. The UN's concerns related to safeguarding international standards for a fair trial and worries about the extent to which the process will be subject to political interference. The result was unsatisfactory. According to Human Rights Watch: '[S]o long as the Cambodian government continues to exercise direct control over the Cambodian judiciary . . . any tribunal with a majority of Cambodian judges and a Cambodian co-prosecutor will fail the most basic test of credibility with Cambodians and the international community.'[40] However, while 'five star justice'[41] might be out of the question, can a measure of justice be achieved that satisfies minimum standards? And is this good enough? After all, as Suzannah Linton points out, Cambodians are not going to get another bite at the cherry.[42] It may already be too late for many, as key leaders of the Khmer Rouge, including Pol Pot and Ta Mok, known as the Butcher and former head of the south-western region, are now dead.

### Peace and reconciliation

Post-conflict justice ought to play an important role in fostering reconciliation, but one must be realistic about what it can achieve and recognize its constraints. The extent to which these courts can achieve peace as well as justice depends not only on the organization and functioning of the judicial process, but also on the context in which they operate. However, as suggested above, locating the trials in the country in which the crimes were committed and involving the local community were thought to increase the chances of making a contribution to peace and reconciliation. Certainly, these factors enhance the profile of such efforts among the local population, especially if supported by a coherent and effective outreach and communications strategy, as was the case in Sierra Leone.

Aside from promoting reconciliation, there are ways in which such courts can impact on more concrete elements of the peace process. In both Kosovo and Timor-Leste, the failure promptly and adequately to address issues of justice was extremely damaging to the overall success of the missions. In the early phase, not only did criminal activity flourish, but much of the evidence of past crimes was destroyed or lost. The Kosovo example demonstrated that successful international intervention in the judicial arena should be 'immediate and bold, rather than incremental and crisis-driven' as it was in this case.[43] Investigation and prosecution of organized crime, terrorism and inter-ethnic crimes, not to mention war crimes and crimes against humanity, may not necessarily be within the capacity of the existing judicial system, especially if its jurists are lacking experience and there is the risk of bias because of past experiences. And yet, the 'failure to address past and ongoing violations promptly and effectively, and to create a sense of law and order, can impede the broader objectives of the operation'.[44] Because of this and other failings, the experiment in Kosovo is largely seen as a 'missed opportunity'.[45]

In Sierra Leone, the case of Charles Taylor demonstrates the pragmatic relationship between peace and justice. As in Bosnia, the removal of certain individuals through indictment and arrest can be highly significant. Taylor's indictment by the Special Court may have been leverage at getting him to step down in 2003 and go into exile in Nigeria, while his handover in 2006 is indicative of forward movement in the peace process in Liberia, notwithstanding the impact it will have in Sierra Leone, where, according to the Security Council Mission to Sierra Leone in June 2004: 'Many believe that lasting reconciliation requires that former President Charles Taylor of Liberia stand trial.'[46] However, in spite of having Taylor now in custody, other obstacles remain. Many in Sierra Leone are critical of the Court's approach, viewing its interpretation of the mandate as too narrow, and criticizing the decision to proceed with the prosecution of 'national heroes', such as Hinga Norman.[47]

## Complementarity

Sierra Leone also demonstrated the complexities of running parallel processes of post-conflict justice/accountability. The reason for implementing parallel processes of transitional justice is that one feature of criminal justice is that it focuses on the individual guilt or innocence of the accused, so does not present the opportunities for participation that another form of accountability, such as a truth commission, might. However, careful thought needs to be given to how these processes can operate successfully in tandem. This was not done in Sierra Leone, leading to a series of clashes between the Special

Court and the Truth and Reconciliation Commission (TRC), established on the basis of the 1999 Lome Agreement.[48] When the Special Court was established, there were concerns about how it would coexist with the TRC process. Some argued that it diverted scarce resources from the TRC (as well as other programmes).[49] If the budget of the Special Court looked small, that of the TRC was miniscule: $6.5 million as compared to the Special Court's $56 million.

There was also confusion between the TRC and the Special Court among the Sierra Leone population: a study of attitudes among former combatants pointed to a blurred distinction between the two bodies and a lack of understanding of their respective mandates among the Sierra Leone population.[50] This confusion soon transformed into mistrust as people refused to testify before the TRC for fear that the information would be turned over to the Special Court. The Chair of the TRC, Bishop Dr J. C. Humper, sought to establish a clear separation between the two bodies, emphasizing the confidential nature of the TRC's findings, but his attempt to persuade people that the Special Court would not be privy to the testimonies given before the TRC were somewhat undermined by Prosecutor David Crane, who stated that while he preferred to build his own case, he would not rule out using TRC testimonies.[51] The potential for conflict between the two bodies came to a head over three Special Court detainees, Hinga Norman, Augustine Gbao and Issa Sesay, who said they were willing to testify to the Commission in September 2003.

In Timor-Leste also, war crimes prosecutions were conducted alongside non-judicial mechanisms for dealing with post-conflict accountability. A Reception, Truth and Reconciliation Commission was established in mid-July 2001 in an attempt to deal with the inability of the judicial system to deal with every alleged perpetrator and to have a process that might make more sense to the affected population.[52] Former militia members were required to confess their crimes to village elders and promise never to commit a crime again. As with Rwanda, where *gacaca* have been instituted in an attempt to clear the backlog of cases in national courts, there is no reason why different processes might not be able to run concurrently, but the relationship between the two must be clearly defined and one must not be seen as a poor substitute for the other. (For more on the *gacaca* system, see box 7.2.)

## Capacity-building and the rule of law

The advantages of situating internationalized courts, such as the SCSL, in the country most affected by the crimes it addresses was set out thus by the Secretary-General in his 2004 Report, 'The Rule of Law and Transitional Justice in Conflict and Post-Conflict Societies':

> There are a number of important benefits to locating tribunals inside the countries concerned, including easier interaction with the local population, closer proximity to the evidence and witnesses and being more accessible to victims. . . . National location also enhances the national capacity building contribution . . . allowing them to bequeath their physical infrastructure (including buildings, equipment and furniture) to national justice systems and to build the skills of national justice personnel. In the nationally located tribunals, international personnel work side by side with their national counterparts and on-the-job training can be provided by national lawyers, officials and staff.

Much has been made of the beneficial legacy of the Special Court, but the fact that the Court will leave behind a state-of-the-art court facility and legal training of those Sierra Leoneans working with it does little to address underlying issues that need to be resolved if a sustainable system of justice and rule of law is to be established.[53] Some complain of a 'spaceship phenomenon', whereby the Court is seen as predominantly international and once it leaves it will have little impact. It is suggested that the few Sierra Leone nationals in professional positions at the Court will not remain in the country after the Court has left, but will seek employment elsewhere. Moreover, with regard to the rule of law, Sierra Leone has only just started to confront fundamental flaws, including widespread corruption, in the police and judicial system.

## Conclusion

Forms of hybrid court have been established elsewhere, including in Bosnia and Herzegovina and the Democratic Republic of Congo.[54] This would seem to indicate that the 'new breed of tribunal' provides a good model. Certainly, as discussed above, internationalized courts offer a number of potential advantages over purely international tribunals and purely domestic courts. They can minimize a number of the problems encountered when using domestic courts to deal with past crimes, while at the same time operating closer to the societies affected and thereby contributing not only to the process of reconciliation, but to rebuilding capacity in the local legal system and respect for the rule of law. As such, *domesticization* of international courts might provide a remedy for some of their defects, most significantly that of remoteness and cost. Meanwhile, *internationalization* can ensure a higher level of legitimacy and impartiality, while limiting the more political processes that are apparent in domestic processes and guaranteeing compliance with international legal standards.[55]

However, as the examples of Kosovo, Timor-Leste, Sierra Leone and Cambodia have demonstrated, the outlook is not entirely rosy. In Kosovo and Timor-Leste, the insertion of IJPs into the domestic system has not been without its difficulties and, in both cases, it has had limited impact. Internationalized courts also suffer from similar difficulties in obtaining state cooperation and procedural and logistic challenges to those encountered by the ad hoc tribunals. All this has to be done on a limited budget and without a Chapter VII mandate, but with high expectations of success. For these reasons, some argue that 'internationalized' courts should be viewed as a 'stop-gap measure', which is 'better than nothing'.[56] All this notwithstanding, there is a pragmatic case for continuing to develop this type of court, based on the potential advantages, which make it a valuable and important development in its own right. Moreover, as was argued with regard to Cambodia, 'insistence on near perfect justice risks losing the good for the sake of the unattainable'.[57]

## Box 4.1: The Special Court for Sierra Leone

The war in Sierra Leone was well documented for its 'breathtaking malevolence'[58] and 'unspeakable viciousness'.[59] It began in 1991, when the rebel group, the Revolutionary United Front (RUF) invaded from across the border in Liberia with the declared objective of overthrowing the corrupt government of Joseph Saidu Momoh. This sparked a decade of brutal civil war in which it is estimated that as many as 75,000 civilians were killed, and 500,000 displaced. Civilians were directly targeted and grotesque atrocities – including mutilation, rape, cutting off of victims' hands and feet, kidnapping children and either forcing them to fight or subjecting them to sexual abuse and wanton destruction of villages and towns – were widespread. After two abortive peace agreements and partly as a result of long-awaited international military intervention, peace was finally declared in January 2002. The extent of the atrocities committed was such that even before the peace agreement, there were calls for some form of accountability. It was felt that without the designation of those responsible – at all levels – and a public acknowledgement of their roles, social structures would remain unsettled and public faith in the solidity of the peace would be undermined.[60]

However, because the domestic legal system was flawed, corrupt and inefficient as a result of years of neglect and abuse, Sierra Leone's own judiciary was unable to address these issues effectively on its own. One solution was to establish a Truth and Reconciliation Commission (TRC) as part of the Lome Peace Agreement in July 1999, but because of the resumption of violence by the RUF, which took 500 UN peacekeepers hostage in May 2000, it did not begin functioning until July 2002. Meanwhile, on 12 June 2000, the President of Sierra Leone, Dr Ahmad Tejan Kabbah, wrote to the Secretary-General asking for UN assistance to set up a court to try Foday Sankoh and other senior members of the RUF. This represented a significant departure from Lome, which had provided for amnesty to be granted to those who testified before the TRC. The Security Council responded in Resolution 1315, 14 August 2000, with a request to the Secretary-General to negotiate with the government of Sierra Leone for the establishment of an independent court. In January 2002, a team of experts travelled to Sierra Leone to finalize arrangements, including granting a Statute for a court, and on 16 January 2002, an agreement was signed between the UN and the government of Sierra Leone establishing the court in Freetown.[61] The agreement was ratified by the Sierra Leone parliament in March of that year and the SCSL began operating in August 2002 when Registrar Robin Vincent and Prosecutor David Crane arrived to take up their posts.

Unlike the ICTY and ICTR, which operate outside the country over which they have jurisdiction, the SCSL is established in Freetown. It was given a three-year mandate and a $56 million budget, not an inconsiderable sum, but small in comparison to the millions that been donated to the ad hoc tribunals. Its 'shoestring' budget has been a point of contention from the outset. The Special Court's mandate is to prosecute those who bear the 'greatest responsibility' for the atrocities perpetrated in Sierra Leone since 30 November 1996 (the date of the Abidjan Accord which temporarily halted the fighting when Kabbah was elected). Given its relatively limited jurisdictional mandate and timeframe, the Court will focus on a limited number of cases only. It is hoped that these cases will be symbolic markers of Sierra Leone's 'emergence from the moral and physical degradation of the war', that it will permit some sense of closure for the victims of the conflict and that it will advance the broader goal of sustainable peace and deter future military and political leaders from regressing to commit similar atrocities.[62] To date, 13 people have been indicted by the Court and 9 are in custody. Hearings began on 3 June 2004 with the joint trial of three former members of the Civil Defence Force, including their leader and former Minister of the Interior, Chief Sam Hinga Norman. The trial of three members of the former RUF began on 5 July 2004, and a third trial, of three members of the former Armed Forces Revolutionary Council (AFRC), began on 7 March 2005.

## Box 4.2: Regulation 64 Panels in Kosovo

Resolution 1244 of 10 June 1999, promulgated after NATO's 78-day bombing campaign, provided for the withdrawal of the Federal Republic of Yugoslavia (FRY) and Serbian security forces and administration and its replacement with the United Nations Mission in Kosovo (UNMIK) and a NATO-led security force (KFOR). The final status of the province was left open. It is ostensibly still part of Serbia and Montenegro, but it operates as an independent entity under UNMIK control. The situation in June 1999 was acute. At the end of the war, almost half of the Kosovo population had sought refuge abroad, mainly in Albania, and as many as 500,000 were internally displaced. In less than a month, more than 650,000 refugees returned, many to villages and towns devastated by Serb forces, creating immense challenges on the humanitarian and security fronts.[63]

Compounding these difficulties, UNMIK was faced with a collapsed judicial system, and escalating crime and violence; UNMIK police estimated that in the first six months, approximately 500 murders and many other serious crimes were committed, including illegal appropriation of Serb property by Kosovo Albanians and politically motivated violence.[64] The Kosovo Liberation Army (KLA; or Ushtria Clirimatare e Kosoves (UCK)) rapidly established itself in the territory and engaged in acts of violence and intimidation against Serbs, including looting, arson, expropriation of property and even killings and abductions, forcing them to leave. The absence of law and order also meant that organized crime was able to take root and flourish, including drug-trafficking, smuggling and trafficking in women. The Secretary-General's report of 12 July pointed to an 'urgent need to build genuine rule of law in Kosovo, including through the immediate re-establishment of an independent, impartial and multi-ethnic judiciary. . . . The security problem in Kosovo is largely a result of the absence of law and order institutions and agencies.'[65]

The main problem was that politically motivated appointments had led to a situation in which, out of 756 judges and prosecutors in Kosovo in 1999, only 30 were Kosovo Albanian.[66] The first priority was therefore to appoint new judges and prosecutors, but it was a challenge to find people who were not only suitably qualified and experienced but also politically acceptable. Many Kosovar Albanian lawyers had left Kosovo to seek refuge elsewhere and those who had stayed were suspected of collaboration with the previous regime.[67] An independent judicial commission was appointed to make the selections, comprising a mix of local and international members: two Kosovar Albanians, one Bosniak, one Serb and three lawyers from international organizations. These appointments were not uncontroversial. The Serb member of the commission was soon forced to leave and joined the exodus of Serbs out of Kosovo.[68]

Most important in the context of this study was the involvement of international judges and prosecutors. Kosovo is unique as a 'hybrid' model in the sense that rather than establishing a sitting court, IJPs become involved in the domestic system on a fairly limited case-by-case basis. They do not apply international law, except in so far as it is part of the domestic law of the province. This model evolved organically in response to developments in the political and social sphere, in particular tensions between the Kosovo Albanian and, now small, Serb communities. In June 2000, the Secretary-General noted that: 'Despite the appointment of more than 400 [local] judges, prosecutors and lay judges and the increased capacity of the courts, the unwillingness of witnesses to testify and the ethnic bias and risk of intimidation of some judicial personnel have hampered the administration of justice.'[69] Albanian judges were subject to a range of pressures, ranging from their own bias and desire for revenge for the years of abuse, pressure from within their communities, and actual threats of physical violence.[70] The objective was therefore to lend 'an air of neutrality' to the Kosovo Albanian-dominated legal system, as well as international skills and expertise.[71] Starting with the appointment of an international judge and an international prosecutor to the District Court of Mitrovica in February 2000, following allegations of judicial bias in cases involving an outbreak of violence in the town,[72] it evolved to a point in December 2000 where the SRSG could exercise the prerogative to assign international judges to form a majority in judicial panels anywhere in Kosovo.[73] These became known as 'Regulation 64 Panels'.

In a separate development, on 13 December 1999, the Technical Advisory Commission on Judiciary and Prosecution Service (TACJPS), a body established by UNMIK to advise on the structure and administration of the judicial and prosecution service composed of ten local and five international members, recommended the creation of a Court for War Crimes and Other Serious Violations of International Humanitarian Law. The Administrative Department of Justice, newly established following a restructuring of the Department of Judicial Affairs in early 2000, was given responsibility for this initiative. The Kosovo War and Ethnic Crimes Court (KWEEC) was established, with jurisdiction for serious crimes committed on grounds of race, ethnicity, religion, nationality or association with an ethnic minority or political opinion committed in Kosovo since 1 January 1998. However, it encountered serious opposition from local population who objected to the types of cases the court would be allowed to try. They wanted KWEEC to try war crimes cases, involving Serbs, and leave other crimes involving Albanians to locally staffed courts.[74] The initiative was abandoned following the decision to allow international judges and prosecutors to participate in all courts in Kosovo.

## Box 4.3: Special crime panels in Timor-Leste

The United Nations Transitional Administration in Timor-Leste (UNTAET) was established on 25 October 1999 and ended when Timor-Leste regained its independence on 20 May 2002. In September 1999, the violent 'scorched earth' campaign of killing, burning houses and looting waged by militia opposed to independence supported by the Indonesian government that followed the 'popular consultation' prompted international intervention in the form of the International Force for Timor-Leste (INTERFET). Entire towns and villages were burned to the ground, forcing many thousands of Timor-Lesteese to abandon their homes and flee into the mountains of Timor-Leste or across the border into West Timor. In just three weeks, 'Operation Clean Sweep' destroyed over 70 per cent of the country's buildings, displaced two-thirds of Timor-Leste's 890,000 population and killed an estimated further 1,100. Although the operation by INTERFET during the critical period of September 1999 to January 2000 is largely judged to have been a success,[75] after this, UNTAET was not effective in planning for and implementing sustainable peace and development, largely because of the failure properly to involve the local population.[76] On 20 May 2002, Timor-Leste achieved its independence, but it remains the poorest country in Asia. Levels of unemployment, illiteracy and instability remain high. A significant area of failure was in the establishment of a justice system and in the implementation of mechanisms for post-conflict justice.[77]

UN Security Council 1272 established UNTAET as the government of the country for a transitional period, with legislative and executive powers vested in the SRSG and the Transitional Administrator, Sergio Vieira de Mello. This was a significant departure. Although in practical terms there was not much difference from the powers and responsibilities of UNMIK, the suspension of sovereignty was new; in Kosovo, sovereignty was vested in Serbia, not in UNMIK.[78] There were four main areas of work relating to post-conflict justice: the evolution of human rights investigations and preparation of cases for prosecution by the UNTAET Serious Crimes Investigation Unit; the establishment of special panels for serious crimes; the negotiations for the return of large numbers of refugees to Timor-Leste; and the establishment of the Commission for Reception, Truth and Reconciliation. It was deemed important to find a way of addressing the widespread violations of international humanitarian law carried out by Indonesian military and pro-integration militias. On 31 January 2000, the UN International Commission of Inquiry on Timor-Leste concluded that, based on 'testimonies surpassing their imagination', the Indonesian military and militia were responsible for 'systematic and widespread intimidation, killings and massacre, humiliation and terror, destruction of property, violence against women and displacement of people'. This was acknowledged by the UN Secretary-General in a speech to the General Assembly: 'Accounting for the violations of human rights which occurred in the aftermath of the consultation process is vital to ensure a lasting resolution of the conflict and the establishment of the rule of law in Timor-Leste.'[79]

Timor-Leste called for the establishment of an ad hoc tribunal along the lines of those for Yugoslavia and Rwanda, but the international community, suffering from tribunal fatigue, thought it preferable to rely on the local justice system.[80] But this was non-existent in 1999. Not only had court buildings been burned down during the violence and equipment looted; more devastatingly, archives, case files and law books were destroyed, leaving little or no written record of pre-existing case law. Legal expertise was similarly lacking; most of the judges, prosecutors and lawyers and judicial support staff fled, fearful that their association with the Indonesian regime or with the intellectual privileged classes would leave them open to reprisals. It is estimated that only ten fully trained lawyers remained.[81] As in Kosovo, an independent commission was established for the selection and appointment of new judges and prosecutors. The first appointments, of eight judges and two prosecutors, were made on 7 January 2000 in the ruins of the courthouse in Dili. The other side of the equation was to ensure adequate provision of legal assistance to defendants, in order to guarantee fair trial standards. UNTAET financed and established a public-defender system, but it too suffered from a lack of experienced and qualified lawyers.

Unlike the administration of justice in general, where international involvement was limited to overseeing appointments and providing training, in relation to past abuses, much greater reliance was placed on international involvement. Initially, however, there was confusion over responsibility for the investigation. Investigations were started by UNTAET and taken over by the UN police forces, but they were not systematically undertaken and were unclear as to the eventual outcome. They were eventually taken over by the Human Rights Unit in March 2000, and then by the Serious Crimes Investigation Unit. The next major initiative was the establishment of special panels of the Dili District Court to try serious crimes. This was an innovative combination of international and Indonesian law and international and Timor-Lesteese judges. The panels had jurisdiction for genocide and crimes against humanity committed between 1 January and 25 October 1999. The first case was concluded in early February 2001 with the conviction of a Timor-Lesteese man for murder. But there was a signal lack of effort compared to what had been achieved by the ICTs and even in Sierra Leone.

## Box 4.4: 'Extraordinary chambers' in Cambodia

The story of the establishment of a tribunal to try members of the Khmer Rouge in Cambodia is a long and tortuous one. It is, according to one commentator, the single most sensitive issue facing Cambodia today.[82]

The Khmer Rouge seized power in Cambodia in April 1975 and were responsible for the deaths of an estimated 1.7 million people during four years of rule (nearly a quarter of the population).[83] They were ousted in January 1979 as a result of Vietnamese intervention and a new Cambodian government was installed (the People's Republic of Kampuchea). The Khmer Rouge retreated to its stronghold along the Thai border and no effort was made to hold them accountable. In fact, the United States and China were at the forefront of international efforts to continue to recognize the Khmer Rouge as the government of Cambodia, and they kept their UN seat until 1991. It was only after a peace agreement was reached in 1991 and Cambodia outlawed the Khmer Rouge in 1994 that international action slowly began to build for accountability. A crucial element was the reversal of US policy in 1994, when Congress passed the Cambodian Genocide Justice Act, pressing for an international tribunal.

In 1997, negotiations between the government of Cambodia and the United Nations began as a result of a letter from the First and Second Prime Ministers of Cambodia (Hun Sen and Norodom Ranariddh) to the Secretary-General on 21 June 1997, which contained a request for assistance in the establishment of an international tribunal.[84] The idea was taken up at the UN by the General Assembly. A Group of Experts was established and recommended in a report of 16 March 1999 that a UN-based tribunal be established under Chapter VI or VII of the UN Charter to try Khmer Rouge officials for homicide and torture under Cambodian law and crimes against humanity and genocide committed between 1975 and 1979.[85] This was welcomed in principle by the Cambodian government, but key elements were rejected, including the recommendation that the tribunal should not be located in Cambodia because of security concerns, lack of facilities and fears of political interference. China also stated that it would veto an international tribunal set up by the Security Council.

A Cambodian taskforce was established which put forward an alternative proposal for a domestic trial process with limited international involvement. A 'mixed' tribunal found support from the United States, which proposed a 'super-majority' formula that would ensure that judicial decisions would require the agreement of at least one international judge. The Law on the Establishment of Extraordinary Chambers in the Courts of Cambodia for the Prosecution of Crimes Committed During the Period of Democratic Cambodia was passed by National Assembly on 2 January 2001 and came into force in August 2001. This required an agreement with the UN but the Law differed in important respects to a draft Memorandum of Understanding with the UN, which set out a framework for an internationalized domestic court. Negotiations broke down in February 2002 when the UN withdrew, stating that they could not move forward until Cambodia was willing to accept the conditions necessary for a fair trial. They were restarted in January 2003 as a result of French and Japanese pressure at the UN and finally, on 17 March 2003, Cambodian and UN officials agreed on a draft framework for a tribunal.

The agreement envisaged a panel of judges with a majority of Cambodians, but retaining the 'super-majority' formula. It was roundly condemned by various human rights groups as containing 'such fundamental structural, technical and political flaws that it is unlikely to provide a measure of justice to the millions of victims of the Khmer Rouge'.[86] Even after an agreement had been reached between the UN and the government of Cambodia in 2003, it took a further two years to gather pledges of sufficient funding for a 3-year mandate. Some eight years after negotiations opened, on 29 April 2005, the UN announced that the legal requirements for the tribunal had been met and that there was sufficient funding committed to sustain operations for a three-year period.[87]

# 5

# Domestic Trials

Domestic prosecution has regularly been used to address past violations of human rights in post-conflict societies. Since the end of the
Cold War, this has taken two forms: either domestic trials without aid
from the international community or, as discussed in the previous
chapter, 'internationalized' domestic trials where the international
community participates in some form in the proceedings.

Domestic trials – where prosecutions against alleged perpetrators
of war crimes and gross violations of human rights take place within
the existing judicial system using domestic laws, judges and prosecutors – have been promoted as a transitional justice mechanism, but
more commonly discredited and claimed to be counterproductive.[1]
They have been criticized because of their potential for bias, unfairness and victor's justice in such processes, and the risk of continued
destabilization. Moreover, the capacity for conducting genocide and
gross violations of human rights trials in post-conflict societies is, in
most cases, extremely limited. Set against these limitations are exaggerated expectations regarding the results of such trials.

Notwithstanding these potential difficulties, domestic trials have
regularly been mounted in post-conflict societies to address past
crimes. In, for example, Latin America, every country that established
a truth commission also held domestic trials,[2] and more recently they
have been held in Rwanda, the Democratic Republic of Congo
(DRC) and Iraq.[3] In light of the fact that there has been a significant
increase in the use of domestic trials to address past human rights
abuses from 1990 onwards,[4] it is crucial to establish under what circumstances they may be useful as part of a process of transitional
justice and to identify the key obstacles as well as the criteria which
need to be fulfilled prior to conducting domestic trials.

The criticisms surrounding the use of domestic trials focus on two broad issues. First, whether or not trials, both 'internationalized' domestic and purely domestic, should be used as a solution to dealing with past human rights abuses or whether other mechanisms promote reconciliation better; in other words a debate over retributive versus reconciliatory justice. The second issue relates to whether a domestic judicial system has the capacity, in the immediate aftermath of conflict, to conduct fair and unbiased human rights trials.

This chapter will begin by briefly highlighting the emerging rights and obligations in international law relating to domestic prosecution, and will outline the key practical and political obstacles to domestic trials as a transitional justice mechanism in a post-conflict society – these include political and financial obstacles, destabilization, issues of legitimacy, witness protection, evidence gathering and victor's justice. It will also underline the potential benefits of domestic trials, arguing that although considerable hurdles need to be overcome, it can be a useful mechanism for addressing past crimes and promoting reconciliation, in so far as certain criteria are in place. Critics of domestic trials have not taken into consideration the potential benefits they offer, including the fact that the use of this mechanism as one of a number of transitional justice mechanisms dealing with past abuses can be constructive – in particular in re-establishing trust in state institutions. That is not to suggest that domestic trials should be conducted in all post-conflict situations, or that there is an obligation to do so, but that it may pose less of a threat than argued by many if it is part of a holistic and complementary approach to transitional justice as long as the minimum criteria for a fair trial are upheld.

## Rights and Obligations in International Law

Although prosecutions have broadly been criticized as being a westernized way of seeking to right wrongs, where the punitive element is crucial, there have been numerous domestic trials for past crimes in countries in transition to democracy or emerging from violent conflict, as noted above.[5] There have also been demands for trials from civil society organizations in a multitude of post-conflict societies since 1990, whether in the domestic, international or 'internationalized' domestic arena.[6] Moreover, as discussed in chapter 1, international law has evolved to support the view that the state has a responsibility to prosecute gross violations of human rights.[7] International humanitarian and human rights law provide often overlapping applicable provisions outlining state responsibility and the need to respect human rights in armed conflict.[8]

The Rome Statute of the International Criminal Court (ICC) has also affirmed the primacy of nation-states in the fight against impunity and re-emphasizes the responsibility of states to ensure justice for crimes committed on their own territory.[9] Under customary international law there are crimes that cannot be ignored in domestic courts, including genocide and gross violations of human rights. In addition, it has been argued that victims have a right to have their case heard and seek redress for wrongs committed against them.[10] However, although there are treaty obligations that bind State Parties to prosecute, there is no agreement among legal scholars that there exists a customary legal obligation to do so, but there is a growing normative trend towards recognizing and upholding the duty of states both to investigate and prosecute human rights violations.[11] Nevertheless, it should be emphasized that even if an obligation to prosecute did exist, this may not solve the problems inherent in a post-conflict society striving for reconciliation and sustainable peace. Demanding or promoting domestic prosecutions of gross violations of human rights will not in any meaningful way begin to solve the problems in a post-conflict society unless two factors are fulfilled: key criteria should be in place enabling domestic prosecution and, crucially, it needs to be the solution sought by the local population to the issue of past crimes. If it is not, the chances of success are considerably limited.

As rights for victims have been established in international law, so have corresponding rights for the accused, including the right to a fair and public hearing.[12] The Office for the High Commissioner of Human Rights has also recognized the establishment of regional and national tribunals and judicial proceedings as measures to combat impunity, at the same time calling upon states 'to ensure that criminal proceedings are conducted in accordance with the right to a fair and public hearing by a competent, independent, impartial and duly constituted tribunal'.[13] If domestic trials are to be used as a transitional justice mechanism to deal with human rights abuse, these rights should be upheld. If they cannot, domestic trials should not be used.

However, the key issue that needs to be addressed prior even to contemplating the potential benefits of domestic trials is the state of the judiciary and the judicial system in post-conflict societies. This is the primary obstacle facing the use of domestic prosecution in post-conflict societies.

## Judicial Reform: A Primary Hurdle for Domestic Trials

In many countries, in the immediate aftermath of conflict the domestic judicial systems are in disarray. In societies that have been marred by conflict for years and even decades, the judicial system has also suffered and requires extensive reform, prior to conducting its ordinary functions, let alone prosecutions against war crimes. There are different ways in which a judicial system might be affected. It may simply have stopped functioning during the conflict or it may not have functioned effectively prior to the conflict. It may have been entirely corrupt, actively encouraging or supporting human rights abuse conducted by government agents, or simply complicit in its failure to deal with such abuses. In all these cases, serious procedural and institutional obstacles need to be overcome prior to conducting prosecutions.[14]

An authoritarian regime is always reflected in its judicial system; the extent of its corruption and/or non-functioning varies according to the regime and conflict, and can be found along a continuum from non-existent/non-functioning to fully functioning containing minor cases of corruption. Three categories that have been suggested are: illegitimate but functional, corrupt and dysfunctional, and devastated and non-functional.[15] It is extremely unlikely, almost certainly impossible, that any post-conflict society will immediately, upon cessation of hostilities, be able to conduct fair and impartial trials. This is not necessarily due only to corruption and abuse, but to the fact that there might no longer exist judges or prosecutors, or even a basic infrastructure such as a courtroom in which to hold trials. In Timor-Leste, for example, the militia in 1999 had burnt and destroyed over 70 per cent of the country's infrastructure. Moreover, most high-ranking posts were held by Indonesians; Timorese in such posts had fled, fearing accusations of collaboration and retaliation. Meanwhile, in Rwanda, it was estimated that 80 per cent of all justice personnel had been killed in the 1994 genocide. In addition, court records, law books and supplies were destroyed or stolen during the genocide – even copies of the penal code and code of criminal procedure were missing – and the judicial system was devastated.[16]

It is therefore somewhat futile to discuss the potential benefits and disadvantages of domestic prosecution if the judicial system is completely flawed – without a functioning judicial system, domestic trials against past crimes cannot be undertaken. If judicial reform is carried out as part of a holistic approach towards the rule of law in a post-conflict setting, then a primary obstacle against using domestic trials to redress past crimes is dealt with. Importantly, judicial reform cannot be viewed as separate or distinct from penal reform and police reform. If domestic trials are to be used to prosecute alleged human rights violators, then police reform – including how the perpetrators are arrested, how they are treated and how evidence is collected – is vital. Moreover, how they are kept until their trial and under what circumstances so as not to violate their rights, and, if punished, how they are confined and treated within their period of confinement – penal reform – is also critical. These three factors are strongly interlinked and need to be addressed as such from the outset in a post-conflict context.[17] A substantial number of the problems encountered in domestic justice systems are linked to deficient enforcement systems.[18] These need therefore to be addressed from the outset.

Judicial reform requires extensive resources and time, which can appear to be at odds with a transitional justice process where demands for justice frequently erupt in the immediate aftermath of conflict. However, as long as the minimum requirements of a fair trial are guaranteed, building and enhancing a rule of law system in a post-conflict society does not necessarily have to be fully completed prior to conducting domestic trials. On the contrary, establishing the rule of law can and should go hand in hand with domestic trials for human rights abuse. These are overlapping and interconnected processes. There needs to be a certain level of judicial reform and development for these trials to be held, but domestic trials can also contribute to the development of rule of law.[19]

However, a number of states that have applied domestic prosecution have done so after lengthy time periods, particularly in Latin America and Central and Eastern Europe, where the greatest number of trials were conducted after nearly a decade.[20] This demonstrates that domestic prosecution does not in all cases need to be started within a short period of time.[21] If a complementary approach is taken towards transitional justice, there might not be a need to have domestic trials at the very early stages of transition. If the government shows civil society that a long-term strategy will be put into place to address past violations, immediate solutions may not be expected.[22] Transitional justice processes may benefit from not taking place immediately after conflict, when all constraints, including political and financial, are most acute. Moreover, it has been argued that a time-lag can give both victim and perpetrator time to 'process their experiences'.[23] This will, however, entirely depend upon the circumstances – the context in which the conflict took place, and the actors involved – all of which will influence whether domestic trials are chosen as a transitional justice mechanism and when and how they are held. Although delaying domestic trials may have worked in the past, this does not mean that it is necessarily a solution – or something that should be promoted in all circumstances. Indeed, in some cases, 'justice delayed is justice denied' if judicial proceedings are put on hold for years. Rwanda is an example in this respect.[24] Perpetrators were arrested immediately after the genocide in 1994, but because of a lack of facilities as well as personnel, by 2002 only 6 per cent of the total number of detainees had been tried. The slowness of the domestic court system led the Rwandan government to begin using *gacaca* courts in addition to the formal system.[25] In addition, delaying a process of criminal justice can be a method by which new regimes avoid addressing the issue altogether, which carries with it the potential dangers of delegitimizing the new government, engendering a lack of trust in the judicial system, contributing to disillusionment among civil society and potentially perpetuating a cycle of vengeance.

Although it is not impossible to put in place minimal standards for a fair trial in a post-conflict society, it is extremely difficult. Critically, it is only in the context where these criteria have been established that it is relevant to discuss whether or not domestic trials can be a mechanism for reconciliation and stability or whether it heightens instability and vengeance.

## Political and Practical Obstacles to Domestic Trials

Domestic trials face multiple challenges if they are to be used as a transitional justice mechanism in post-conflict societies, even if the minimum standards of ensuring fair and unbiased trials are in place. Several of these challenges are also faced by 'internationalized' domestic trials, though international intervention in such trials can often alleviate them to some extent.[26] The following section will outline the key practical and political obstacles confronting domestic trials.

### Political realities and destabilization

The enabling and constraining factors, outlined in the Introduction to this book, including the context of the conflict, history, personalities of key actors and type of abuses committed, will influence whether or not domestic trials are or can be chosen. For example, Argentina held domestic trials after an official investigation had taken place into the fate of the disappeared after the end of the 'Dirty War'

in 1983. Conversely, Chile chose not to conduct trials after the military regime, but to hold an inquest. In many ways this was a compromise, affected by the power still retained by the military, where the
government supported the work of the truth commission, thereby
averting conflict with the military by promising not to follow up with
prosecutions.[27] In Uruguay the government called for neither an
inquest nor trials, but a sweeping amnesty was granted to the military,
which was justified on the grounds that it would be safest for the
country.[28] The circumstances of the conflicts reflected in many ways
the choices in these cases; whereas in Argentina disappearances
resulting in deaths was common, in Uruguay torture with long-term
imprisonment was the choice of state terror.[29] The policies chosen in
regard to transitional justice have also been shown to be significantly
influenced by the preferences of the heads of state, their convictions,
priorities and agendas.[30] The political realities and landscape of a
post-conflict society is therefore crucial in dictating whether or not
domestic trials will be chosen as a mechanism to deal with past crimes
or if, indeed, it is a viable option. Trials are often shunned because
the new government is not in a sufficiently strong position to promote
domestic trials. The situation in a post-conflict society is precarious
and trials are frequently viewed by policy-makers as jeopardizing reconciliation. There may also be an unwillingness to agree to domestic
trials by the parties to the conflict because they do not want to
acknowledge the crimes committed by their own side.

Moreover, it has been argued that the political situation in post-
conflict societies can be such that trials may destabilize the peace
agreement or obstruct the transition to democracy.[31] This view was
endorsed by a high-ranking Ministry of Justice official in the DRC,
who argued in 2005 that although it was imperative that the crimes of
past human rights abuses should be dealt with in the domestic courts,
in the transitional phase it could risk the foundation of the transition
and would most likely lead to destabilization.[32] He emphasized,
however, that it should be addressed in this forum after elections had
been held, and that this would be an issue to be determined by the
elected parliament.[33]

Many new regimes have avoided using retributive justice because
they do not want to put into jeopardy their relatively delicate positions
by angering the outgoing regime and its supporters, who can incite
violence if they feel persecuted. However, set against this there is an
expectation of change in post-conflict societies, and if no mechanisms
are implemented to address impunity, this may undermine the new
regime and stability. Accountability for violations of human rights

underpins democratic society, and, if this is absent, it may threaten stability and reconciliation, at the same time emphasizing to the perpetrators the non-existence of rule of law. Accountability for human rights abuse does not have to be established through domestic courts, but it needs to be addressed in some way – the significance of the transition from authoritarianism to democracy is one of accountability and should not be ignored.

However, the need for the government to have a working relationship with all parties to the conflict can mean new governments are faced with a choice that precludes domestic prosecution. For example, President Xanana Gusmao in Timor-Leste argued against any form of trials because it might create problems for Timor-Leste's relationship with Indonesia.[34] Nevertheless, since 1999 civil society in Timor-Leste has demanded trials for the abuses committed both during the Indonesian occupation and during the violence of 1999. This is an issue that has repeatedly been observed in many post-conflict societies where politicians and the government avoid prosecutions and use mechanisms such as truth and reconciliation commissions, in particular, to silence the cries for any other forms of justice process.

In some cases, avoidance of holding domestic trials by the political leadership may reflect their emphasis on national reconciliation rather than individual or community reconciliation. However, while national reconciliation is imperative – since it is often the elites that have started internal and external conflicts in the past and not populations, and it is essential that tensions between these groups are reduced[35] – ignoring the need for individual reconciliation is dangerous. After all, since it is the populations that have been used to perpetuate the stereotypes, vilification and conflict created by the elites, individual and community reconciliation also needs to be addressed. There has to be a balance between the two. This does not mean that this has to happen through domestic courts, but focusing exclusively on national reconciliation will rarely suffice.

All choices regarding transitional justice are shaped by political realities, and the context in which the conflict took place. It is regularly a compromise between what is morally compelling and what is practically feasible. It is important to underline, however, that while the *choice* of whether or not to use trials as a mechanism to address human rights violations is influenced by political realities, politicization of the process of domestic prosecution must be avoided at all cost. It is when there is a fear of political destabilization that amnesties are often given, which then creates a further obstacle for domestic trials.

*Amnesties*

Amnesties have often been used by political leaders as a means of not disturbing a fragile peace in a post-conflict society and to avoid a process of justice by perpetrators. Amnesties have been a very common tool in different types of post-conflict settings. They were granted, for example, in Argentina and Chile to military officers who had committed human rights violations. In Haiti, amnesties for the key perpetrators of the military regime were part of the agreement prior to the international intervention in 1994, and in South Africa conditional amnesties were granted in conjunction with the Truth and Reconciliation Commission (TRC). It has been suggested that amnesties can be a very effective way in which to curb abuses 'when implemented in a credible way' and that they can strengthen the peace process.[36] In such cases, amnesties are taken to be necessary, reflecting political realities on the ground, and they can be a useful tool in the inevitable bargaining process that goes on after conflict to build a stable society.[37] This seems to support the argument that, far from contributing to peace and reconciliation, the system of trial and retribution might actually be detrimental, fuelling destabilization of society. But critically there are numerous examples where amnesties have been accompanied by continued abuse.[38] One comes from Sierra Leone, where amnesties were included in the 1999 Lome Peace Agreement, but were followed by appalling atrocities.[39] This was also the case in Haiti, where the amnesties granted by and for the military and the absolute lack of accountability for any other human rights perpetrators exacerbated violence and breaches of human rights by the police, the special riot police and private security forces, as well as former military and paramilitary forces.[40]

Moreover, even if potential destabilization caused by the perpetrators of past crimes is reduced, amnesties can enrage the victims of that violence, hence fuelling instability and conflict. Ignoring the calls for justice – if there are such calls – within a post-conflict society can not only have a detrimental effect on people's confidence in the rule of law and democracy; they can also be potentially destabilizing if victims feeling let down by amnesties take it upon themselves to right wrongs. Amnesties can foster a culture of impunity where perpetrators, knowing that no action will be taken against them if they commit acts of violence and abuse, will continue to do so. This does not only increase fear and instability in a post-conflict setting, where the perpetrators can roam with impunity in the neighbourhoods of their victims, but it can renew conflict and violence because there has been no change.

Because of political realities and expediency it has been argued that 'amnesties should be recognized as a legitimate tool when it serves the broader interest in establishing the rule of law'.[41] However, granting broad amnesties in post-conflict societies can undermine the establishment and strengthening of rule of law. When none of the perpetrators of gross violations of human rights is in any form held accountable for their offences, it becomes very difficult to try to establish an accountable rule of law system in a post-conflict society in which the previous rule of law systems also protected abusers, violated the rights of the population and were corrupt and brutal. Furthermore, the complications become exacerbated if there is a failure to address past human rights abuses. If no one is held accountable for the crimes perpetrated, the legitimacy of the new system can be undermined and it can encourage further abuses or indicate impunity for such abuses. It is therefore complicated, if not impossible, to 'build a rule of law system while allowing complete impunity for major violations of human rights'.[42] Trust needs to be created in the rule of law system, and granting general amnesties can undermine this trust.

The examples of Algeria and Mozambique illustrate some of the dilemmas surrounding amnesties. After a referendum on 29 September 2005 in Algeria, more than 97 per cent of those who voted (of a voter turnout of 79 per cent) endorsed an amnesty granting exemption from prosecution to any member of armed groups for crimes committed since the conflict began in 1992, which, according to official estimates, left more than 200,000 killed.[43] The referendum was held after a protracted campaign by President Bouteflika for an amnesty, and has been severely criticized by numerous international organizations.[44] Victim and human rights groups in Algeria have also raised doubts concerning the amnesty law, particularly if it will lead to never knowing the truth about what happened to the victims and the disappeared, of which estimates vary at between 6,000 and 18,000.[45] It has since been claimed that opposition to the amnesty law was largely silenced by the government,[46] and that the referendum was 'the fruit of a gross manipulation exercise'.[47] It is too early to say what effect this will have on reconciliation and reintegration of Algerian society. Nevertheless, it is significant that such a vast proportion of the population has supported this effort. If amnesty is a true choice by the population in any given post-conflict society, then it should be respected by the international community, as long as it does not contravene international law. Interestingly, however, in Algeria the initial reaction from the largest insurgency group that would benefit from the amnesty was to ignore the offer.[48]

Mozambique is often referred to as an example where widespread amnesties were given after the conflict, with no subsequent violence, leading to reconciliation of society. This however ignores a number of vital factors. Traditional healing and justice mechanisms were put into place in the post-conflict setting as a transitional justice mechanism to deal with the violations perpetrated during the conflict. Moreover, the choice of amnesties was a decision made not only by political leaders, but by members of the society at large, who then played an intrinsic part in the reintegration process. It was a post-conflict situation in which a choice was made where one type of transitional justice was preferred over others. Furthermore, the choice reflected the nature of the conflict in Mozambique, which should be viewed in the context of the Cold War as a proxy war. When it ended, all parties were keen simply to return to the situation prior to the war.[49] Mozambique cannot therefore be held up as an example of the success of amnesties; other factors were vital in ensuring peace.

Crucially, arguing *against* general amnesties is not arguing *for* the use of domestic trials in all circumstances and contexts; to the contrary, what is best for each different situation must be sought and the solutions tailor-made. The obstacles facing domestic trials are, even in a context without amnesties, plentiful, and may complicate rather than ensure a path to justice.

### Financial obstacles

Even if there is considerable political will to choose a sytem of domestic trials as one of the mechanisms to address past crimes, post-conflict societies rarely have the financial capabilities to prosecute. They are often ravaged by years of war, and there are scarce resources for reconstruction, let alone conducting trials which may take several years. Moreover, if resources are allocated for this purpose, it may undermine work in other crucial areas. This is one reason which frequently renders domestic trials an unfeasible option.[50]

There has also been a continuous unwillingness on the part of the international community to support domestic trials, because of the view that they may be unfair and biased. However, where transitional justice forms part of the reconstruction of society, and if the minimum standards of a fair trial are ensured, then the international community has a duty to support whatever transitional justice mechanism is chosen by the post-conflict country. In Haiti, donors refused to support a process of prosecutions because there had been a truth commission, even though civil society had demanded justice in the form of prosecutions.[51]

It is important to emphasize that domestic trials pose substantially less of a financial strain than international tribunals, which are extremely costly for the international community. For example, the cost of the ICC for Rwanda is estimated to have amounted to $1 billion by the end of 2006.[52] Supporting domestic trials can therefore not only potentially support greater judicial reform and enhance rule of law, but it is also less costly than large international tribunals.

### Victor's justice or vengeance

A key argument against domestic trials without the influence of the international community is that they can turn into victor's justice. Where one party to the conflict has won an outright victory, domestic trials can be used not only to legitimize the new regime and dispel the other parties, but also to create a new mythology and rewrite the past through the judicial process – if only the losing parties are put on trial. Yet, an assumption should not be made that prosecution in post-conflict societies automatically leads to vengeance. All societies prosecute crimes because they do not wish to see crimes go unpunished, but this does not indicate vengeance.[53] Nor should it routinely be viewed as such in post-conflict societies where gross violations of human rights have taken place, although the risk is considerably higher.

International law has, however, evolved in recent years to pressure governments to ensure the fair and unbiased nature of domestic trials by reinterpreting the principle of *non bis in idem*, the principle that a person cannot be tried twice for the same crime. The statutes of both the ICTY and the ICTR (Articles 10 and 9 respectively) allow an alleged perpetrator to be prosecuted again if 'national court proceedings were not impartial or independent, were designed to shield the accused from international criminal responsibility or the case was not diligently prosecuted'. The Rome Statute reinforces this by stating in Article 20 that a perpetrator can be retried if the domestic trial had 'the purpose of shielding the person concerned from criminal responsibility for crimes within the jurisdiction of the ICC' or if the trials 'were not conducted independently or impartially in accordance with the norms of due process recognised by international law and were conducted in manner which in the circumstances was inconsistent with an intent to bring the person concerned to justice'. This exerts further pressure upon governments which opt for domestic trials to address past human rights violations to ensure that they are fair and unbiased, since, if they are interpreted not to be fair, the alleged perpetrators may still be prosecuted in an international forum.

In addition, a fair and unbiased judicial process can reduce the chances of vigilante justice and a spiral of popular vengeance and violence, because civil society sees that the judicial system is dealing with the alleged perpetrators. It can also heighten the perceived legitimacy of the judicial system among the population, since, commonly, prior to and/or during the conflict the judicial system has not addressed such issues at all. Hence, focusing on such issues signals a change not only in the judicial system, but in society at large, towards democratization and good governance. In other words, it 'transfers the individual's desire for revenge to the state or official bodies',[54] which in turn reduces the need for vigilante justice or popular vengeance. There is a higher chance of vigilante justice where there are few or no attempts at dealing with past crimes.

## Selectivity

Another criticism of domestic trials is that local judicial systems are not able to handle the potentially vast number of cases and hence only a few will be heard and the process will seem arbitrary and unfair.[55] There will always be an element of selectivity in the process of prosecutions; however, this is not necessarily a problem as long as there is no discrimination as to how investigations and prosecutions are carried out. Moreover, selectivity is present in truth commissions as well, but it is a problem that is largely ignored by their proponents.[56] Although criminal justice systems are not structurally able to deal with all crimes committed during a conflict, this does not automatically delegitimize prosecution and what role it can play in addressing gross violations of human rights.[57]

An attempt to circumvent the problem of selectivity was made by the Rwandan government, which sought to deal with all perpetrators of the genocide through a process of criminal justice.[58] Putting a whole country on trial not only leads to immense practical and ethical problems, but also raises the questions of the usefulness of such an approach and what can be achieved. The case of Rwanda exemplifies that using domestic trials in this manner can exacerbate problems rather than solving them.[59] The domestic trials in Rwanda have not been a success, and this has been recognized by the Rwandan government; putting the whole country on trial in the context of a devastated judicial system proved impossible. However, it is not necessary to deal with all the perpetrators of a conflict in one mechanism of justice. Prosecuting a number of key perpetrators for ordering and/or committing human rights violations – which may include the chief of police, head of militia movements, military commanders – will serve as a significant symbol that impunity no longer reigns. Cases should be prioritized according to the level of human rights abuse and where there is sufficient evidence to prosecute.[60] This type of selection will not undermine the judicial system or the process of transitional justice, since inherently there is selectivity in all criminal proceedings. Nevertheless, it is acknowledged that there are two potential problems. First, if only the high-ranking perpetrators are prosecuted, the lower-ranking violators may assume that they can continue to act with impunity.[61] Second, if only those who committed the most horrific abuses are prosecuted, they might be perceived as scapegoats.[62] But this argument assumes that domestic trials will be the only mechanism of transitional justice in a post-conflict society. If a complementary approach to justice is taken, where other mechanisms are employed alongside, addressing other perpetrators, there will not be such a danger of a perception of impunity for the vast majority, and the minority who are prosecuted will not be perceived as scapegoats

A combination of methods is necessary for reconciliation to begin to come about in any post-conflict setting. Crucially, prosecution is only one potential response to human rights violations, and, if used, can only ever be a partial response.[63] One method of transitional justice will rarely suffice to bring about reconciliation, sustainable stability and peace. It is the combination of different forms of justice that will have a greater probability of achieving the rather large objective of reconciliation, at both national and individual level. The so-called arbitrariness of prosecuting a few rather than all can serve several purposes, assuming that they are unbiased and fair – namely, that key individuals are dealt with in this manner thereby limiting impunity, and it can enhance rule of law and the legitimacy of the judicial system. Other perpetrators can be dealt with by the traditional methods, and some referred to in the context of a truth commission. It is not helpful therefore to see such issues dichotomously in terms of peace versus justice, reconciliation versus justice and trials versus truth commissions. It is not necessarily a choice between one or the other; it is a plurality of complementary mechanisms that will be more effective in establishing sustainable peace and reconciliation.

## Revictimization

Additional criticisms against domestic as well as 'internationalized' domestic trials emphasize that they focus on the perpetrator not the victim, that they can lead to revictimization, exacerbating the hostile feelings between perpetrator and victim,[64] and that they focus on individual guilt rather than patterns of widespread abuse.[65] Unfortunately, there is little doubt that trials can lead to revictimization and reliving of trauma, and that they complicate the process of individual healing. Truth-telling is always a risk, which, as will be discussed in the next chapter, is also present in giving testimony to truth commissions. Whether the risk is greater in local trials than in truth commissions is something that needs to be further researched in countries that have had both a truth commission and local trials to establish the extent of retraumatization in both groups. Nevertheless, in both instances there are advantages of finally being able to tell the truth to an authoritative body, which may change the victim's own situation and, in the case of a trial, punish the perpetrator. Although courts are not able to deal with the traumas experienced by the victims, they are a vehicle to reduce fear. If perpetrators are punished, it may reduce the general fear in civil society which may be present when perpetrators of past crimes continue to live alongside their victims.

Moreover, it is not necessarily bad that trials focus on the perpetrator. In fact, that may be exactly what the victims want. The courts' job is to establish individual guilt; truth commissions are there to establish patterns of abuse. The *primary* objective of trials in any context is not reconciliation, although individual reconciliation can come about as a result of trials. Victims often feel the need to establish individual guilt. The acknowledgement of violations, the public record of abuse, the emphasis that this was wrong and should not have been perpetrated, and the individualization of guilt can all serve as tools in the complex process of individual reconciliation. As has rightly been pointed out, a trial is not a vehicle to obtain forgiveness.[66] Trials demand accountability and punishment, and reconciliation is often equated with forgiveness, but it is only one part of the reconciliation process, which, if it comes at all, will come very late in the process. To forgive is an extremely individual and personal decision, which will not come about simply by revealing the truth – and sometimes not at all.

Reconciliation can come about as a result of seeing that impunity is no longer present in society and by the fact that the violations have been acknowledged. Acknowledgement is crucial for reconciliation, whether this takes place in a judicial or a non-judicial forum. In addition, individualizing guilt eradicates the perception that whole ethnic groups or communities are responsible for the abuse; it removes the stigma from the innocent members of the communities,[67] which can lead to reconciliation on a national level. If communal responsibility can be eradicated, the chances of promoting segregation and vilification of ethnic groups are limited. Therefore, individualizing guilt is not by default negative; on the contrary, it can serve to support reconciliation.

### Evidence and witness protection

For domestic trials to be held, there needs to be availability of evidence and a capacity to collect it, yet in the context of a post-conflict society this can be extremely difficult. Where mass violations of human rights have taken place, evidence needed in a court of law can often be absent, because of the scale of atrocities and lack of documentation. Even where such evidence might have been in existence, it may have been destroyed during the conflict. In both Cambodia and Sierra Leone, such evidence has been hard to find.[68] Ethiopia was an exception, where violations were meticulously documented and evidence easier to come by, yet it did not lead to a large number of trials.[69] A complaint raised in the DRC was that evidence, although sometimes in existence, disappeared.[70]

In cases where the evidence does exist, the gathering of it can often be fraught with difficulties. This is related to the police and investigative capacity, which is often lacking. Reform is frequently needed, and without reform and heightened capacity the collection of evidence may be jeopardized. Evidence-gathering must follow the correct procedures. If it doesn't, the cases run a risk of being thrown out of court. This is a challenge for domestic prosecutors and investigators when domestic trials are chosen in a post-conflict environment. It can be made easier by international assistance, but even then it can be problematic. International human rights investigators working in the context of domestic and 'internationalized' domestic trials are not necessarily lawyers or police investigators, and do not always have adequate knowledge on how to collect evidence that can be used in a court of law.[71] They gather evidence of human rights abuse, but often they do not fulfil the criteria needed for a trial,[72] which complicates matters in domestic trials.

Protection of witnesses and victims is also something that has been lacking in domestic trials.[73] This is a result of a combination of factors. The main problem is that, frequently, there are not sufficient resources to adequately protect victims and witnesses who come to testify. In a post-conflict society, where resources are lacking, witness protection becomes deprioritized. Lack of capacity prevails on all levels in a post-conflict reconstruction phase, which can be another factor hindering witness protection. Moreover, witnesses may not be given much protection or support in normal criminal proceedings and it might not therefore be emphasized during human right trials. It can also reflect an unwillingness to conduct proper trials, which was the case in Indonesia. Although Indonesia eventually bowed to international pressure and established a human rights court to hear crimes against humanity committed during the violence of 1999 in Timor-Leste, witness protection was severely lacking, especially for witnesses who were called from Timor-Leste to give evidence. The witnesses were frightened of testifying in case of repercussions, but this was largely ignored by the court, and sufficient protection procedures were not put in place. The witnesses had been traumatized by their experiences at the hands of the Indonesian security forces and militias, and therefore needed guarantees for their security. As a result, several important witnesses refused to partake in the proceedings and the case for the prosecution suffered substantially. During trials in the DRC, victims and witnesses received death threats and were very frightened of reprisals.[74] The problem in the DRC was that domestic trials took place early on when the conflict was still ongoing. Protection was therefore particularly difficult. Witness protection needs to be given adequate priority and support if domestic trials are to be an option of transitional justice.

## Benefits of Domestic Trials

The potential advantages of domestic trials must not be undervalued in the face of the many obstacles described above. Domestic prosecution can particularly enhance trust in a judicial system that has had limited or, in many cases, no trust during previous regimes. Judicial systems during times of conflict, war or authoritarian regimes habitually engender minimal trust by the civilian population, because it is frequently used against them, violating rather than protecting their rights. Using domestic courts as a vehicle for promoting and protecting civilian lives may therefore boost trust in the judicial system and the government, because it is their own government taking control of the process, signalling a commitment to accountability, which may not previously have existed. Domestic trials can therefore have a positive effect on the rule of law, strengthening accountability and transparency, because civil society sees that their demands are met in a judicial forum. Moreover, when the government acknowledges that the violations perpetrated should not have taken place, an important message is relayed to the public;[75] the crimes are no longer kept silent, but made public in a judicial forum, and recognized. The violations are accepted as part of the larger truth about the conflict, which can lead to individual reconciliation and acceptance of what took place. Acknowledgement and recognition are central to reconciliation and eventual healing.

Domestic trials also ensure greater local ownership of the process than a purely international mechanism, which is crucial to the continued success of the process. A major criticism of international tribunals has been the lack of local ownership. Furthermore, when the trial is situated in the country where the abuses took place, it can have a much more direct effect upon victims and potential reconciliation of society than international tribunals and courts situated elsewhere.[76] In addition, domestic prosecution can reinforce human rights norms and strengthen democracy[77] by implementing human rights rules in the judicial process through fair and unbiased trials.

It has also been argued that deterrence is a positive consequence of domestic and 'internationalized' domestic trials.[78] Instinctively, it might seem that a punitive mechanism will provide a higher deterrence effect than a non-punitive mechanism. However, the level of deterrence by trials for human rights abuse during conflict and war has been questioned. As Justice Jackson stated: '[P]ersonal punishment, to be suffered only in the event the war is lost, is probably not to be a sufficient deterrent to prevent a war where the war-makers feel the chances of defeat to be negligible.'[79] The deterrence effect of local trials may lie not in deterring future conflicts or wars on a massive scale, but in deterring further acts of violence in a transitional post-conflict society, by individuals and former combatants recognizing that there is a transition to another type of regime, where accountability is the rule not the exception. It can strengthen civil society's resistance towards renewed conflict and authoritarian regimes.[80]

However, what is crucial in this context is that although individual trials may not serve to adequately deter violations of gross abuses of human rights in the next conflict, it has not been proved that 'a policy of forgiving and forgetting automatically deters future abuses'.[81] Where demands for justice are not satisfied, it can encourage impunity and continued violations of human rights. Although the deterrence effect of individual trials may be questioned as to their ability to deter future conflict or war, this is most certainly the case when issues of justice are not addressed in any meaningful way. In the case of Indonesia and Timor-Leste, the absence of any real efforts of justice with regard to the Indonesian military troops who had been stationed there meant that the military continued to commit atrocities in other parts of Indonesia, such as in Aceh.[82]

## Conclusion

It has been stated that 'retributive justice, especially in the context of a post-conflict society, is at best plagued by certain shortcomings and at worst may endanger reconciliation and democratisation processes'.[83] All mechanisms of transitional justice are beset by shortcomings and are by their very nature not flawless, and in certain contexts they might all endanger reconciliation and democratization. However, it is crucial to bear in mind that reconciliation will very rarely be brought about by any type of transitional justice mechanism on its own, and will not appear in the immediate aftermath of a transitional justice process. It is also not something that can be easily measured since it takes place over a very long period of time and requires different types of action and intervention. Furthermore, reconciliation is a tall order, since it requires 'fundamental psychological adjustments in individual and group identity'.[84]

It is a common misconception that prosecutions lead to destabilization and further conflict, rather than to peace and reconciliation.[85] Prosecution can lead to reconciliation, particularly on an individual and community level, *as long as* the trials are strictly fair and unbiased. This does not mean that a post-conflict society emerging from violent conflict should choose domestic trials as the method by which to address past crimes, but that in certain contexts it may be a viable option that does not *necessarily* lead to instability and further conflict, and may serve to strengthen reconciliation. In particular circumstances, contrary to what many currently argue, local trials can be one of the many ways of redressing crimes committed during conflict. Four conditions which should be met prior to conducting domestic trials have been cited:

> A workable legal framework through well-crafted statutes of criminal law and procedure; a trained cadre of judges, prosecutors, defenders and investigators; adequate infrastructure such as courtroom facilities, investigative offices, record keeping capabilities and detention and prison facilities; and a culture of respect for the fairness and impartiality of the process and the rights of the accused.[86]

Assuming that these conditions can be met in a post-conflict society is perhaps somewhat unrealistic. There must therefore be a realistic standard of what can be achieved in the circumstances. This does not derogate from the right to a fair and unbiased trial and due process, which must be upheld. However, in spite of shortcomings in the infra-structure, domestic prosecutions may still be an option.

The extent to which domestic trials promote stability and peace is dependent upon a range of enabling and constraining factors, as outlined in the Introduction. There is no single best way for *all* post-conflict societies to deal with past crimes – it must be tailored to that specific context and country, with local ownership being the crucial ingredient. Yet, the extent of the symbolism of prosecution in a society where accountability has been absent should not be ignored or mini-mized. Using ad hoc solutions, hybrid courts and a combination of justice mechanisms may seem arbitrary to well-established democra-cies with long traditions of rule of law. Nevertheless, a transitional society must be recognized for its differences and that work must be undertaken within the restrictions that this framework ultimately provides.

## Box 5.1: Rwanda

After the genocide in Rwanda in April–June 1994, which resulted in nearly one million dead, the Rwandan government took the view that to ensure peace and stability there had to be a process of crim-inal prosecutions of the perpetrators of the genocide. The aim was to prosecute all who had been involved with the genocide.

However, the domestic trials have faced numerous problems. There were vast numbers of accused; between 100,000 and 150,000 people were detained. The rule of law system was non-functional and the police did not have the capacity to arrest – this was conducted by the military force, the Rwandan Patriotic Army (RPA). In addition, there were no proper facilities in which to house the accused so they were held in overcrowded prisons where deaths from malnutrition and disease have been rife.[87] Many in detention have been held without trial for as long as ten years. Although arrests were made in the immediate aftermath of the genocide, the first domestic trials did not take place until December 1996. There was a huge shortage of personnel after the genocide. It is estimated that over 80 per cent of those working within the justice system were either killed or had become refugees. The trials were also heavily influenced by the extensive lack of resources, external agents and some degree of corruption.[88] Donor commitments to domestic judicial reform in Rwanda were reportedly US$10 million per year (in the first five years after the genocide), whereas the budget for the ICTR was US$90 million.[89]

Between January 1997 and 2002, more than 7,000 individuals were tried, but, by 2003, this had just amounted to just 6 per cent of all who were at the time detained for genocide offences. The Rwandan government acknowledged that the vast number of accused within a crippled justice system, and the lack of prosecutors, judges and defence lawyers, would mean that 'at the present rate it would take over 200 years if Rwanda was to rely on the conventional court system to deliver justice'.[90] Therefore, to solve the crisis in the domestic system that Rwanda faced while trying to put all those accused of genocide-related crimes on trial, they adopted a categorization system whereby suspects were put into four different categories. Category 1 consists of the planners, organizers, instigators, supervisors and leaders of the genocide and these were still to be dealt with in the domestic formal judicial system. However, if a suspect was in category 2, 3 or 4, with less serious offences, they would be tried in the *gacaca* courts.[91]

The domestic trials also had a complicated relationship with the ICTR, in particular since the domestic court used the death penalty, which was handed down in 20 per cent of the cases;[92] the ICTR, on the other hand, which handled some of the worst perpetrators of the genocide, did not.[93]

## Box 5.2: The Indonesian ad hoc Human Rights Court

After much international pressure, Indonesia established the Human Rights Court (HRC) to address human rights crimes committed in Timor-Leste in 1999, so as to avoid having their security personnel potentially face international prosecution. It was riddled with problems from the beginning. The process was continuously postponed – the prosecutor named 23 suspects in January 2000, but it was not until January 2002 that indictments against 18 suspects were issued by the HRC. Large segments of the Indonesian government were non-supportive of the process, particularly President Megawati. Her attitude was underlined by her statement to the armed forces on 29 December 2001, when she stated: '[D]o your work in the best possible way without worrying abut accusations of human rights violations. Do your job without hesitation.'[94]

A key problem with the Court was the appointment of the judges. President Megawati did not approve the judges until 15 January 2002. There were 30 judges, including 12 practising judges and 18 academic professors, none of whom had any experience in hearing cases under international human rights law. In addition, the low wages and a requirement to work on the cases for five years excluded the most experienced judges.[95] This had a very negative effect on how the cases were conducted.[96]

The HRC's jurisdiction severely limited what it could achieve. The Court was only allowed to hear cases that had occurred within three districts of Timor-Leste: Dili, Liquisa and Kovalima – and only in the months of April and September 1999. This excluded hundreds of cases of torture, rape and killings. Because of this mandate, it became impossible for the Court to say anything meaningful regarding systematic violations and policies of human rights abuse. Moreover, the Prosecutor did not 'acknowledge the connection between the birth of the militia groups . . . and the Indonesian military and security policy enforced by the Indonesian army in Timor-Leste'.[97]

Of the 18 people indicted by the Court, 12 were acquitted and 6 were sentenced, receiving less than the legal minimum sentence. Abilio José Soares, the former governor of Timor-Leste, was found guilty of crimes against humanity and sentenced to three years' imprisonment. The former Regional Police Commander, Brigadier-General Timbul Silaen, responsible for security during the ballot, was acquitted, as were five Indonesian military, police and government officials accused of failing to prevent the massacre in Suai in September.[98] The former chief of the Dili police was sentenced to three years in prison and Dili's military commander was given five years. However, the sentences of four of the six sentenced were overturned in 2004 by the Appeals Court, leaving only two Timorese with sentences, and no Indonesians. All these factors strengthen the view that it was never the intention of Indonesia to provide justice for the crimes committed in 1999 in Timor-Leste. This is also underscored by the fact that the Indonesian government has repeatedly refused to cooperate with the Serious Crimes Investigation Unit and Special Panels in Dili when asked to extradite persons wanted for crimes in Timor-Leste.

## Box 5.3: The Supreme Iraqi Criminal Tribunal

The Supreme Iraqi Criminal Tribunal (SICT) was established by the Iraqi Governing Council to try Saddam Hussein and the Ba'ath Party leadership for genocide, crimes against humanity, war crimes, disappearances and summary and arbitrary executions committed during Saddam Hussein's dictatorial regime. It came about after the war with the coalition forces in which they ousted Saddam Hussein's regime. The government of Iraq announced in September 2005 that the SICT would begin the prosecutions of Saddam Hussein and his close supporters that same autumn.

The US had promoted and supported an international tribunal for Iraq, but the Iraqis made it clear that they wanted an Iraqi court to prosecute Saddam Hussein and his associates. However, they indicated that they wanted external help with the setting up of the tribunal. At the time of writing, there are numerous problems with the tribunal, including the application of the death penalty, the question of a fair trial and its politicization and, moreover, a concern that it will be viewed as 'victor's justice' and that it is significantly influenced by the US.[99] The tribunal's jurisdiction extends to the crimes of genocide, war crimes and crimes against humanity committed in the period 1968–2003. However, it cannot hear complaints against non-Iraqis, even those who have committed such crimes on Iraqi soil; ordinarily it is within the sovereign nation-state's jurisdiction to hear such claims, and this has raised doubts as to the independence of the SICT from the occupying powers.[100]

Although the SICT draws upon the experiences of previous tribunals, such as the Special Court for Sierra Leone, it relies heavily upon the 1971 Iraqi Code of Criminal Procedure, under which there may be problems concerning the treatment of the accused and the rights of the defence, which may not conform to international standards.[101] Several of the defendants have boycotted the trial, arguing that their rights are not being upheld. In January 2006, the Chief Judge Rizgar Mohammed Amin resigned, protesting over government interference and harsh public criticism. The new Chief Judge decided to continue with the trial, although the majority of the defendants and their defence lawyers refused to appear in court. Three defendants were at one point barred from the proceedings because of unruly behaviour.

Critically, three defence lawyers have been killed since the start of the trial proceedings. As a result, Saddam Hussein and three co-defendants went on hunger strike from 7 July 2006 to ensure better security for their lawyers.[102] After 16 days of hunger strike, Saddam Hussein was taken to hospital and force-fed and the trial continued without him.[103] He was returned to court in late July, while his defence team continued to boycott the proceedings. The court was adjourned at the end of July and on 5 November 2006 Saddam Hussein was found guilty of crimes against humanity and sentenced to death by hanging. He was executed on 30 December 2006. Three of his co-defendants were also sentenced to death by hanging.

# 6

# Truth Commissions

Establishing a truth commission (TC) in a post-conflict society has become increasingly popular. Since 1974, more than 25 such commissions have been established around the world, and often the first thing that newly elected politicians call for in a country making a transition from authoritarianism to democracy or from war to peace is the establishment of a truth commission. TCs, as we currently perceive them, stem from the numerous Latin American commissions held in the 1980s;[1] however, they have evolved and changed since that time, particularly in the context of a post-conflict society which has experienced international intervention.

A wealth of literature has grown up as a result of this expansion, which includes detailed analysis of a number of cases.[2] However, a large proportion of this literature focuses on a few key cases only – in particular the South African Truth and Reconciliation Commission (TRC) and the various Latin American commissions – and makes recommendations for the design and operation of such a mechanism.[3] There is an underlying assumption in much of the literature that TCs are a path to reconciliation and peace for all post-conflict societies, and that they are to be preferred to other transitional justice mechanisms. However, more recently, they have come under criticism even from their erstwhile supporters in the human rights community.[4] Increasingly, it has been recognized that this approach to transitional justice has its shortcomings as well as its advantages. Moreover, as with all transitional justice mechanisms, the aims, mandate and what can be achieved by a TC are context-dependent.

In addition to truth commissions, other types of truth-seeking mechanisms have been established throughout the years. These have included historical commissions which have looked into abuses that took place many years ago – these serve to set the historical record straight, but do not affect the sitting government. There have also been commissions of inquiry, which tend to focus narrowly on abuses that took place at a specific event, and have typically been less independent of the political process.[5] In addition, there have been numerous non-governmental commissions, particularly by human rights organizations, uncovering violations and abuses committed. These are especially important in contexts where it is impossible to have an official truth-seeking mechanism.[6] In this chapter, however, the primary focus will be on truth commissions.

The following discussion focuses on the benefits and limitations of TCs as a tool of transitional justice, drawing on numerous cases.[7] It will be argued that TCs are not the answer to all post-conflict societies' transitional justice demands and that they face several problems that have often been underestimated. The first part of the chapter discusses issues of truth, reconciliation, healing and retraumatization. It moves on to emphasize the importance of local ownership and argues that establishing a truth commission should be a choice made by the population. Perhaps most importantly, TCs should not be viewed as an alternative to trials and/or other justice mechanisms, but as one of a range of approaches that can be used in a complementary manner in a post-conflict society.

## Definitional Clarity

Truth commissions are established to investigate human rights abuses perpetrated in a specific time period, usually during conflict and civil unrest, and ranging from assault to mass killings. Critically documenting the disappeared is an important function of TCs. They investigate abuses perpetrated by military, government or other state institutions or non-state actors. They are non-judicial bodies, which do not have the authority of the courts and cannot punish, although they may in some cases be mandated to make recommendations – whether or not these are implemented is entirely dependent upon political will.[8] TCs allow victims and their relatives to disclose human rights abuses; some commissions also let the perpetrators give their account of events. Typically, they are established and given authority by the local governments or international organizations, in some cases by both. They exist for a specified time period only, but can have a multitude of different procedural and organizational arrangements.

The focus of a truth commission is not so much on the individual, but on establishing a pattern of human rights abuse committed within a given timeframe.[9] TCs have different official names – for example, truth and justice commission, truth and reconciliation commission, historical clarification commission, etc. These names reflect the different contexts, backgrounds and objectives of the individual commissions and what is seen as their essential aims. A TC cannot determine culpability of the individual, and it cannot punish or sanction perpetrators of human rights abuses. It can give recommendations for broad reforms of state institutions based on its findings, and suggest reparations for the victims, which a court cannot. In some cases, it may also make recommendations for criminal trials. Primarily, however, it is a vehicle for truth-telling, and for establishing and voicing the victims' stories – stories which may otherwise remain untold.

The aims and objectives of TCs are broadly to determine and create an historical record of human rights abuses, while at the same time giving the victims an opportunity to be heard and instituting by its process an official acknowledgement that these acts took place; making recommendations for reform and change; bolstering and legitimizing the new political authorities; providing a measure of accountability; and ultimately leading to or assisting in healing and reconciliation of the post-conflict society.[10] These objectives are extensive and have been shown to be beyond the reach of many truth commissions.

## Design and Resources

The design and composition of truth commissions can take many shapes and forms; they will be structured by the context of the conflict as well as the country's political, historical and cultural framework – and they should be uniquely tailored to the specific context of the post-conflict society. Nevertheless, minimum standards should always be followed.[11] The mandate and the way in which commissioners are elected to sit on the commission can vary extensively, both of which greatly influence the potential successful outcome of the commission. It is, in particular, the political context within which a TC is set and the individual commissioners elected that has a significant impact upon the outcome of the commission. In many cases foreigners have been chosen to sit on commissions because it has been felt that it would make it more fair, impartial and unbiased. For example, in Guatemala the chair of the commission was a non-national, and El Salvador, Haiti and Sierra Leone each had three non-nationals on their commissions.

In a number of cases, commissioners were elected without any consultation with civil society; this was the case in, for example, Argentina, Chad, Chile, Haiti and Uganda.[12] Extensive consultation with civil society to garner support for the process is essential and, in recognition of this, there has been a trend towards more extensive consultation with the population in later TCs, South Africa being one pertinent example, as well as Sierra Leone and Timor-Leste. The Commission of Reception, Truth and Reconciliation (CAVR) in Timor-Leste was the result of an initiative taken by the congress of the National Council of Timorese Resistance (CNRT) and all the commissioners were Timorese, although they were supported by international experts.[13] Meanwhile, the Truth and Reconciliation Commission Act in Sierra Leone provided for 'broad consultation with a cross-section of Sierra Leonean society'.[14] These TCs were part of an evolution regarding consultation with civil society, which it was hoped would become a feature of subsequent TCs. However, in the DRC there was no such consultation with civil society, and, consequently, the commissioners were chosen along party and faction lines.[15] The selection mirrored political realities on the ground and was conditioned by the fact that the commission was established while the conflict was still ongoing, rather than reflecting the demands of civil society for the truth.

The mandate and the powers bestowed on a TC are crucial in determining the impact the commission is able to have on reconciliation. The mandates typically specify how long the commission will be working, which varies, but is often not much beyond two years; and what time period the commission will conduct inquires into. This can either be very broad, encompassing the whole period of the conflict or previous regime (as in Timor-Leste, where the TC was mandated to look at violations committed from the beginning of the Indonesian occupation in April 1974 until the withdrawal in October 1999), or be more limited in scope. It is important to select a time period that is as broad as possible rather than restricting it to certain dates or specific events. If only selected dates or events are investigated, the legitimacy of the process can potentially be undermined, since what might have happened during the rest of the time period in question is not considered. Similarly, if the TC is mandated to investigate the conduct of only one side in a conflict, or only the government's conduct and not that of opposition forces (or vice versa), it can lead to a lack of trust in the TC and scepticism as to the government's desire to uncover the whole truth about what took place.

The mandate of a TC also sets out what violations are under investigation and what powers the commission has, which govern its ability to take testimony from victims, witnesses and perpetrators. For example, South Africa's TRC had substantial powers, including the power to subpoena, and subsequent commissions were keen to follow this example. Ghana's National Reconciliation Commission (NRC) was also given the power to subpoena, as well as equivalent powers to the police 'for the purposes of entry, search, seizure and removal of any document or article relevant to any investigation', and the right to question any person.[16] Sierra Leone's TRC, which emulated the one in South Africa, also had broad powers, including the power to subpoena.[17] Apart from these few examples, however, extensive powers have been rare in TCs. In Guatemala, for example, the Historical Clarification Commission (CEH) had no power to subpoena, no search and seizure powers, was not able to hold public hearings or name names, and it was preceded by amnesty laws.[18] The TRC therefore set a milestone in regards to the powers of commissions, and although some have followed this example not all have chosen to do so. Morocco's Equity and Reconciliation Commission (IER) had a more limited mandate, whereby the commission could investigate and gather information, but had no power to compel testimony.[19]

A weakness of many TCs is that they have not been given the power to compel victims and perpetrators to testify and cooperate, or to impose sanctions if cooperation has not been forthcoming. This can lead to only a partial truth being uncovered. The mandate also commonly states the potential for follow-up by the government once the commission has published its report.[20] However, the TC has no power to ensure that there is a follow-up process – this depends entirely upon the prevailing political climate and willingness of the government to implement the commission's recommendations, which may be absent.

As with all transitional justice mechanisms, having sufficient resources is vital to ensure its successful implementation. Compared to other mechanisms, TCs are not wildly expensive undertakings and this is one of their many benefits, especially when set against the huge costs of international courts. But post-conflict societies may still not have sufficient funds to conduct such a process. For example, although the budget of the TRC in Sierra Leone was a relatively meagre $6 million, compared to the $56 million assigned to the Special Court, it was still a significant sum when set against the wide range of other demands of post-conflict reconstruction. Earlier TCs rarely exceeded $5 million, but since the Guatemalan and South African commissions, budgets have generally increased. Both these two commissions stand out in regard to the size of their budgets: South Africa spent $18 million per year for the two and a half years the commission was operational, and the budget of the Guatemalan Commission was $11 million. Where there is more international involvement and interest, there is also more funding forthcoming. In Guatemala most of the funding came from other governments, namely the US, Norway, Sweden, Japan, The Netherlands and Denmark.[21] Where international interest is low, it will be less easy for a post-conflict government to establish a truth commission.

## 'Truth' and 'Reconciliation'

Its very name establishes that what a truth commission seeks is the 'truth'; 'reconciliation' is sometimes also an explicit goal and almost always an implied objective. Both, however, are complex concepts and objectives. Truth in the form of narratives is never simply uncovered, but is partially constructed and affected by numerous processes and actors. This is even more the case in the aftermath of conflict.

A typology of truths has been suggested.[22] The list includes factual/forensic truth, which only details what can be verified, such as the number of bodies, how they were killed, what weapons were used, etc.; it does not try to establish why the atrocities were committed or the political context, and nor does it place the violations within a moral framework. Second, personal/normative/narrative truth, a subjective form of truth, is needed where written records do not exist and oral retelling becomes a must. And, third, dialogue truth, where truth comes through discussion between perpetrators and victims; however, such a dialogue can be difficult to establish and, even though it can serve to clarify *what* happened, it might not establish *why*. There is also restorative truth, which may come through acknowledgement of the past; and others have added historical and moral truth to this list.[23]

Most TCs have not acknowledged the complexities of 'truth'. The South African TRC is an exception in this regard. The TRC outlined four different types of truths that could exist – namely, factual, personal, social and healing.[24] Although this did acknowledge the complexity of 'truth', it may not have made it less problematic when applying it in the TRC's process. Unfortunately, numerous commissions have not even acknowledged the problematic nature of 'truth', but assumed that one truth could be established, and must be established so that reconciliation could ensue. Defining the truth as merely factual may be one method of circumventing becoming entrapped in the complexities of its meaning. That said, many among the military in Latin America felt they were fighting communist expansion, which they thought justified the use of extraordinary security measures. They did not deny the facts of what took place, but felt it was justified under the circumstances, hence 'shared facts do not necessarily conduce to shared truths'.[25] There might therefore be agreement as to the facts concerning gross violations of human rights taking place, but to agree on what these facts mean can be more difficult.

A truth commission cannot solve the inherent problems of the concept of truth, which has been debated by different academic disciplines for years without any answers being forthcoming. A TC will not be enhanced by returning to an endless debate of the 'true' meaning of 'truth'. Yet, since the very premise upon which a TC is built is that of truth, it makes it vital that the problematic nature of the concept is acknowledged. The commissioners should pay particular attention to the different levels of truth, while underlining the very subjective element in narrative truths. Importantly, regardless of the complexities of the concept, the fact remains that when such truths have been voiced they can no longer be denied, which may lay the foundation for a process of reconciliation.

Reconciliation is also central to truth commissions; in fact, as stated above, numerous TCs have the very concept in their name and nowhere perhaps was it as strongly emphasized as in South Africa, where the name Truth and *Reconciliation* Commission was chosen deliberately, since reconciliation was the objective of the commission, and forgiveness and *ubuntu* were underlying the whole process.[26] Here the distinction between national and individual reconciliation becomes important. TCs, because they are bodies where individual testimonies are heard, can indicate to the victims that individual reconciliation is the objective. Individuals are interviewed and testimonies recorded of the abuses perpetrated against them; it therefore seems like an individualization of the abuse. This is also what is promoted as one of the great strengths of a TC in comparison to trials, namely that the focus is on the victim rather than the perpetrator. Victims therefore commonly expect individual reconciliation as a result of a TC. However, a TC tracks the overall general pattern of human rights abuse and investigates the social and political factors leading to abuse – the focus is that of national reconciliation. This can inevitably lead to disappointment among the victims who had anticipated, or hoped for, a solution to their individual cases.

Since truth commissions focus on patterns of abuse, individual victims may be disillusioned by such a process and want more, while others may feel content that the violations committed against them have been established as part of a wider pattern. Hence, establishing a case within the wider context of a pattern of abuse may also lead to individual reconciliation. It serves the purpose of placing the suffering of one in the context of many; it can create an understanding of why the individual had to suffer and make sense of the violations that were committed against the individual by placing the suffering in a larger framework and relating it to the fact that this was part of violations perpetrated by state institutions on, in many cases, a vast scale. Reconciliation is a highly individual process and whether or not it will come about as a result of placing the abuses in a larger framework will vary according to the personal experience of violations. Individual reconciliation is hard to achieve and perhaps even harder to measure through a TC, especially because forgiveness, healing and reconciliation are such personal experiences.[27]

It is frequently asserted that for reconciliation to come about, knowledge of the truth is essential. The chair of the TC in Honduras emphasized that 'only after truth is known and justice rendered are pardon and reconciliation possible'.[28] A UN principle states that 'every people has the inalienable right to know the truth about past events and about the circumstances and reasons which led, through systematic, gross violations of human rights, to the perpetration of heinous crimes'.[29] Knowing and establishing the truth might be a right in post-conflict societies, yet that does not mean it is the best solution for all; moreover, they can choose not to exercise that right. The process of reconciliation can be started without establishing a TC and detailed analysis of past abuses. Mozambique and Cambodia chose not to establish TCs, because they did not want to relive the historical facts, fearing in part what the consequences of such a process might be.[30] Although there has been consistent international pressure for truth-seeking to take place in Cambodia, the idea has found little resonance within the population. If a country's approach to reconciliation is not that of truth-telling then this should be accepted by the international community.[31] It should be kept in mind, however, that, although Mozambique and Cambodia are examples of cases where the absence of truth-telling has not led to renewed conflict, denial may nevertheless lead to further conflict and impunity.[32]

Truth is in many circumstances essential to start the process of reconciling the parties of the conflict, but not in all. There are multiple different ways to begin reconciliation, of which truth is but one – whether or not truth is crucial for reconciliation is dependent upon several factors, including the context of the conflict, the parties to the conflict and their aims, the international community and their involvement, particularly since they emphasize the importance of a truth-seeking process. Crucially, what must be recognized is the diversity between post-conflict societies and that their needs to recover after conflict will be different.

## Restorative Justice: Healing and Retraumatization

Truth commissions are a restorative justice process, which eschews the punitive elements of trials. It is commonly argued that, because of its non-punitive core, it is of more use in a post-conflict society, and in particular that it will lead to reconciliation of societies after war, more so than different types of trials, whether in the form of international tribunals, special courts or domestic trials.[33] It is in the context of TCs that the concepts of forgiving, healing and reconciliation are most often heard. Moreover, because TCs are often purported to be the primary vehicle of restorative justice, since traditional justice mechanisms have received much less attention,[34] it is here where this particular discussion is found. Promoters of restorative justice as the solution to the post-conflict transitional justice dilemma tend to emphasize the healing potential of TCs,[35] and that they 'may even be structured to enhance the therapeutic benefit of testifying'.[36] However, it can be questioned how much individual healing can come about as a result of a truth commission process.

A truth commission's healing potential, as all transitional justice mechanisms, may be limited. Healing at an individual level indicates restoring mental health to individuals who have suffered and been traumatized perhaps for a period of several years. This is a much more difficult and vaster objective than establishing patterns of abuse and the political and social reasons for these violations. Emphasizing healing also shifts the focus from a justice to a health issue. There is an implicit assumption that healing can automatically come about as a result of truth-telling in the context of a TC. Yet healing is an extremely personal experience, which will take different forms and length of time for each individual. Research has shown that healing can often come about through a process of talking about what has happened.[37] But this tends to reflect an individual therapy environment. A TC setting is very different.[38] TCs cannot equal the relationship built over time between a therapist and a victim. Victims will commonly only meet a statement-taker – and that only once – or testify in front of the whole commission, in public or private; either way it is very different from a therapy setting. Without professional therapists to support them individually, the question becomes how much healing can take place in such a setting? As has been pointed out, to be therapeutic, a statement needs to move beyond the plain fact and involve the emotional reactions.[39] This may be difficult in the context of a truth commission.

It would perhaps be an advantage if the discussion of the benefits of TCs stopped being couched in the medical language of healing. This language also ignores people who do not consider themselves to be victims, but survivors – they do not necessarily feel the need for healing, but may, rather, emphasize the need for justice. Perhaps the emphasis should be less on healing and more on acknowledgement of past abuses and reconciliation, and what that can begin to do for healing in the long term. Healing cannot be achieved in the short term or by a TC. It may be essential to face, rather than forget, trauma,[40] but a TC may not be the most appropriate forum in which to do so as far as individual healing is concerned.

To expect any transitional justice mechanism to achieve individual healing is expecting too much, particularly in circumstances where therapy and victim support are scarce. Truth commissions should have more limited and realisable criteria, focusing on accountability, letting the victims come to terms with what has happened, whilst emphasizing the acknowledgement of the gross violations of human rights that have taken place. A process of healing may begin for some who testify in front of a truth commission, but rarely on its own will it achieve individual healing, nor is it meant to.

Opposed to the purported healing propensities of TCs is the issue of revictimization and reliving the trauma of horrific abuses. It is important to emphasize it in this context because TCs are always highlighted as being restorative in nature and the potential for revictimization is frequently underestimated. Yet, they can also retraumatize. Crucially, it has been found that reliving trauma through truth-telling can serve to slow down the healing process.[41] Whether the testimonies are conducted in public or given in confidential statements, the experience can be difficult. It can be extremely traumatic to relive past abuses in public and over radio and television, especially for women. Whether in public or private, women of many cultures do not want to detail the crimes committed against them. This was evidenced in Morocco, in that the testimonies were quite general, and more importantly, silent on the subject of rape.[42]

Victim and witness support are rarely substantial in post-conflict societies, which is a problem in all types of transitional justice mechanisms.[43] Most TCs have not had the capabilities or resources to provide adequate support, although, again, South Africa was an exception in this respect. The only person that the victims will usually meet is the statement-taker, who is not necessarily trained to deal with people who have experienced vast trauma. Yet, so much relies on these statement-takers and whether or not the telling of the victims' stories will lead to revictimization and also how the TC is perceived. For many, the perception of the TC will be based solely on their experience with this one person. It is therefore crucial that the education and training of statement-takers is conducted in a thorough fashion prior to beginning the work of the TC. For many, even talking confidentially about the violations will be an ordeal, and it is essential that the statement-takers do not exacerbate this in any way. In Timor-Leste, the CAVR staff were given a three-week course in how to conduct the statement-taking and relate to the victims.[44] This may be sufficient to gather information for a TC, but for most victims the statement-takers' capabilities will most probably not suffice in terms of individual healing.

## Additional Benefits and Limitations of Truth Commissions

### Acknowledgement and local ownership

Truth commissions give a voice to the voiceless, to the people who have for years been persecuted by abusers, but the trauma and pain they suffered has never been recognized. The acknowledgement that this took place and what effect it has had on the people testifying is crucial. Moreover, it serves an educational function in that it instigates awareness of what took place during the time of conflict among all people in society, which leads to acknowledgement of past abuses. TCs can educate regarding the whole spectrum of political and social reasons for the abuse and violations conducted by state institutions – they can be a 'most powerful tool to inoculate a society against dictatorial methods'.[45] Not forgetting, but establishing a written record and acknowledgement of the past, is one contributing factor in ensuring that such atrocities are not repeated. The aim of a TC is to establish not only the truth, in its many forms, but also accountability for human rights abuses; in this way, it can complement trials. By starting a process of acknowledgement and potential reconciliation, a TC can strengthen democratic transition in the aftermath of war. It can signal a change from an authoritarian, brutal regime and conflict to a transparent, accountable form of government.

In addition, TCs have the potential to have complete local ownership of the process of transitional justice – in fact this is critical to their success.[46] International assistance in creating and setting up a truth commission can be important, but it must be a locally owned process and not viewed as something imposed from the outside. If it is locally owned, and properly implemented, then a TC can have a significant effect upon civil society – it can demonstrate that the government is taking responsibility and acknowledges past abuses and is willing to do something about it. This is particularly so if the recommendations that follow from the TC are implemented. The positive impact of local ownership is enhanced by the fact that a TC takes place within the borders where the conflict took place. The population that suffered the abuse has the opportunity not only to partake directly in the proceedings, but also to see the direct effect of it, in terms of perpetrators acknowledging what took place, recommendations and reform put into operation and in some instances reparations paid out.

### Amnesties

Conditional amnesties can potentially hinder the overall aim of reconciliation in the context of a truth commission. South Africa was the first TC to incorporate an amnesty clause in its mandate, where a perpetrator would not risk prosecution if he/she told the truth about past abuses. This has since been discussed by other commissions. This approach – very different from other TCs and unique at the time to South Africa – has raised complications. The question of conditional amnesties is a controversial issue, particularly because the perpetrators may tell their stories without remorse and with impunity. It also abrogates the rights of victims to seek redress and is 'inconsistent with a state's obligation under international law to punish perpetrators of serious human rights crimes'.[47] The result of a structure that incorporates conditional amnesty is that the perpetrator immediately walks free after testifying, whereas the victims are left waiting for reparations which may never come.[48] This can delay or hinder individual reconciliation and reinforce impunity by establishing that actions will not have consequences.[49] This in turn can increase fear, instability and insecurity. Not all victims will be satisfied with knowing what happened to their loved ones, or that the perpetrators acknowledged that they committed particular crimes or gave the order to do so. It can become especially difficult, since perpetrators giving testimony in return for amnesty do not necessarily believe that it was wrong to commit these atrocities, but that they had legitimate reasons to do so – for example, in cases of threats to national security. If this is the case, it will not further reconciliation, but simply be a way for the perpetrators to avoid prosecution by providing a factual account of events. For reconciliation to begin, the victims need to find the claims of remorse, if they are uttered, to be credible. Conditional amnesties may serve the larger national reconciliation process, but on an individual level people may still feel wronged. Therefore, conditional amnesties should only be incorporated into a TC mandate with great caution. Although the South African TRC was successful in many ways,[50] particularly in relation to the number of victims, witnesses and perpetrators who testified before the commission, it was also controversial by its inclusion of conditional amnesties. Critically, this has led some, including Bishop Tutu, to call for the prosecution of perpetrators.

### Due process and naming names

In cases where amnesties are not incorporated in the mandate, the findings of the commission can potentially lead to criminal prosecutions after the end of its mandate. The commission in Argentina, which documented the disappeared between 1976 and 1983, handed all its files over to prosecutors, and these provided the grounds for the subsequent prosecution of the junta leaders.[51] However, because of an absence of political will, the difficulty of conducting such trials and the question of due process and naming names, this has not been a common occurrence. The political will and ability to conduct trials are often absent in a post-conflict society.[52] More importantly in the context of the potential to follow up with trials after or in conjunction with a truth commission are the issues of due process and naming names. Because a truth commission is not an official judicial forum, it does not need to follow the proper procedures of due process, nor does it have to follow the same strict evidence procedures as a court of law. Consequently, the evidence gathered might be sufficient to establish that human rights violations occurred and that a pattern of such abuse was conducted by, for example, the military forces or police services. However, the evidence might not be adequate for individual prosecution in a court of law, and might be deemed inadmissible.

Issues of due process and naming names further complicate a truth commission process. Due process demands that the accused are given the opportunity to defend themselves once accused of a crime, but if the perpetrators are named in the report of the TC, they are not given this chance.[53] A commissioner on the Chilean truth commission, which did not name names, stated that 'to name culprits who had not defended themselves . . . would have been the moral equivalent to convicting someone without due process'.[54] On the one hand, the rights of the accused must be protected, but on the other, uncovering the truth without naming perpetrators may lead to it being a less effective tool of transitional justice. The mandate of the TCs in El Salvador, Chad and South Africa explicitly allowed the commissioners to name names. In El Salvador the commission concluded that 'not to name names would be to reinforce the very impunity to which the parties instructed the commission to put an end'.[55] This did not lead to prosecutions; on the contrary, five days after the report of the commission was published, full amnesties were given to the perpetrators who had been named in the report.[56] However, a number of top-ranking military officials were forced to retire from government positions, but they were given full pensions.[57] This had a negative effect on reconciliation since the perpetrators were, in the eyes of the victims, rewarded for their crimes, although they had lost their positions. Morocco's IER chose not to name names, perhaps not so much out of respect for due process, but because of the absence of political willingness to follow up with prosecutions.[58] The CEH in Guatemala was also not allowed to name names, which was criticized and led to the chair of the commission stating that this stopped them from 'penetrating the heart of evil'.[59]

This is a difficult conundrum to solve for a TC, particularly since, if perpetrators are named, but no further action is taken in the formal judicial system, it may lead to popular vengeance and violence. It is only a de facto not a de jure pronouncement of guilt, but it is doubtful whether this distinction will be relevant to the victims, who might want to see the perpetrators punished, which could then lead to vigilante retribution. In Haiti they found another way to ensure individual culpability without naming names in the report. A confidential appendix with the names of perpetrators of human rights abuses was attached to the final report, so that they could be prosecuted in a court of law, depending on the evidence produced.[60] But this can only be a solution if there is political will and a judicial system capable of dealing with trials. Insufficient action was taken after the release of the report in Haiti, and thereafter the judicial reform process and security sector reform rapidly unravelled.[61] Hence action based on the findings of the TC was minimal to non-existent.

## Deterrence

There is also an assumption that documenting past abuses will deter abuses in the future. When abuses are recorded, they can be acknowledged, which ensures that what happened will not be forgotten. The deterrence effect of such a process can, nevertheless, be questioned. Even though it is vital that these abuses are acknowledged and recognized, the extent to which a TC's revelations of the truth of a particular conflict can deter a potential conflict elsewhere, with different parties, actors, reasons and causes, may be limited. There is no inherent deterrent within the framework of a TC in a post-conflict society. What it does do is ensure that perpetrators know that if they do trespass, it can become public knowledge. Moreover, if it is followed by a process of reform of government ensuring transparency and accountability of the security forces, the chances of such abuses reoccurring within the institutional framework can be minimized. Therefore remembrance is vital. Also, providing 'an accurate record can serve as a powerful deterrent to later revisionism'.[62] Yet, this does not mean similar acts will be deterred in the future. What is important is that revelations of the truth can function as an 'insurance against collective amnesia'.[63] A TC is a tool of remembrance and acknowledgement; empowered with this knowledge, civil society can work against the return of such regimes.

## Political obstacles

Although TCs are potentially much less destabilizing than domestic trials and less contentious among both outgoing and new regimes, they too can be deemed politically sensitive, and therefore the recommendations are not always implemented by the sitting government.

In post-conflict societies the outgoing regime wants to avoid prosecution, civil society wants truth and justice and the new regime wants to stay in power.[64] Because of the truth commissions' non-ability to punish, they are much less politically sensitive than trials and tribunals and are, for this reason, often chosen as the primary or only vehicle of justice. Their limited power serves as no direct threat to the outgoing authoritarian regime and as a result they can often be used by new governments as the only process of dealing with the past. They do not have to be an alternative to prosecution, but have been so in many cases.[65] For some governments, it is not a desire to set the historical record straight that drives them to choose a TC as the preferred transitional justice mechanism, but a strategic political choice that sees a TC as the least disruptive transitional process and, moreover, the fact that its findings and recommendations can be ignored. But a TC should not be used to avoid accountability.[66] The weak mandate of the Guatemalan commission was a result of the political and fragile situation of the government.[67] It was given few powers out of a fear that it could lead to destabilization. The TCs in Bolivia and Ecuador were disbanded prior to finishing their work because they were deemed too politically sensitive. Bolivia did not issue a final report.[68] The discussions following the publication of the National Commission for Truth and Reconciliation report (the Rettig report) in Chile were cut short when three assassinations took place and it was felt that the risk of instability was too high for the discussions to continue.[69] In December 2005, Afghanistan endorsed an Action Plan for Peace, Reconciliation and Justice, but this was not launched until December 2006. The Action Plan includes according dignity to victims, institutional reform, truth-seeking, reconciliation and establishing a task force to advise on an accountability mechanism. This could lead to a TC or a tribunal. Initially, it demanded a tribunal, but this changed, since it was feared from many quarters that it would lead to destabilization.[70] As of March 2007, no transitional justice mechanism was in place in Afghanistan.

The level of media attention can be a reflection of the emphasis put on the truth commission by the regime. For a TC to ensure a modicum of success, there must be a high level of national media focus. In Argentina, the TC's report, *Nunca Más*, was widely published and became a best-selling book. The South Africa's TRC had extreme national, as well as international, media attention, and testimonies were often shown on television. Ghana followed this example, and all proceedings were broadcast live on television and journalists and the public could come and watch. Some proceedings were held behind closed doors if this was judged necessary by the commissioners, or if the victims wanted it that way.[71] In Morocco, hearings were public and the victims' testimonies broadcast on television.[72] However, this level of attention is a recent development. More often, attention has been limited. In Haiti, initially only 75 copies of the commission's final report were published; it was not until much later that it had wider circulation when 1,500 copies were published with the help of the UN International Civilian Mission in Haiti. Reports in the media were almost non-existent.[73] This led people to ask where the report was and if the commission had happened at all, since there were simply too few visible results from it.[74] In Sierra Leone, too, the delay in publishing the report of the TRC led to disgruntlement among civil society groups who had been eagerly awaiting it.

The level of media and government attention reflects the circumstances surrounding the conflict and also international pressure – limited government and media attention can often be a deliberate strategy in the post-conflict setting, where government actors fear that too much truth may destabilize the political situation. However, high public visibility is a crucial ingredient in ensuring the success of TCs. Although there might be high public, government and media attention during the process of collecting statements and evidence, it is also vitally important that the findings of the commission be made public and widely disseminated, or disillusion with the process may set in. In Timor-Leste, questions were raised among the people who gave statements to the commission regarding what happened to the information they gave, because it took longer than they anticipated for the report to be published.[75] Unless this is addressed swiftly, people may turn against the process.

One result of a lack of political will, combined with a fear of destabilization and absence of power by the TCs to enforce their decisions, is that the recommendations of the commissions, for example reparations, can be and often are ignored. It is fundamental that victims have a forum in which to tell their story, but if the recommendations put forward by the commission are ignored, then disillusionment, not reconciliation, can follow. All the recommendations of the National Truth and Justice Commission in Haiti were ignored. In his report on Haiti in 1997, the UN Secretary-General pointed out that neither the Follow-Up Committee nor the Compensation Committee to help victims of the coup, which the report had recommended be set up, had been created.[76] The Follow-Up Committee did begin working in January 1998, and forwarded numerous demands to the government, but these were never met – they included the suggestion of a special tribunal to try the accused from the coup era.[77] But there was lack of will by the Haitian government to pursue the recommendations given by the commission, together with an absence of international donor funding to do so. The international community had no interest in pursuing or supporting trials in Haiti. It was deemed sufficient that a process of truth-telling had taken place. This led to profound disillusionment among the population, who had expected far more from the commission and subsequent follow-up.[78]

If recommendations are not followed up and the report is not widely disseminated, a truth commission can become a means of avoiding properly addressing transitional justice. Yet the government cannot be accused of inaction, because it had done its duty.[79] In Chile, for example, it was hoped that the TC would lead to prosecutions, but this was not accepted by Pinochet.[80] There is a very real risk that if TCs are chosen by the new government as the *only* vehicle for justice in a transitional justice process because it lacks certain powers, then not only will the process itself fail, but reconciliation will not take place. Rather than leading to stability, disillusionment with the new government may be enhanced and the risk of further instability and violence will be greater. Victims who perceive the lack of account-ability as an affront to their suffering may take justice into their own hands, thereby perpetuating a cycle of vengeance. More assuredly, it will engender a lack of confidence in the new regime and undermine the transition to democracy. However, it should be acknowledged, as discussed in the previous chapter, that many transitional societies do not have the capabilities or resources to conduct prosecutions, but they are able to set up a truth commission – in some post-conflict set-tings, it is not a choice between a range of judicial or non-judicial mechanisms, or a complementary approach, but between a truth commission or nothing.[81]

## Conclusion

Truth commissions can in many contexts make a positive contribu-tion to the overall process of reconciliation. However, for a TC to be successful, it needs to be impartial and unbiased, like all transitional justice mechanisms, and given sufficient resources and sufficiently broad mandates. National focus and dissemination of findings are crucial, as is the political will to ensure the implementation of the recommendations. If these variables are lacking, so too will be the chances of a successful outcome of a truth commission. Truth-telling is often seen as a first step in the process of achieving justice and rec-onciliation on an individual level. Yet, TCs without any other process of justice, as evidenced by numerous cases, will not be sufficient for many of the victims.[82] Moreover, although they are in effect estab-lished for the victims of abuse, it has been questioned whether or not they have helped them.[83]

There is a right for all to know the past and have human rights abuses documented. However, there should not be a blanket obliga-tion to establish a truth commission in every post-conflict or transi-tional society.[84] There are different ways of establishing a record and the decision regarding what type of transitional justice mechanisms should be applied needs to be related to the specific context. A truth commission may not necessarily be the answer in all cases. They undoubtedly contribute, especially to reconciliation and stability, but they are not the only transitional justice mechanism. Furthermore, if they are conducted in the absence of other justice mechanisms they are unlikely to lead to national *and* individual reconciliation.

Choosing the most appropriate transitional justice mechanisms for each particular post-conflict society depends upon the several enabling and constraining factors, described in the Introduction to this book. These include the context, history and background of the conflict, which encompass peace agreements and political will and ability to cooperate; the support of the international community for transitional justice; and the culture of the country, and how this affects rule of law. As emphasized throughout these chapters, these factors are essential when discussing all transitional justice mechanisms. Mere truth-telling will often not be enough; it can be part of the process towards reconciliation, but will not on its own satisfy all victims or survivors. The discussion on TCs should incorporate these factors. It is not possible to state that a TC is or is not the right tool in all circumstances. The solution to dealing with past crimes in one post-conflict society will differ significantly from that of another. A holistic approach to reconciliation, which may or may not include truth commissions, should be promoted.

### Box 6.1: The Truth and Reconciliation Commission in the DRC

The Democratic Republic of Congo has experienced what has been termed Africa's equivalent of the First World War, which began when Laurent Kabila toppled the Mobutu regime in 1997 with the help of Rwanda and Uganda. A bloody war began, mainly fought over the mineral wealth of the DRC and involving Angola, Zambia, Zimbabwe, Namibia, Chad and Sudan. Kabila was assassinated in January 2001 and his son Joseph Kabila was chosen as his successor by political and military leaders. In February 2002, peace talks – the Inter-Congolese Dialogue – began in Sun City, South Africa, with participants from all the parties to the conflict. These talks established the Truth and Reconciliation Commission. A transitional government was set up in July 2003 headed by Joseph Kabila as President, with four vice-presidents from the rebel movements and political opposition. The UN Mission in Congo has been present since 1999.

Although the TC was created by the Sun City agreement in 2002, it was not formally established until July 2004. Its mandate states that it can deal with political, economic and social crimes committed between 1960 and 2003. At the time of writing, it was seen as completely unsuccessful by Congolese civil society, some Congolese government officials and numerous members of the UN Mission in Congo.[85] There are several reasons for this. There was a lack of consultation of civil society in the establishment of the TC, and no consensus as to its mandate or design.[86] Moreover, arguments were raised that the process was started too early. There was still conflict raging in many parts of the country when the TC was put into operation, which made its mandate much more difficult to implement. Moreover, the composition of the commission was flawed: it was politicized and has been severely criticized by civil society.[87] The commissioners reflected political affiliations and represented parties to the conflict. The commission is in effect formed of people whose political factions committed the abuses that the TC is mandated to investigate. It has from the beginning therefore seriously lacked legitimacy.

The TC, in addition, decided to focus on reconciliation before truth. However, doubts have been voiced in Congolese civil society whether you can have reconciliation before the truth is known.[88] Moreover, the commission began to focus on reconciliation of the problems occurring during their operation, looking more at conflict resolution, which is not their primary mandate. They had at the time of writing not undertaken any investigations into war crimes.

The commission was originally given the power to grant amnesties on 'crimes and large-scale violations' where the motivation was of a political nature, but not for crimes of genocide or crimes against humanity.[89] However, this was changed and what was initially adopted by the National Assembly was the power to give amnesties for political crimes. There is no amnesty law at present, but it is proposed that *faits de guerre* will be amnestied, but not *crimes de guerre* – yet there has not been a proper definition of this difference. If *'faits de guerre'* only incorporate acts of war, then they need not be amnestied, since they are legal in war. The potential passing of such an amnesty law must be observed carefully so that it is not turned into an amnesty for war crimes.

The TC had, at the time of writing, no trust or legitimacy within the population, it focused on conflict resolution and mediation rather than uncovering historical abuses, and it comprised representatives of fractions who had committed the abuse. One solution mentioned in mid-2005 was to create a new TC after the elections. However, civil society seemed no longer to trust the TC process and the new constitution makes no mention of a truth commission, so it would be necessary to make a change in the law – which could be achieved – but, more importantly, people would need to be convinced that a TC would be of value to them. There is the potential of re-establishing a TC, since the second round of elections were held in the autumn of 2006; however, by March 2007 steps to do so had still not been taken.

## Box 6.2: The Truth and Reconciliation Commission in South Africa

The TRC in South Africa came as a result of more than 30 years of armed struggle and resistance to a brutal and repressive apartheid regime. South Africa's TRC has been extensively analysed and documented and is by far the most famous and well known of truth commissions. Its mandate began in 1996 and ended in 1998, and it looked at crimes committed during the apartheid era from 1960 to 1994. Although it is the most widely known TC, it is perhaps not the most representative, since it stands out in numerous ways.

In South Africa, the mandate, resources and size of the TRC were extensive; it was at the time the largest truth commission ever undertaken. When the report was submitted, 21,297 victims had given statements, more than 8,000 perpetrators had applied for amnesty and the report was contained in five volumes covering abuses over 34 years.[90] The commission had search and seizure powers, the right to issue subpoenas, a witness protection programme and the power to grant amnesties from prosecution to perpetrators in return for giving testimonies to the commission. It also had the support of both Nelson Mandela and Archbishop Desmond Tutu, who argued for the importance of forgiveness, reconciliation and *ubuntu*. The budget was enormous compared to previous truth commissions: $18 million per year and a staff of 300.[91] It had extensive media coverage, again unprecedented in so far as previous truth commissions were concerned. The commission held public hearings, which were televised and also commented upon in other forms of news media.

At first, commentators seemed to underline the extraordinary success of the TRC. Later on, however, more critical voices were raised. In particular, the power to grant individual conditional amnesty upon telling the truth to the commission is what has raised the most controversy.[92] For many, hearing the key perpetrators admitting guilt was a great relief; to others, who wanted a further process of criminal justice, this was not the case. The expectations of the commission's work were very high, particularly emphasizing that its objective was to obtain reconciliation. Doubts have been raised whether this has been achieved.[93] This seems to be reflected in a poll in South Africa, which reported after the end of the TRC's work that two-thirds felt it had fuelled their anger and contributed to deterioration in race relations. Only 17 per cent predicted that forgiveness would be a result of the TRC.[94] Yet, importantly, there were no revenge killings reported in the period of the TRC.[95]

The TRC has undoubtedly had positive results in South Africa. Of vital importance was the fact that it had extensive international and national attention, sufficient resources, a vast mandate and key symbolic figures supporting the process. However, it is doubtful that it can be held to have led to reconciliation of South African society, where divisions between the communities are still large. Interestingly, ten years after the end of the TRC, Archbishop Desmond Tutu acknowledged that perhaps prosecutions should have been conducted in conjunction with the truth commission.[96]

## Box 6.3: The Commission on the Truth for El Salvador

After a 12-year-long civil war which began in 1980 and ended in 1991, the UN brokered a peace agreement between the parties to the conflict: the government and the Farabundo Marti National Liberation Front (FMLN). These 12 years saw thousands of political killings, disappearances, torture and massacres of civilians. In the peace agreement, the Commission on the Truth was set up to deal with the aftermath of violence that had plagued El Salvadorian society for so long.

The mandate of the TC was broad, and outlined in the peace agreement, namely to investigate 'serious acts of violence that have occurred since 1980 and whose impact on society urgently demands that the public should know the truth'.[97] However, it was only given eight months to finish its work. In that time, it collected information from 2,000 victims and witnesses detailing more than 7,000 gross violations of human rights.[98] There was extreme pressure upon the commission, which concluded that it was the government, or government forces, that had conducted the vast majority – 95 per cent – of human rights abuses.[99]

The El Salvadorian TC was rare in that it allowed for the naming of names of perpetrators of violence. The commission chose to do this because of the peace agreement's emphasis on knowing the whole truth and a belief that it could not be known without naming names. This could have led to prosecution of the perpetrators, but, at the time, the judicial system was corrupt and inefficient. The commission expressed a belief that if this had not been the case, it could have handed the names over to the courts without publishing them, for the courts and police to take appropriate action.[100] The TC was criticized for naming only some names and it was unclear what criteria were set for which to choose. Only five days after the publication of the report, a sweeping amnesty law was passed, which included all who had been named in the report. Subsequently, the military officers who had been identified as having committed gross violations of human rights were retired from the armed forces with full pensions; this was to the great dismay of civil society in El Salvador.

The recommendations of the commission were broad and included reform of the armed forces, public security and the judicial system, as well as dismissal from the armed forces and civil service of the persons mentioned in the commission's report and a disqualification of those who had committed abuses from holding public office.[101] These recommendations were, however, not all implemented.

# 7

# Traditional Informal Justice Mechanisms

The application of traditional methods of justice to address gross violations of human rights in post-conflict societies has long been ignored. It is only very recently that such mechanisms have begun to be mentioned in the international community.[1] In his 2004 report, *Rule of Law and Transitional Justice in Conflict and Post-Conflict Societies*, the UN Secretary-General stated that 'due regard must be given to indigenous and informal traditions for administering justice or settling disputes' in relation to transitional justice in post-conflict societies.[2] In practice, UN staff have promoted and supported such mechanisms on an ad hoc basis in several contexts, but without a coherent policy or guidelines, as was done, for example, in Timor-Leste[3] and Mozambique.[4]

It seems, therefore, that there is an acknowledgement that traditional mechanisms can contribute to the process of transitional justice, peace and reconciliation in a post-conflict society.[5] However, what traditional mechanisms consist of, how they can contribute to reconciliation, what the key positive and negative factors are when it comes to applying these mechanisms to gross violations of human rights, whether they can be transferred at all onto such crimes and how they relate to formal state and international mechanisms for addressing such crimes are all issues that have not been properly analysed. There is a gap in the discourse concerning the applicability of these methods to past crimes in post-conflict societies. The support of these mechanisms, therefore, seems to be based more on an assumption that they will create further stability and reconciliation than on a thorough analysis of their potential. However, it has been recognized that this is something that needs to be tackled, because of its increasing importance in the international community.[6]

One of the main reasons why traditional mechanisms are proposed as a potential source of addressing past human rights violations is that in many societies these types of mechanisms deal with the vast majority of crimes, conflicts and disputes.[7] The UNDP estimates that as many as 90 per cent of all conflicts are resolved in such forums.[8] Yet most of the focus on traditional mechanisms has tended to be in relation to judicial reform of the formal justice system.[9] Because of their prevalence within so many developing societies, they are viewed as having a high potential for dealing with past crimes. This chapter will aim to establish if this premise is true. It will emphasize that these justice mechanisms are used in both the retributive and restorative sense. It will not focus to any significant degree on their dispute resolution and prevention activities, but on their suitability to address human rights crime and further national and individual reconciliation of a post-conflict society. It is repeatedly stressed that these mechanisms are restorative in nature, but traditional mechanisms frequently incorporate some sort of punishment, and hence are also retributive.[10]

This chapter will also discuss traditional informal mechanisms of justice, starting by outlining the definitional problems of the different terms, and moving on to discuss the positive and negative attributes of such mechanisms in general when dealing with both crime and conflict resolution, and in particular when dealing with gross violations of human rights in a post-conflict context, and elaborating what should be in place for such mechanisms to serve as a complementary tool of the process of justice when addressing past crimes.

## Conceptual Clarity

Traditional mechanisms exert some type of non-state judicial authority. This authority may be exercised in various forms: religious or secular, restorative or retributive. Several concepts have been and are used to denote the different forms of non-state judicial authority. These include customary, indigenous, informal, primary, traditional and religious justice mechanisms.[11] Many of these raise definitional problems.[12] The vast number of different terms reflects the equally large number and diverse types of justice mechanisms. Nevertheless, there are commonalities that can be established in many of these mechanisms, as will be discussed throughout the chapter.

The 'traditional informal justice mechanisms' (TIJM) term adopted here has been chosen for a number of reasons. It is important to emphasize that the mechanisms are traditional in the sense of not only having a link with the past, but also having been established and applied over some length of time, although they may have changed with time.[13] At the same time, it should be noted that all traditional laws and mechanisms are constantly changing, and were also doing so during pre-colonial times.[14] Tradition is not static. Moreover, 'traditional' in this context incorporates community-based justice structures, as well as traditional leaders and councils; it refers not only to rural mechanisms, but also to urban and religious justice mechanisms. It is used to differentiate between mechanisms that may be informal justice mechanisms, but have been established and applied only recently. There is a tendency in post-conflict societies in particular for so-called 'traditional' rites and customs to spring up, which are actually recent innovations. This happened in Timor-Leste, where new ways of dispersing justice were introduced, but were argued to be traditional.[15] It has also been the case in parts of Afghanistan, where the term 'traditional' is used to justify vigilante-style justice processes and/or where it has been appropriated and manipulated by wartime or post-conflict power-holders and misused both during and after the conflict.[16] The use of the term 'TIJM' seeks to not include these types of 'traditional' mechanisms. The definition uses 'informal' to distinguish it from formally established justice systems; however, it is acknowledged that the state often has significant influence upon these mechanisms in different contexts. They do not necessarily operate completely independently from the state; they may be supported by the state, or the people involved in the informal mechanisms may have a dual role in that they may be representatives of the state at some other level. 'Informal' does not therefore indicate a complete separation from the state, but denotes the absence of a formal structure created solely by the state. Hence, 'informal' rather than 'non-state' is used: the latter indicates a stricter separation from the state than is in many cases present. 'Mechanisms' are used rather than 'systems', since systems suggest much more specialized and formal establishments.[17]

Traditional methods of justice can take many different forms, and vary extensively from community to community. Yet, there are commonalities between them. In the international discourse they are generally perceived as providing restorative justice, but they can also be retributive. On a broad and general level they are mechanisms for solving disputes, conflicts and crime at community level. In some developing and post-conflict societies these mechanisms are arranged at three levels. First, where the community administers justice via village leaders, councils and/or influential individuals. Second, where these TIJM are modified and supervised by NGOs. Third, where the mechanisms are modified and administered by a local government body. This is the case in, for example, Bangladesh, where *shalish*, a non-state dispute resolution technique, comes in these three forms, and in several African countries.[18] On all these three levels the TIJM are political – law and politics are frequently highly intertwined. This chapter will focus primarily on the first level, since this is frequently the most relevant in relation to post-conflict societies. If there has been prolonged conflict, the state has not been able to modify and administer such justice and the level of NGO intervention in TIJM is also significantly less than in a non-conflict developing country.

TIJM at the first level are where a village or tribal council or court, community meeting or council of elders are convened to deal with crimes perpetrated towards the community and individuals. It can also play a mediation role, focusing on resolving conflicts such as marital disputes and domestic violence, and addressing land disputes, inheritance and other financial issues, gender and family concerns and violence. In cases concerning wrongdoing by an individual, the council, elders or group decide what is to be the punishment for the perpetrator. The punishment can vary extensively depending not only upon the seriousness of the crime or transgression, but also on the culture of the country and community. It can include public humiliation of the perpetrator, paying fines, community labour or physical punishment. It is often focused on the fact that the perpetrator is part of the community and although he/she can be punished for the crimes committed, punishment does not usually involve incarceration. The perpetrator may serve the community and make reparation for his/her crimes. The rationale for this is that it serves the greater good of the community rather than separating the perpetrator from the community, and enhances reconciliation to a greater extent.

It is also important to note that there are highly different definitions of justice among communities using TIJM, and that these seldom conform with a Western view of justice. For example, among Native Americans in Canada, 'justice' as a concept understood by the Western view does not exist, and the elders have problems in understanding what is meant by it.[19] In particular, justice often reflects the importance of the community and crimes are viewed in terms of how they negatively affect the community rather than the individual. Hence, in some societies adultery and assault will be considered a minor offence because they are directed at the individual not the group.[20] In many societies, such as in Mozambique, healing and reconciliation are a primary goal of TIJM; in other societies the punitive element is at the fore if the community has suffered as a result of the transgression.[21]

## The Context of TIJM

TIJM have been in existence for longer than formal mechanisms of justice, and customs have been central to the formation of formal law, namely 'as tribe became state, so custom became law'.[22] How to deal with and relate to these mechanisms have therefore been a focus among a wide variety of actors for a long time, particularly during colonialism and in the immediate post-colonial era. The attitude towards TIJM in colonial times varied extensively from country to country, depending on who was the imperial power. In the British territories in Africa, for example, the attitude towards TIJM went through several stages, from toleration to recognition, followed by control and reorganization.[23] However, regardless of how tight control was, TIJM continued to be practised during colonialism and after.

In post-colonial times during times of conflict and authoritarianism, what has repeatedly been seen is a heightened use of these mechanisms. There are several reasons for this. First, when there are long periods of conflict or authoritarian regimes, the judicial system can often be unfair and corrupt at best, or, at worst, used as a tool in the systematic abuse of the population.[24] There is therefore a lack of trust in the judicial system, and TIJM are used more extensively. This is the case in, for example Afghanistan, where the formal judicial system lacks credibility because of complaints about corruption, and TIJM are preferred.[25] Second, as a result of the conflict there might not be a functioning formal judicial system at all; it might have completely broken down and the role of TIJM therefore becomes essential. Third, it may also reflect the frequent lack of accessibility to formal judicial systems in terms of geographical distance to courts, understanding the language spoken in the courts, or lack of resources to make use of the existing formal system.

In the immediate aftermath of colonialism, particularly in Africa, the role of TIJM was discussed as a central issue. It was acknowledged that although there were great variances in these mechanisms throughout the continent it could be looked at in a wider African context.[26] During a conference on local courts and customary law in Africa, it was recognized that: '[T]hese informal proceedings would inevitably continue and that they had an extremely valuable function to perform.'[27] Moreover, it was concluded that these informal proceedings should be encouraged and could continue alongside the court system.[28]

Presently, how these types of mechanisms are dealt with varies substantially in the different contexts. In many countries, traditional or customary laws are referred to in the formal law and/or constitution, as in, for example, South Africa[29] and Bolivia, where state recognition was seen as the most effective way of tackling the issue.[30] In Papua New Guinea, the constitution states that when deciding which principle of law to apply, custom should always be looked at first and common English law second.[31] The constitution in Peru also recognizes the right of *certain* TIJM to administer their own law, but within the limits of the constitution – in stark contrast, they have tried to severely control other TIJM, even by prosecuting and imprisoning the people conducting them.[32] Codification of customary law was particularly emphasized in certain countries in Africa, including Ethiopia, the Ivory Coast and Madagascar, in the immediate aftermath of colonialism.[33] However, codification is not necessarily positive in that in effect it 'freezes' a living law, and is not at the moment being encouraged by development agencies.[34]

Current research on TIJM has focused on customs and their relation to law, legal traditions, how TIJM may influence common law and ideas and procedures in TIJM – to mention but a few.[35] The most relevant research for the purpose of this book is the increasing development literature on access to justice, which attempts to outline various TIJM and their use in relation to ordinary crime, disputes and conflicts.[36] There is, however, a gap in the discourse in relation to these mechanisms' suitability to address gross violations of human rights.

Unlike international courts, truth commissions and other mechanisms for transitional justice discussed in the previous chapters, these TIJM are in constant use for present crimes and conflict resolution; they are not mechanisms created or developed to deal particularly with past crimes of human rights abuse in a post-conflict setting. Because of their focus on reconciliation and their restorative *and* retributive function, they can be valuable in the context of post-conflict/transitional justice. However, several cautionary notes must be struck before unequivocally embracing all traditional mechanisms in all their forms as ways of dealing with past crime.

## Dealing with Past Crimes: Challenges of TIJM

There are several arguments in favour of using TIJM – and a growing tendency to promote them in a UN peace operation context[37] – but there are also strong reasons for exercising caution when promoting the use of traditional mechanisms to address past crimes in a post-conflict setting. Internationally, they have taken on a greater significance, but it has not been established exactly what it is they can achieve. They are often promoted as a means of fostering reconciliation and as a tool of conflict resolution, and it is in this role they are put forward as a vehicle for dealing with human rights abuse in post-conflict societies. There are, however, a number of potential drawbacks that need to be addressed.

## Legitimacy and accountability

There is an underlying assumption in all of this that TIJM are inherently more legitimate than either a formal domestic legal system, which may have been imposed on society, or newly established bodies, such as truth commissions. However, simply because a justice mechanism is traditional and informal, it does not automatically mean that it has legitimacy in the local community or in the larger population. It varies substantially from region to region, country to country and community to community.

These mechanisms are not only methods used to address issues of justice, but are closely linked with the political systems in the community and village. In effect, they are frequently political systems where political patronage is common. The fact that they are habitually consulted by the vast majority in developing countries does not mean that in all cases they are perceived as legitimate, nor does it necessarily indicate satisfaction with their processes; rather, it may reflect the weaknesses of the formal justice system.[38] Moreover, solutions in TIJM may be arbitrary and only respected because of the political, social and economic power that the council/court/elders are able to exert in the communities. These leaders have complex relations outside the TIJM, which may determine the outcome or form of the proceedings. Legitimacy can be further eroded by the fact these mechanisms are sometimes viewed as corrupt. In East Africa, several of them are perceived to be corrupt by the public.[39] Some TIJM in Bangladesh and their judgements are 'designed to ensure continuity of [their] leadership, to strengthen [their] relational alliances'.[40] The issue of legitimacy is often not addressed in TIJM, because of an assumption of validity by the members of the mechanisms who decide upon punishment or dispute resolution.

The level of legitimacy will vary, but it should not be automatically assumed that TIJM have a legitimacy that the formal system does not possess. Naturally this will differ substantially from case to case. In addition, the level of legitimacy will also be affected by the type of

TIJM that is adopted, as outlined above, whether it is a traditional community-based mechanism, supported by an NGO or administered and monitored by the state. If monitored by the state, their legitimacy is intimately linked to the legitimacy of the state and will therefore in most cases vary according to public perception of the state and the formal justice system. An NGO-supported TIJM may be seen as fairer because it tends to train participants of the councils, encourage women to participate and introduce record-keeping.[41] Yet this does not necessarily induce a public perception of legitimacy, especially since it may be viewed as an external actor intervening in the process.

Accountability is an essential part of ensuring legitimacy. However, the more informal the structure, the harder it can be to ascertain accountability. Since TIJM are defined by their informality, it can be very difficult to create oversight and accountability mechanisms for them. The more organized a TIJM is, such as those sponsored by NGOs and the state, the easier it is to put accountability structures in place. In spite of these inherent difficulties, many TIJM have inbuilt accountability structures that function well.[42] It is important not to assume that, because these mechanisms are informal, they are not accountable to the population they serve. As stated above, it is often because of a lack of accountability in the formal justice system that they have been strengthened during times of conflict and/or occupation. This is of particular importance in a post-conflict society, where the formal judicial system in the vast majority of cases is in dire need of reform and therefore where the TIJM may take on a role in addressing human rights abuse during conflict.

If a TIJM lacks legitimacy and accountability, it creates a problem for applying such a mechanism on past violations of human rights in a post-conflict society. For TIJM to be used on past crimes, they must be perceived as legitimate by the population. Most importantly, the people conducting the process, whether it is retributive or restorative in nature, need to be accountable for their actions. If they are not, these mechanisms cannot be applied to past crimes. Before the international community lends its support to such mechanisms, therefore, there needs to be a thorough assessment of the degree of legitimacy they enjoy, including such elements as accountability.

### Fairness of trials

A significant drawback in using TIJM is that they regularly deny the perpetrator the right of a fair trial, as the African Commission on Human and Peoples' Rights has pointed out: 'It is recognised that traditional courts are capable of playing a role in the achievement of peaceful societies and exercise authority over a significant proportion of the population of African countries. However, traditional courts are not exempt from the provisions of the African Charter relating to a fair trial.'[43] Because solutions are frequently arbitrary and identical cases do not receive the same treatment or resolution, the fact that these mechanisms are heavily influenced by politics and that there is sometimes no possibility to defend oneself means that they habitually do not adhere to the principles set out to ensure a fair trial. This may be exacerbated by the fact that sometimes the proceedings of such trials are not written down, and therefore the judgements will be based not on precedents, but on particular circumstances surrounding the trial. The trial may also be much more subjective than what is expected of a trial in a formal system. It is important to emphasize, however, that this is not the norm in all TIJM, and it will vary substantially between the different mechanisms.

If the international community is to endorse the use of TIJM in a particular post-conflict context, the fairness of the procedures needs to be ensured. These processes are too significant to be invalidated by unfairness and bias. The mechanisms might be 'traditional', but this does not necessarily confer fairness or legitimacy.

## Human rights and gender discrimination

Another dilemma is that the punishments delivered in TIJM can contradict international human rights law and standards. They may, in particular, not respect women's rights. Also TIJM are frequently incompatible with the laws of the country.[44] A good example of this concerns some traditional customs for dealing with rape. In several countries, a man accused of raping a woman will be forced to marry her and pay her parents. In other countries, the woman will be blamed for the rape and punished by lashes or killed by a male relative for dishonouring her family.[45] In one case in Timor-Leste, a man who raped a woman was sentenced by the village council and chained to her bed as punishment.[46] Arguably, the victim in this case suffered more from this punishment than the perpetrator, since she had to endure the trauma repeatedly until he was no longer chained to her bed. The solutions outlined above are not appropriate in any situation where rape has occurred, but they are even less appropriate in cases of mass rape, where it has been deployed as a deliberate tactic linked to strategies of genocide or ethnic cleansing. The view that these particular types of punishment might be a solution to *any* form of rape accentuates the problems of using these mechanisms to deal with human rights violations. Moreover, when such crimes are committed on a vast scale, the issue is further complicated because of the limited jurisdiction of TIJM. Importantly, state oversight might not ensure heightened conformity to human rights norms, because the state in many cases itself violates such standards, in particular where discrimination and human rights abuse may also be enshrined in the formal law.[47] In a post-conflict society, where previously state control has regularly meant state abuse, this is very pertinent.

In addition, there is a tendency in several TIJM not to include women in the decision-making processes. In many developing countries, where a reliance on TIJM is prevalent, the society is based on patriarchy. This is reflected in the TIJM, where, for instance, they may consist of only male members,[48] or where females are left out of the proceedings altogether even if they are witnesses or victims. This male domination can lead to bias against women, which becomes notably evident when punishment is meted out. One example is where refusal to marry, demanding a divorce or failing to serve a meal on time leads to so-called honour killings, practised in many different cultures and religions. Frequently, the perpetrators are not punished; in certain cultures it is not even considered a crime.[49] However, male domination is not a consistent feature of all TIJM. For example, in Lesotho men have been delegating power to women, and consequently decisions on, for instance, inheritance have begun to favour women.[50] Gender discrimination also varies when the TIJM are mentored by NGOs. NGOs tend to emphasize equality and gender mainstreaming, thereby attempting to limit gender discrimination in the TIJM. However, state-sponsored mechanisms may not be any better at reducing discrimination, because numerous countries' formal justice mechanisms also discriminate against women, so having state control over TIJM will have limited impact.

It is important to highlight that not all TIJM violate human rights when they punish. For example, in Peru, Bolivia, Ecuador and Colombia, they tend to respect fundamental human rights. However, in the rare cases when human rights were violated, they attracted a disproportional amount of media attention.[51] The violation of international human rights standards is the foremost argument raised against the use of TIJM for past crimes.

Because of their non-adherence to international standards of human rights, the ability of some traditional mechanisms to deal with large-scale abuse is extremely problematic. Applying mechanisms whose punishments may contradict international human rights laws in order to deal with breaches of those very same laws should not be encouraged by the international community, which should also be wary of gender discrimination within certain mechanisms when it promotes TIJM as a way of redressing past wrongs. Mechanisms that persistently discriminate against women, particularly when it is reflected in punishments, should not be supported. This is not to argue against using traditional mechanisms. But blanket support of *all* justice mechanisms termed 'traditional' should not be given just because there is an assumption that, by their very definition, these will be superior to any other mechanism because of their local ownership and cultural relevance. Assessments not only of the mechanisms in each case and country, but also of when and to what crimes they can be most successfully applied, need to be made.

### Linkages with formal judicial systems

There are limited linkages between informal and formal justice mechanisms in most developing countries. Establishing effective linkages could enhance the capacity of the decision-makers in the TIJM, and in some cases ensure greater accountability and oversight and also provide more opportunity for people to address their grievances in both formal and informal mechanisms. If there are few linkages between the mechanisms, this opportunity is significantly reduced. More linkages could strengthen, and be valuable for, both formal and informal mechanisms in addressing crimes at all levels. And although this is crucial to the development, reform and sustainability of these mechanisms, it is of particular significance in relation to using these forums for redressing past violations of human rights in a post-conflict society.

When a complementary approach to post-conflict transitional justice is chosen which incorporates TIJM and domestic trials, there need to be linkages between them to oversee both procedures in order that victims may have recourse to the formal system even if, in the first instance, they are dealt with at the local level. They need to have recourse to both types of solutions for their grievances. If there are greater linkages between the two it will also ensure that what happens at the domestic court level can be fed back into the local communities, thus enhancing the process of justice at both levels.

### The number of TIJM and limited jurisdiction

An argument sometimes raised against the use of TIJM for past crimes is that there are so many different types within one country that applying just one type would not be fair. In the DRC, this was an argument raised against the use of TIJM for violations of human rights during the war.[52] It was repeatedly stated that there was too much variation among the various tribes/communities. However, this assumes that these mechanisms would have a retributive function were they to deal with past crimes. The number of different TIJM is irrelevant in so far as dealing with past crimes is concerned if the focus is restorative. Different strategies among the various groups handling violators of human rights are irrelevant if there is no punishment involved. It does not matter if different forms of healing mechanisms and types of reintegration are applied. It is only where punishment is involved at any level that there needs to be a coherent structure followed throughout the territory to ensure fairness of the process. In the DRC there were, however, some who argued that, although there were numerous different TIJM, they were not necessarily fundamentally different on all levels. Several commonalities could be found between them. They could, therefore, if this option was chosen to redress the crimes committed during the war, use TIJM even when it involved punishment.[53]

In connection with the number of TIJM within a country, there is also the question of their limited jurisdiction. Frequently, these mechanisms only have jurisdiction within their village or area, and to crimes committed within a specific district and by locals and people in the immediate neighbouring area. This has been heralded as problematic in relation to dealing with gross violations of human rights, because some see it as crucial that such violations are addressed on the wider scale and not only in limited local arenas. However, the limited jurisdiction may serve individual and community reconciliation well. If the TIJM are to deal with past crimes, they would only address crimes and perpetrators in and of their area, and, as will be discussed below, only a limited number of types of crimes. Therefore, limited jurisdiction of TIJM would not necessarily adversely affect the process of justice in any country, but could potentially lead to reintegration and reconciliation

### Attitudes of the members of the formal systems towards TIJM

A central challenge to using TIJM in relation to past human rights abuses is the fact that lawyers, judges, prosecutors, magistrates and government officials may be hostile or indifferent to these mechanisms.[54] This may be due to general concerns about potential human rights abuses in TIJM or a reluctance to admit that the formal systems possess similar problems of legitimacy, accountability and human rights abuse. It could also be due to a desire to show that their country has a developed justice system, and that using and supporting such mechanisms obstructs development,[55] thereby hindering the perception of the country as a modern nation which applies 'modern' law. Another reason for antipathy is that international support of these mechanisms means that donor resources are diverted from the formal judicial systems. Therefore it might serve both the government and formal systems better to emphasize the drawbacks of TIJM rather than underlining their role as a way of reconciliation in a post-conflict society.

In the DRC, this was underlined by many lawyers who emphasized that the country had come a long way since the reliance on traditional methods of justice and that there was no need to use such mechanisms in dealing with past crimes.[56] They did not believe this would be a viable strategy. It was made very clear that the DRC had the capabilities in its judicial system to deal with such crimes, although it would need external assistance and reform. There was great reluctance to accept that there might be a role for TIJM in this connection. Only grudgingly was it accepted that, if used on very minor trespasses, it could lead to greater reconciliation among the communities.[57] It was viewed as an internationally promoted idea, and perhaps something that was being supported because it would cost less money for the international community. It was also suggested that the DRC had far too many different tribes, and corresponding TIJM, so that this would limit the use of these mechanisms for past crimes. This, as discussed above, shows a limited knowledge of these mechanisms and does not reflect the reality. It has for a long time been recognized that 100 tribes do not equate to 100 TIJM, and that many 'resemble each other more than they differ'.[58]

The negative attitude found among many members of the formal justice system may inhibit the use of TIJM in post-conflict societies as a means to redress war crimes. It is certainly a challenge that needs to be met when promoting such mechanisms post-conflict by the international community. Although the above factors may potentially severely limit the use of TIJM in certain contexts to deal with gross violations of human rights – and these criticisms should be carefully evaluated before implementing TIJM in post-conflict societies as a tool to deal with large-scale atrocities – there are several positive factors of using TIJM as an instrument of addressing past crimes, as discussed below.

## Promoting Reconciliation

There are numerous advantages to using TIJM in developing and post-conflict societies, but there is a vast difference between using these methods to deal with petty crime and domestic disputes and applying them to war crimes and gross violations of human rights. Although it is important that the above discussed challenges and problems are analysed and taken into consideration when deciding whether or not to apply these types of mechanisms to address gross violations of human rights after conflict, the various positive outcomes of TIJM must also be emphasized. There seems to be too much of an acceptance of the unquestionable advantages of TIJM so that they are rarely discussed in much detail, but the question in this connection is whether these advantages will also be relevant in relation to transitional justice in a post-conflict society, and if they will outweigh the challenges outlined above.

### Low cost, accessibility and speed

The cost of taking cases through the formal justice system is, in any country, very high, which limits accessibility to justice for the vast majority of the population in any given developing country. In sharp contrast to this, traditional informal mechanisms of justice tend to be free or very cheap.[59] This expands the access to justice for large parts of the population. However, a note of caution must be struck: this mechanism might be chosen because it is free, not because it is everyone's preferred option. In a post-conflict society, low cost is also crucial. Even if domestic courts were to waive the fees for lawyers and all surrounding expenses in a court case for addressing human rights violations during conflict, there would still be the expenses of travelling to and from the court and staying in the city or town where the court case was held, potentially limiting the number of people who would be able to take advantage of such a recourse to justice. In many cases, a vast number of victims reside at some distance from a court, because there are huge rural populations and there are rarely courts in every town. Therefore, the low cost of TIJM is relevant in the context of past crimes.

The accessibility of TIJM is also a positive factor. People who otherwise would be on the outside of the justice process have access due to the fact that these mechanisms are situated within their local communities. They do not have to travel to reach the formal court system. It is on, this level, an inclusive mechanism of justice. In relation to past crimes it would mean that a greater number of people would have access to justice, since it could potentially take place in all communities.

Moreover, in general, TIJM are quicker than formal mechanisms of justice. This means that, rather than waiting for months or perhaps even years for a decision, it can be made quickly and both victims and perpetrators can get on with their lives. There are exceptions to this where, for example in Bangladesh, the *shalish* can take several months to come to a decision.[60] In a post-conflict situation where rebuilding relations, reintegration and reconciliation are all essential parts of ensuring sustainable peace, faster processes of justice can be positive as long as they are fair and unbiased, and not so fast that they do not consider the perpetrators' rights. However, the quicker the emphasis on reconciliation can begin, the less likely it is that conflict will be renewed.

### Cultural relevancy and local ownership

The cultural relevance of TIJM to the local community is another factor that must not be overlooked. Within the same country there are often numerous different cultures, norms and traditions, and a common or civil law tradition may feel alien to vast numbers of people. This is also why there is a preference for TIJM in many communities. It is based on and reflective of their own norms and traditions. It can therefore also feel more appropriate that perpetrators are treated within these TIJM. Furthermore, the process is conducted in the local language, which makes the process feel safer and less distant, and interpreters, who can often complicate the process, are not needed. This is crucial when dealing with post-conflict processes of justice. International forums can feel especially alienating and removed from both the local context and culture. For example, in Sierra Leone, certain communities have found their own way of dealing with the atrocities and the truth commission was seen to disrupt this process.[61]

Addressing certain levels of past crimes within TIJM can therefore ensure that justice is culturally relevant, and can *potentially* heighten the chances of reconciliation. The Sudanese government stated that it would use traditional mechanisms, in addition to its national courts, to deal with the violations of human rights that took place in Darfur, arguing that one reason for this was that 'we have traditional ways of solving problems on the ground'.[62] Traditional mechanisms in Sudan often take the form of tribal conferences, but doubts have been raised whether this can be adequate to address the crimes committed in Darfur, which have been determined by the UN to constitute grave crimes against humanity,[63] in a conflict that has left thousands dead and displaced more than two million people.

In addition to being culturally relevant, the local population sees an immediate and direct effect of the process of justice and reconciliation taking place in their midst. It is not distant, and can therefore potentially have a more direct impact upon reconciliation than many other of the transitional justice procedures. International processes are far removed from the local communities and often lack an efficient feedback mechanism whereby local communities can be informed about the progress of the process of justice. This means that they will not get sufficient information about what has been going on or details of the results of the tribunals or trials. Both truth commissions and domestic trials take place either in capitals or in the larger cities and are therefore removed from large parts of the population. TIJM have an immediacy the importance of which should not be ignored.

It has been shown that local ownership is crucial for the successful outcome of any process that involves international intervention at any level. Of the various mechanisms of transitional justice, truth commissions, domestic trials and TIJM boast the highest potential for allowing local ownership of the process. International processes, including hybrid or internationalized courts, typically have more limited local ownership and are also frequently geographically removed from the communities they are serving, whereas TIJM are not. However, although truth commissions and domestic trials have the potential for greater local ownership, this may vary depending upon the circumstances; where, for example, there is heavy external involvement in setting up a truth commission and determining the scope and participants of the TC, local ownership is more limited.[64] Domestic trials may limit local ownership because of the fact that the judicial systems are usually in grave need of reform and reliant on external assistance to do so.[65] Traditional informal justice mechanisms therefore have an additional advantage. They are perceived to be entirely in the ownership of the local population. It is not something that is enforced from the outside, and they decide how to deal with the perpetrator without external interference, whether this is in a retributive or restorative manner, or a combination of the two. In this way they can contribute to the process of reconciliation with each other, the past and with the crimes committed.

*Reconciliation*

Traditional mechanisms undeniably enable and promote reconciliation in certain circumstances. In the case of Mozambique, which rejected both trials and a truth commission, traditional methods of healing were used with great success.[66] The combatants of the conflict returned to their communities and went through traditional healing and justice processes. Reasons for Mozambique's success included the particular context of the conflict, the focus on not reawakening the traumas of the war, and society's desire for healing.[67] It is important to underline that, as with trials and truth commissions, the extent of the potential for success of these mechanisms is dependent upon the numerous enabling and constraining factors outlined in the Introduction, including the context of the conflict, the culture of the country and the international community's role.

Traditional mechanisms are designed, in general, to deal with relatively minor crimes; if therefore they are to be applied in a post-conflict society dealing with past crimes, it may be better to utilize them at this level to deal with, for example, house burning, assault and minor altercations and violence on property and person. For more serious crimes, including crimes against humanity, war crimes and genocide, other mechanisms might better serve the purpose of reconciliation. In Timor-Leste traditional mechanisms were used for militia members who had burned houses and conducted minor assault. They were asked by the community to rebuild houses and perform community services and thus were reintegrated into the community. However, the community often did not want people who committed major human rights violations to return, and they were transferred to other parts of the country.[68] Yet again, it is entirely dependent upon context, since in Mozambique the healing rituals worked even in more severe cases – in particular the reintegration of boy soldiers was successful.[69] Traditional mechanisms can therefore, depending upon circumstances, promote reconciliation at many different levels.

## Conclusion

There has been a tendency in international interventions to equate the concept of 'traditional' with 'fair', 'good' and 'impartial', particularly in situations where international interveners are sensitive to stepping on the culture and customs of the country. Nevertheless, care should be taken so that in the pursuit of supporting and protecting a country's cultural norms and values, international human rights standards are not sidelined or obliterated altogether.

Although traditional mechanisms can be an invaluable part of dealing with past crimes in post-conflict societies, where there is international intervention several factors should be taken into consideration, assessed and dealt with. First, it must be established what the traditional mechanisms are prior to supporting them unconditionally, so that human rights, public security forces and the rule of law will not be undermined. Second, if they are retributive, the mechanisms must be implemented in a consistent way throughout the area, and they should not deliver punishments which are a violation of international human rights. If they focus solely on reconciliation and healing, they may vary according to community. Third, it must be decided what crimes can be dealt with in this manner. This must be decided through a consultation process with the local government and not enforced by the intervener, thus ensuring local ownership. Fourth, the TIJM should be run in conjunction with the court system, so that they can complement one another. Fifth, education in the new type of judicial system must be established so that trust can be created. It should not be the case that the judicial system is not used because of a lack of trust, but rather because the choice is made at certain times and for particular crimes to apply traditional mechanisms.

The criteria for deciding whether TIJM should be applied to these crimes in a post-conflict setting should include an assessment of the legitimacy of such mechanisms in that particular context and whether or not the mechanisms violate international human rights norms and standards. TIJM should only be encouraged by the international community if they respect human rights; if they do not, they should not be supported by the international community, although this does not mean that they will not and cannot be used by the post-conflict society in question to deal with past crimes.

Moreover, before promoting TIJM in any context, it must be determined how adaptable they are to addressing these new issues and what may block this adaptation. Typically, these mechanisms have been used on lesser crimes in the community. For these to become effective mechanisms of transitional justice, it is preferable to have them deal with cases at the same level in cases of retributive justice. However, when they are purely restorative, they can with ease be used at all levels of crime if that is so chosen by the local population. It then becomes a matter of reconciliation and healing, where retribution plays no part, as Mozambique so clearly exemplifies. Yet, where there is a mix of wanting both retribution for larger crimes and reintegration of perpetrators who have committed lesser crimes, then using TIJM only on the minor infractions might be preferable because of the many challenges that face these mechanisms in adaptability towards gross violations of human rights.

Applying TIJM to gross violations of human rights can be facilitated if there are references to them in formal law, and there are already linkages between the formal system and informal mechanisms. However, in post-conflict societies, such a pre-existing linkage may be rare. It has been argued that sometimes TIJM with flaws 'are better than nothing'.[70] This may be true for access to justice in general, but not when it concerns transitional justice and gross violations of human rights; if they violate human rights, these mechanisms should not be used to address such crimes. TIJM can be vital to ensuring reconciliation and sustainable peace in a post-conflict society, but in each case these mechanisms should be assessed and evaluated to see whether or not they can play such a role. Therefore, a more stringent focus on what role TIJM can play in what contexts is crucial.

### Box 7.1: Timor-Leste

Traditional mechanisms of justice for solving disputes, conflicts and crime have always been prominent in Timor-Leste, and there are a number of different types throughout the various districts.[71] Usually they take the form of a village meeting, where the perpetrator must do community work or is forced to pay a fine. Depending on the seriousness of the crime, this can mean paying with chickens, water buffaloes or land. It also focuses on reconciliation and resolving conflicts, including marital disputes and domestic violence. These mechanisms grew particularly strong during the Indonesian occupation, as a reaction to what was seen as an abusive justice system.

This traditional system did not change with the UN Transitional Administration in Timor-Leste (UNTAET) or with the presence of UN civilian police (UNPOL) throughout the territory. There were several reasons for this. First, the endemic problems within the judicial system. There were simply not enough resources or possibilities to deal with all crimes in the judicial system. These traditional methods were therefore supported as a means of alleviating the strain on a judicial system in creation. Second, there was a desire by the population to continue to deal with some of the crimes in this way. Third, it was supported and used by UNPOL, particularly in the districts, as a way of solving crimes.

There was an apparent tension in UNTAET between establishing a functioning justice system and the use of traditional methods. There was support generally for using the TIJM both for ordinary crime and for past crimes conducted during 1999, but these mechanisms were not critically evaluated and it was not established what crimes they could be applied to. The conflict seemed rooted in a fear of receiving criticism for not respecting Timorese society and culture, while trying at the same time to establish a Western-style judicial system. In Timor-Leste, the consequence of this conflict was to some extent an uncritical acceptance and support by UNPOL and UNTAET of the traditional mechanisms.

The traditional system was supported by UNPOL officers at senior levels and in the districts.[72] It was mainly used for minor crimes, but no definition of what constituted such a crime was offered. Different officers allowed a variety of crimes, such as thefts, land disputes, threats to kill and common assault, to be dealt with by the traditional system,[73] but the way it was used varied from district to district. There were no guidelines outlining when or when not to use it. In relation to past crimes conducted in 1999, perpetrators were brought back to the villages where they originated, frequently by UNPOL, and the village council then decided upon a punishment. This usually took the form of community service, such as rebuilding houses that the perpetrator had burnt down or other services that benefited the whole community. In this way the perpetrator was reconciled with society. However, if the crimes had been too brutal, the village repeatedly refused to take the perpetrator back and he/she was then relocated to another part of the island.[74]

A key concern was that this traditional system did not protect the rights of women. Timor-Leste is a patriarchal society, and in this traditional system of justice it manifested itself even more distinctively. In cases of rape, the perpetrator has been forced either to marry the victim, or to make a payment to the victim's family, in most cases the father. The victim would never receive any of the payment, and would remain stigmatized because of the rape. Punishments given by the traditional system in many cases also contravene international human rights law. UNPOL officers were present during rape cases and, by their presence, endorsed the process.[75] This set a very negative precedent and did not encourage women to come forward and make complaints to UNPOL; instead, it reinforced the patriarchal system of traditional law. Human rights representatives at the time were very worried that UNPOL might be using this system too extensively and readily without quite understanding what they were endorsing.

In some contexts TIJM were able very successfully to reintegrate the perpetrators of crimes in 1999. However, for those perpetrators who were moved on because the community did not want to deal with them in this manner, there was a void of justice. Moreover, there was no assessment conducted to ensure that the TIJM, when dealing with past crimes, complied with international human rights standards.

## Box 7.2: *Gacaca* courts in Rwanda

The *gacaca* courts are perhaps the most widely known example of what has been termed by many as 'traditional mechanisms'. Although they are mentioned here in the context of TIJM, they are in fact a hybrid of domestic trials and traditional mechanisms, which evolved especially to deal with the perpetrators of the genocide. It is important to emphasize that *gacaca* as used to deal with the *genocidaires* is a far cry from the original traditional justice mechanism upon which it was based. The original *gacaca* – the word literally means grass or lawn – is a dispute resolution mechanism devised to deal with minor crimes, marital disputes and property rights.[76] However, in the context of dealing with gross violations of human rights after the genocide, the *gacaca* evolved into a mechanism which included both traditional and more formal methods of justice.

After the genocide in 1994, more than 130,000 people were detained in prisons; eight years later, 125,000 were still in detention. The Rwandan government decided upon a path of criminal prosecution of all perpetrators involved in the genocide. The use of the *gacaca* system was a response to the inability of the Rwandan formal judicial system to complete such an enormous task.[77] Therefore the Rwandan government decided to use the model of the traditional mechanism to reach their objective of criminal prosecution, although originally the *gacaca* was a dispute and conflict resolution mechanism. More than 10,000 courts were established, with 250,000 judges to deal with the crimes committed during the genocide.[78] The judges are non-professionals, elected by members of the community, and they sentence those who are found guilty. It was argued that there were several advantages to this system: it would result in a faster process than in the formal judicial system, thereby leading to the release of a vast number of accused from long-term detention; it would reduce the cost of trials to the government; it would be a participatory process with continued discourse; and it would aid the reconciliation process of Rwandan society. Reaching these objectives has been far from successful.

There is a reported consensus among Rwandan government leaders and the international community that the process is flawed; in particular, it does not incorporate international standards guaranteeing a fair trial.[79] Moreover, an accused person who has been acquitted in national courts can still be tried in gacaca courts. It is also extremely problematic because of the number of judges, some of whom reportedly were themselves involved in the genocide. For example, one of the judges of the gacaca courts was accused of having used a machete on a young woman because she had refused to sleep with him (this act was said to have taken place within the context of the genocide); the judge admitted this act and explained that 'it was OK' because she then 'agreed' to live with him.[80] The level of agreement as opposed to that of enforcement is here questionable at best. There have also been questions raised regarding corruption and doubts about judges' impartiality.[81] In addition, this process was meant to speed up the deliverance of justice to both victims and perpetrators, but it has taken much longer than anticipated.

This hybrid of traditional and formal mechanisms, although flawed, was an inventive way of trying to deal with past crimes. However, its problems were perhaps not a reflection of the methods as much as of the Rwandan government's insistence that all had to be prosecuted – which necessarily resulted in the traditional mechanism becoming more like a formal process of prosecution.

# Conclusion

Transitional justice has come a long way in the last two decades. It has developed significantly as an area of academic enquiry, policy and practice. There is an implicit recognition of the link between justice and peace, and some form of transitional justice mechanism has become an important tool of UN post-conflict reconstruction and peace-building efforts.[1] However, a note of caution should be struck. Simply ticking the 'transitional justice' box on the 'to do' list for a new regime or interim administration is not enough. Far more thought needs to be given to exactly how these processes are going to work, to setting realistic objectives for them, and to making sure they are coordinated with other aspects of post-conflict reconstruction – most importantly in the area of judicial and security sector reform, demobilization and reintegration programmes, and establishing the rule of law.

The examples of the ad hoc tribunals, the ICC, the range of hybrid courts, domestic courts and non-judicial mechanisms offer up important lessons, many of which may not yet be fully understood. We have not arrived at a perfect solution – nor should we assume that there is one. Dealing with past abuses in a delicate post-conflict setting can be at best complicated and at worst calamitous. As the examples discussed in this book have demonstrated, there are various merits and drawbacks of different approaches and there is a range of factors that need to be taken into account: from pragmatic considerations about the state of the existing infrastructure and available resources, to cultural and historical factors relating to the way in which society views issues of justice and reconciliation, the nature of the conflict and the extent of abuses committed, and the range of actors involved, and political factors – crucially the extent to which transitional justice mechanisms are backed by political will, both domestically and internationally.

Most important is understanding the *context* in which transitional justice operates and managing *expectations*. We need to be realistic about what transitional justice can achieve and be honest about what it cannot. Here, a framework is set out which might help guide decisions on what form or forms of transitional justice might be appropriate in a given setting, based on the experience of events since the 1980s. The framework is organized under six main headings, which consider aims and objectives in terms of peace, justice and reconciliation; capacity-building and the rule of law; contextual factors; the importance of engaging the local population; the implementation of integrated and complementary approaches; and the management of expectations and setting realistic goals.

## Justice, Peace and Reconciliation

The record here is patchy and incomplete. While we can point to concrete ways in which transitional justice mechanisms have contributed to peace, the situation with regard to reconciliation is less clear. As discussed in chapter 2, the ad hoc tribunals were established to maintain and restore *international* peace and security and in this they have had some degree of success. Most important was their contribution in establishing a new norm of accountability over one of impunity and their numerous contributions to the further development of international criminal law and procedure. The ICC might be able to make a similar contribution internationally and the referral of the situation in Darfur by the Security Council in 2005 was testament to that body's potential role as a 'perfect symbiosis' of international peace and security and international criminal justice. The ICTY has also shown how indicting individuals and thereby removing them from the political process can make a concrete contribution to the restoration and consolidation of peace on the ground, and this may again be an important role for the ICC. International trials can also be significant in terms of recognizing the scale of abuses and the importance of dealing with them, not only for establishing international norms of impunity, but for satisfying the needs of victims to have their suffering acknowledged and drawing a clear line under the past.

However, as discussed, ICCs suffer from a number of drawbacks that make their contribution to national and individual reconciliation more doubtful. Most problematic is that the trials largely take place in settings far removed – geographically, culturally and psychologi-cally – from the location in which the crimes they are dealing with were perpetrated. Additional problems of funding, the length and complexity of trials, state cooperation and the lack of an effective out-reach and communication programme have also hampered their ability properly to engage the local population. But it should be noted that this is not only the responsibility of the court, whose mandate is one of justice primarily, albeit as a tool of peace; the extent to which an international court can or cannot influence the domestic arena will depend upon the context in which its messages are being received. If, as in the case of both Rwanda and the former Yugoslavia, the governments of the affected state are hostile, there is little that can be done.

More direct access to trials increases the feeling of justice, account-ability and transparency for the local population. Since the govern-ment sets up these trials, it ensures official acknowledgement of the violations that have taken place, acknowledgement that is a first crucial step for both national and individual reconciliation. Critically, because domestic trials take place within the communities where the abuses occurred, they have a more direct effect upon reconciliation and stability, thus ensuring that vengeance and retribution are not sought by victims of violence. But, as discussed in chapter 5, domes-tic courts might not always be appropriate or desirable, because of a lack of infrastructure, capacity, political will or ability to conduct fair and unbiased trials. Internationalized courts were therefore estab-lished to take advantage of some of the merits of international trials, including expertise, funding and legitimacy, whilst at the same time avoiding some of their pitfalls, most importantly by being based in the country concerned, and therefore being more accessible to the local population and potentially also more unbiased. As discussed in chapter 4, the numerous difficulties attending these 'hybrid' courts indicate that they are a less than perfect solution. Political and logis-tic difficulties have dogged efforts in Sierra Leone, Cambodia, Timor-Leste and Kosovo. Nevertheless, there is evidence that, at least in the case of Sierra Leone, the Court's extensive outreach programme has, on the whole, ensured effective communication of its work to the population of Sierra Leone.

Truth commissions and TIJM have a critical role to play in satisfy-ing goals that criminal justice cannot. Truth commissions provide a comprehensive historical record of past abuses, ensure that the truth about the violations is known, and provide a victim-centred forum, but alone they have rarely been sufficient to bring about reconciliation or justice. As discussed in chapter 6, since the focus of TCs is broader – establishing patterns of abuse – national reconciliation becomes the main aim, while individual reconciliation is sidelined and can thus lead to a desire by some victims for further action and demands for prosecution. The emphasis by some policy-makers and academics on truth commissions as the only tool of reconciliation, and particularly their healing propensities, has been exaggerated. They are not the perfect solution in all contexts, especially since they have been used as a tool for avoiding other forms of accountability. Yet they can play an important part in establishing the truth about the past, critically hindering collective amnesia.

TIJM have in several cases, for example Mozambique, contributed significantly to reconciliation of populations ravaged by war. They closely reflect local norms and customs and potentially have an immediate impact upon the reconciliation taking place in the communities where the violations took place. However, as discussed in chapter 7, they suffer from a number of flaws, particularly that in their proceedings they may abuse the very same human rights they were meant to address. When they are applied as a non-punitive measure, on minor crimes, by focusing on reconciliation only, they are less likely to breach human rights standards. For TIJM to have a positive impact upon reconciliation, peace and justice, careful assessments of the different mechanisms in each case should be made so as to ascertain the beneficial impacts of incorporating this system in a transitional justice process.

## Capacity-building and the Rule of Law

Much has been made of the contribution that transitional justice can make to building local capacity and helping fill the rule of law vacuum in the aftermath of conflict. This is seen as an increasingly important function of transitional justice, and recent efforts, focused on 'hybrid' courts, are explicitly aimed at fulfilling this goal. It was also hoped that internationalized courts, whether established outside the normal domestic judicial system as in Sierra Leone, or involving the insertion of international legal personnel into parts of the existing system as in Timor-Leste and Kosovo, would contribute to building local capacity in a weak or failing local judicial system. This was to be achieved on a practical level through international and local staff working together, allowing for the transfer of skills and practices, and more generally through the encouragement of dialogue on judicial reform and disseminating norms and values relating to the rule of law.

The Special Court for Sierra Leone is in the process of developing its 'legacy programme', but, as discussed in chapter 4, the fact that the Court will leave behind a state-of-the-art court facility and legal training of a handful of Sierra Leoneans working with it, who may take their skills abroad when the Court closes down anyway, does little to address fundamental flaws in the local justice and security sector, such as a responsive and non-corrupt police, and obstacles to local access to justice. Nonetheless, it is an improvement on the ICTs, where people from the region were excluded from working at the court and, in the case of the ICTY initially, were treated with a great deal of suspicion.

Domestic trials may in certain circumstances have the potential for influencing rule of law in post-conflict and transitional societies. By choosing domestic trials – as long as it can be ensured that they are fair and unbiased, which is a difficulty, as we have seen in chapter 5, in itself – the new post-conflict government has shown that it is taking accountability and rule of law seriously: it is drawing a line between the past and the present and establishing a new rule. This can have a positive impact not only upon the local population, but also upon the judicial system. Yet, without external assistance it is doubtful whether such trials will serve to help build capacity within the judicial system. But the positive impact these trials may have should not be under-estimated in face of the considerable challenges.

The non-judicial mechanisms, as opposed to international and hybrid courts, have not been especially promoted as creating capacity in the local communities. Nevertheless, they may influence the rule of law. As with domestic trials, because they establish accountability for past crimes, these mechanisms can strengthen the rule of law in a post-conflict society. They will not by themselves build capacity in the judicial system, although personnel in truth commissions may enter the judicial system later on, and hence in some small way contribute to capacity-building. However, it is more in the creation of a belief in change from authoritarianism and abuse of powers to one based on accountability and the rule of law that the contribution of these mechanisms can be made.

It is questionable whether rule of law and capacity-building are realistic objectives for transitional justice, which has its work cut out simply handling the complex and difficult process of dealing with past abuses. Alone, clearly, it is unrealistic to expect one single mechanism, often operating under strict budgetary restraints, to do this, but there is significant overlap and scope for cooperation with other elements of post-conflict reconstruction or peace-building aimed at judicial and security sector reform. It is more realistic, therefore, to look for ways in which transitional justice might contribute and be complementary to these processes, rather than expect it alone to achieve capacity-building and the rule of law. For this to work, it needs to be fully incorporated into an overall strategy of post-conflict reconstruction, not seen as a side issue.

## Context

The goals set out above – of peace, justice and reconciliation and building local capacity and the rule of law – are ambitious, to say the least. Achieving all this in societies emerging from violent conflict, where domestic institutions may be devastated or destroyed, resources are stretched, security is tenuous at best, and the population divided, is a colossal task. A lesson that comes through clearly from the cases discussed in this book is the need to take into account a range of pragmatic, political, cultural and other considerations when determining the best way of dealing with a legacy of large-scale abuses.

On a pragmatic level, an assessment needs to be made of the capacity of the local justice system to deal with such abuses. As discussed in chapters 3 and 5, domestic courts are the court of first resort, even with the establishment of the ICC. But, in many cases, domestic courts may be unable, because of a lack of infrastructure, personnel and finance, to deal with transitional justice, or they may simply be unwilling. Political constraints – ranging from a lack of will to reform, or difficulties because of a relatively fragile power-sharing arrangement, or the residual power of institutions like the military, or simply a desire to focus on other apparently more pressing needs – might push the issue of dealing with past abuses to the bottom of the agenda. It is here that the international community might step in, either through the ICC, by supporting domestic capacity, or by supporting and encouraging non-judicial means. However, as has become increasingly clear, with the best will in the world, international involvement often requires more in terms of political commitment and resources than external actors are willing to provide.

Of equal importance when contemplating transitional justice are historical, social and cultural factors. It has been suggested that imposing criminal trials amounts to a form of Western imperialism. However, on the evidence presented, this judgement is unwarranted. It is patronizing to suggest that developing countries are not suited to criminal trials; in fact, in several cases, the initiative for international or internationalized trials has come from the states themselves. (Rwanda requested an international tribunal, although it was opposed to the form it took; Cambodia and Sierra Leone requested international assistance, resulting in the establishment of Extraordinary Chambers in Cambodia and the Special Court for Sierra Leone; and Uganda and the DRC referred their situations to the ICC. In other countries including Timor-Leste and Haiti, there has been a demand for international tribunals – a demand that went unmet.)

Nevertheless, it is important to recognize the needs of different sectors of society for different forms of justice. Justice does not only mean criminal trials; it encompasses a range of approaches discussed in this book aimed at ensuring accountability and fairness. An approach that combines restorative and retributive justice might best suit a situation where there may be a cadre of leaders who 'bear the greatest responsibility' and a majority of others for whom the line between victim and perpetrator is less easy to determine. As discussed in chapter 7, in some contexts TIJM can have more to offer than criminal trials. But we should be careful about falling into cultural relativism, supporting such mechanisms just because it reflects cultural norms without a prior assessment of the suitability of applying them to the particular set of past crimes. TIJM may be all well and good when dealing with minor crime, but in cases of mass murder, rape, sexual assault, torture, mutilation, etc., it may not provide the best or most appropriate solution. Yet, if the choice of the population, as it was in Mozambique, is to focus on healing and non-punitive measures of justice, then the international community should not insist on criminal trials or any particular type of transitional justice.

In all this, it is important to have a full understanding of the nature of the conflict, the extent of the abuses, the degree of organization, the levels of responsibility and the role of the different actors. As discussed in chapters 3 and 4 in relation to Uganda and Sierra Leone in particular, child soldiers present a dilemma, especially where they have been coerced into taking part in hostilities and forced to carry out horrific acts of violence, in some cases against their families and neighbours, which was a way of ensuring that they severed their ties with their communities and shared the shame of the group they were joining. Moreover, certain sections of the population (for example, women) might also be more vulnerable than others; in such cases, it is important to make sure that transitional justice addresses their needs as survivors as well as victims, and does not exacerbate their suffering.

## Engaging the Local Population

The importance of effective communication and outreach and of involving the local population has already been noted as a crucial element in the success or failure of transitional justice in fulfilling the objectives set out for it.

The ad hoc tribunals are a stark lesson in how not to do this. As discussed in chapter 2, while they may have had an important impact internationally, domestically they leave a lot to be desired. Part of the problem was the lack of engagement with local people at an early stage. In the case of the former Yugoslavia, this was made all but impossible by the ongoing conflict; in Rwanda, the lack of consultation with the government resulted in a tribunal that was rejected by both the government and many of the people of Rwanda.

It is in the context of local ownership and engagement that domestic trials, as well as TCs and TIJM, are critical – these are all transitional justice mechanisms that have the most engagement with and ownership by the local populations. Yet, in many circumstances even domestic trials can be distant in geographical, psychological, monetary and cultural terms. Many districts in Timor-Leste felt cut off from the domestic trials taking place in Dili, and the TIJM offered a much more immediate access to engagement in and ownership of the justice process.

Extensive consultation with a range of actors is a requirement irrespective of the transitional justice mechanism chosen and applied. Although the needs of different groups might complicate matters, suggesting a range of approaches enhances understanding of those groups, and the context in which transitional justice is sought.

## Integrated and Complementary Approaches

There is increasing recognition that, while one type of transitional justice alone might not be sufficient to meet the various needs of post-conflict societies, equally, adopting a piecemeal approach will not bring satisfactory results. There is no reason that trials cannot be conducted alongside a truth commission process, or alongside TIJM, or that international trials may not be conducted alongside domestic trials. But the experiences in places like Sierra Leone and Rwanda indicate a need for careful planning in order to ensure that the processes work in a mutually reinforcing fashion, not against one another. Critically, the experience of Timor-Leste showed that TIJM worked well alongside domestic trials, although the domestic trials left a lot to be desired in terms of lack of victim protection and suffering from bias and unfairness.

The clash between the Special Court and the TRC in Sierra Leone provided a harsh lesson in how not to conduct apparently contradictory processes. This manifested itself in suspicion towards both institutions among the population, because of a lack of understanding of the relative roles of the two bodies and the suspected extent of collusion between them. It could also be seen in public rows about whether or not suspects at the Special Court could testify before the TRC, which were unedifying for both institutions. In Rwanda, the contrast between the international tribunal, where higher-level perpetrators were tried, and the overloaded domestic judicial system was stark. These experiences do not, however, indicate that such processes are incompatible, merely that careful thought should be given in advance to how they might operate in a complementary manner.

Careful thought should also be given to how transitional justice fits into an overall strategy of conflict transformation and/or post-conflict reconstruction. The interests of justice and the interests of peace are mutually reinforcing, but the relationship is rarely straightforward. A careful balancing act needs to be performed in order to satisfy long- and short-term objectives and in order to juggle successfully the needs of disparate groups for accountability, truth, reconciliation, retribution, reintegration and the building of a society based on the rule of law.

## Managing Expectations and Setting Realistic Goals

As we have seen, the goals of transitional justice are ambitious. Often, they are imposed from elsewhere and it not in the power of those working within such processes to deliver them. It is important therefore to find a way of managing expectations. That is not to say that transitional justice should aim merely at securing the lowest common denominator, but that we need to be realistic when setting objectives and careful to ensure that those objectives are accurately transmitted.

On a more positive note, just because something has not brought about a perfect society, where warring factors are living side by side in a state governed by the rule of law and abiding by democratic norms, it does not mean that transitional justice has failed. Myriad other factors influence the extent to which a process might be successful in fulfilling goals of peace, justice and reconciliation.

It has been a recurrent theme of this book that there is no single template, no one-size-fits-all solution that can be happily applied to every situation. All the experiences discussed here have their own merits as well as their own disadvantages, which are a result as much of the context in which they are operating as of the design of the model of transitional justice applied. However, as discussed above, some broad lessons can be drawn from these experiences. Managing expectations, setting realistic goals and communicating those goals to the local population are crucial, as are engaging the local population in the process and taking into account local preferences. Also critical is proper understanding of the historical, cultural, political and social context in which transitional justice is going to operate. The most important lesson is that peace and justice are mutually reinforcing, not incompatible, goals. We cannot abandon one in favour of the other. There is an international legal imperative to ensure justice is done, as well as a moral imperative to ensure that perpetrators of widespread and egregious abuses of human rights face some form of justice, and a pragmatic and political imperative based on the potential contribution to the process of peace-building and post-conflict reconstruction. What form this justice should take is open to debate and should be tailored to suit circumstances, but failure to deal with past abuses only lays the foundations for future instability, insecurity and war.

# Notes

## Peace and Justice: An Introduction

1 This term was first used by David Scheffer, former US Ambassador at Large for War Crimes, in his 'International Judicial Intervention', *Foreign Policy* (1996): 34–51. See also Rachel Kerr, 'International Judicial Intervention: The International Criminal Tribunal for the Former Yugoslavia', *International Relations* 15/2 (August 2000): 17–26.

2 *The Rule of Law and Transitional Justice in Conflict and Post-Conflict Societies*, Report of the Secretary-General, 23 August 2004.

3 Draft report, Wilton Park Conference, 24–26 January 2005, 'Transitional Justice and Rule of Law in Post-Conflict Societies: The Role of International Actors', p. 2.

4 See, for example, Luc Huyse, 'Justice After Transition: On the Choices Successor Elites Make in Dealing with the Past', *Law and Social Inquiry* 20/1 (Winter 1995); Chandra Lekha Sriram, 'Truth Commissions and the Quest for Justice: Stability and Accountability after Internal Strife', in A. Adebajo and C. L. Sriram (eds), *Managing Armed Conflicts in the 21st Century* (London: Frank Cass, 2001), pp. 92–3.

5 For an excellent survey of the debate, see Jack Snyder and Leslie Vinjamuri, 'Trials and Errors: Principle and Pragmatism in Strategies of International Justice', *International Security* 28/3 (Winter 2003/4): 5–44. Also see: Priscilla Hayner, *Unspeakable Truths: Confronting State Terror and Atrocity* (New York: Routledge, 2001); Carla Hesse and Robert Post (eds), *Human Rights in Political Transitions: Gettysburg to Bosnia* (Boston: MIT Press, 2000); Neil J. Kritz, *Transitional Justice: How Emerging Democracies Reckon with Former Regimes* (Washington, DC: United States Institute of Peace, 1995); Rama Mani, *Beyond Retribution: Seeking Justice in the Shadows of War* (Cambridge: Polity, 2001); Juan Mendez, 'Accountability for Past Abuses', *Human Rights Quarterly* 19/2 (1997); Martha Minow, *Between Vengeance and Forgiveness: Facing History after Genocide and Mass Violence* (Boston: Beacon Press, 1998); Diane Orentlicher, 'Settling

Accounts: The Duty to Prosecute Human Rights Violations of a Prior Regime', *Yale Law Journal* 100 (1991): 2537–615; Chandra Lekha Sriram, *Justice vs Peace in Times of Transition* (London: Frank Cass, 2004); Ruti G. Teitel, *Transitional Justice* (Oxford: Oxford University Press, 2002).

6 Theodor Meron, 'The Case for War Crimes Trials in Yugoslavia', *Foreign Affairs* 72/3 (1993): 122–35.

7 Aryeh Neier, 'Rethinking Truth, Justice and Guilt after Bosnia and Rwanda', in Hesse and Post (eds), *Human Rights in Political Transitions*, p. 49.

8 Antonio Cassese, 'Reflections on International Criminal Justice', *The Modern Law Review* 61/1 (January 1998): 1–10.

9 Orentlicher, 'Settling Accounts', p. 2542. See also Malamud-Goti, 'Transitional Governments in the Breach: Why Punish State Criminals?', *Human Rights Quarterly* 12/1 (1990); Samuel P. Huntington, *The Third Wave: Democratization in the Late Twentieth Century* (Norman: University of Oklahoma Press, 1991).

10 Cited in Brandon Hamber, 'Past Imperfect: Dealing With the Past in Northern Ireland and Societies in Transition', paper presented at the 'Moving Towards Pluralism Conference', 4th International Conference of the Ethnic Studies Network, 8–11 June 1999, Institute of Ethnology and Anthropology at the Russian Academy of Science, Leninsky Prospeckt, Moscow. See <http://www.brandonhamber.com>.

11 Joseph Monteville, quoted in K. Avruch and B. Vejarano, 'Truth and Reconciliation Commissions: A Review Essay and Annotated Bibliography', *The Online Journal of Peace and Conflict Resolution* 4/2 (Spring 2002): p. 4.

12 David Crocker, quoted in J. D. Tepperman, 'Truth and Consequences', *Foreign Affairs* (March/April 2002): 7.

13 Denis Thompson, quoted in ibid.

14 John Lederach, quoted in A. Odendaal, 'For All Its Flaws. The TRC as a Peacebuilding Tool', *CCR* 6/3–4 (December 1997): 1.

15 See also Winslow, quoted in Avruch and Vejarano, 'Truth and Reconciliation Commissions', p. 4.

16 Kenneth Roth, 'Human Rights in the Haitian Transition to Democracy', in Hesse and Post (eds), *Human Rights in Political Transitions*.

17 The civil wars and security and development literature has examined these issues. See, for example, S. Stedman, 'Spoiler Problems in Peace Processes', *International Security* 22/2 (1997): 5–53.

18 Tadeusz Mazowiecki, quoted in Mendez, 'In Defense of Transitional Justice', in James A. McAdams, *Transitional Justice and the Rule of Law in New Democracies* (Notre Dame: University of Notre Dame Press, 1997), p. 7.

19 Mendez, 'In Defense of Transitional Justice', p. 1.

20 Orentlicher, 'Settling Accounts', p. 2539.

21 Ibid., p. 2540. Although Additional Protocol II to the 1949 Geneva Conventions, 1977, Article 6, para. 2, allows for a broad amnesty to be

granted to 'persons who have participated in the armed conflict, or those deprived of their liberty for reasons related to the armed conflict', this provision seeks to encourage the release of individuals who might be subject to criminal proceedings under domestic law for the fact of having taken part in hostilities and should in no way be read as supporting amnesties for war crimes or other international offences committed in internal armed conflict. See Yasmin Naqvi, 'Amnesty for War Crimes: Defining the Limits of International Recognition', *International Review of the Red Cross* 851 (2003): 583.

22 Anonymous, 'Human Rights in Peace Negotiations', *Human Rights Quarterly* 18 (1996): 249–58.

23 Mark Osiel, 'Why Prosecute? Critics of Punishment for Mass Atrocity', *Human Rights Quarterly* 22 (2000): 125.

24 Ibid., p. 129.

25 'Tutu Urges Apartheid Prosecutions', BBC News, 16 December 2005.

26 Jane Alexander, *A Scoping Study of Transitional Justice and Poverty Reduction* (London: Department for International Development, January 2003), p. 43.

27 The UN Human Rights Committee has stated that general amnesties are inconsistent with the International Covenant on Cultural and Political Rights (ICCPR) because they 'create a climate of impunity' and deny victims the right to a remedy. Office of the High Commissioner of Human Rights, Impunity, Resolution 2004/72. The Inter-American Commission has found *all* amnesties that it has had under its consideration to be incompatible with the American Convention. See Diane Orentlicher, *Independent Study on Best Practices, Including Recommendations, to Assist States in Strengthening their Domestic Capacity to Combat all Aspects of Impunity*, E/CN.4/2004/88, 27 February 2004.

28 Quoted in ibid.

### Chapter 1    The Nuremberg Legacy

1 M. Cherif Bassiouni, *A Draft International Criminal Code and Draft Statute for an International Criminal Tribunal* (London: Martinus Nijhoff Publishers, 1987), p. 2.

2 Hilaire McCoubrey, 'The Concept and Treatment of War Crimes', *Journal of Armed Conflict Law* 1 (1996): 123. The defence of superior orders, i.e. immunity on the basis of acting in furtherance of an order is well established for military trials, but, as Nuremberg established, it is not available as a defence for crimes against humanity, war crimes and genocide.

3 Ibid., p. 124.

4 Barrie Paskins and Michael Dockrill, *The Ethics of War* (London: Duckworth, 1979), p. 266.

5 Ann Tusa and John Tusa, *The Nuremberg Trial* (London: Macmillan, 1983), p. 487.

 6 Telford Taylor, *The Anatomy of the Nuremberg Trials* (London: Bloomsbury, 1993), p. 42.
 7 Judith N. Shklar, *Legalism: Law, Morals and Political Trials* (Cambridge, MA: Harvard University Press, 1964).
 8 Documents on German Foreign Policy, Series D, vol. I, no. 19.
 9 Robert K. Woetzel, *The Nuremberg Trials in International War* (London: Praeger, 1960), p. 183.
10 Taylor, *Anatomy of the Nuremberg Trials*, p. 627.
11 Richard H. Minear, *Victor's Justice: The Tokyo War Crimes Trial* (Princeton: Princeton University Press, 1971), p. xiii.
12 Ibid., p. 180.
13 Ibid., pp. 10–13, 19.
14 See Madoka Futamura, 'Revisiting the "Nuremberg Legacy": Transformation and the Strategic Success of International War Crime Tribunals: Lessons from the Tokyo Trial and Japanese Experience'. PhD dissertation, Department of War Studies, King's College London, 2005.
15 Taylor, *Anatomy of the Nuremberg Trials*, p. 4.
16 Department of State Report of Robert H. Jackson, US Representative to the International Conference on Military Trials (US Department of State, 1945). Cited in Virginia Morris and Michael P. Scharf, *An Insider's Guide to the International Criminal Tribunal for the Former Yugoslavia*, vols I and II (New York: Transnational Publishers, 1995), p. 8. The Nuremberg Judgement has succeeded in providing an historical record, but it has not been wholly undisputed.
17 Lyal Sunga, *Individual Responsibility in International Law for Serious Human Rights Violations* (Dordrecht: M. Nijhoff, 1992), p. 48.
18 Address by the Honourable Justice Richard Goldstone to the David Davies Memorial Institute of International Studies, Institute of Directors, London, 6 June 1996, p. 3.
19 S/PV. 3175 (1993), 22 February 1993.
20 A/RES/95(I) (1946), 11 December 1946.
21 See M. Cherif Bassiouni, *International Criminal Law*, vol. III: *Enforcement* (New York: Transnational Publishers, 1986), p. 61.
22 Joseph L. Kunz, 'The UN Convention on Genocide', *American Journal of International Law*, 43 (1949): 738.
23 A/RES/95(III) (1948), 9 December 1948.
24 M. Cherif Bassiouni, *A Draft International Criminal Code and Draft Statute for an International Criminal Tribunal* (London: Martinus Nijhoff Publishers, 1987), p. 9.
25 Roger S. Clark, 'The Influence of the Nuremberg Trial', in R. Clark, R. and M. Sann, *The Prosecution of International Crimes: A Critical Study of the International Tribunal for the Former Yugoslavia* (New Brunswick: Transaction Publishers, 1996), p. 254.
26 James Crawford, 'The ILC's Draft Statue for an International Criminal Court', *American Journal of International Law* 88 (1994): 141.

27 See chapter 3 for a detailed account of the process of establishment and analysis of the Statute.

28 Jean Pictet, *Development and Principles of International Humanitarian Law* (Dordrecht: Martinus Nijhoff Publishers, 1985), p. 3.

29 See, for example, Nicholas Wheeler, *Saving Strangers: Humanitarian Intervention in International Society* (Oxford: Oxford University Press, 2000) and the report of the International Commission on Intervention and State Sovereignty, *The Responsibility to Protect* (December 2001); available at <http://www.iciss.ca/report2-en.asp> [14/03/07].

30 GA Res. 217A (III) (1948), 10 December 1948.

31 Sydney D. Bailey, *The UN Security Council and Human Rights* (London: St Martin's Press, 1994), p. xi.

32 10 December 1998. Cited in Geoffrey Robertson, *Crimes Against Humanity: The Struggle for Global Justice* (London: The Penguin Press, 1999), p. 32.

33 S/RES/232 (1966), 16 December 1966. N. D. White takes the view that denial of the right of self-determination, or a significant deprivation of human rights, has the potential in itself to ignite international violence, and is therefore a threat to international peace and security. See White, *Keeping the Peace: The United Nations and International Peace and Security* (Manchester: Manchester University Press, 1993), p. 43.

34 S/RES/418 (1977), 4 November 1977.

35 Nagendra Singh, 'The UN and the Development of International Law', in Adam Roberts and Benedict Kingsbury (eds), *United Nations, Divided World: The UN's Roles in International Relations* (Oxford: Clarendon Press, 1993), p. 395.

36 S/PV. 3175 (1993), 22 February 1993.

### Chapter 2    Ad hoc International Criminal Tribunals: The ICTY and ICTR

1 See David J. Scheffer, 'International Judicial Intervention', *Foreign Policy* (1996); and Rachel Kerr, 'International Judicial Intervention: The International Criminal Tribunal for the Former Yugoslavia', *International Relations* 15/2 (August 2000): 17–26.

2 Jack Snyder and Leslie Vinjamuri, 'Trials and Errors: Principle and Pragmatism in Strategies of International Justice', *International Security* 28/3 (2003/4). Ralph Zacklin, 'The Failings of Ad Hoc International Tribunals', *Journal of International Criminal Justice* 2 (2004): 541–5.

3 See chapter 4.

4 The first manifestation of this shift occurred in the context of the Gulf War, when, on 5 April 1991, Resolution 688 found the persecution of Kurd and Shi'a minorities in northern and southern Iraq to be a threat to international peace and security. Following this, tentative measures were taken in response to the outbreak of violent conflict in Yugoslavia in 1991, and in Somalia in 1992. On 31 January 1992, a meeting of the Heads of Government of Current Security Council Members in New

York issued the following statement: '[T]he absence of war and military conflicts among states does not in itself ensure international peace and security. The non-military sources of instability in the economic, social, humanitarian and ecological fields have become threats to peace and security.' See James Gow, 'A Revolution in International Affairs: Governance, Justice and War', *International Relations*, 15/1 (2000): 1–10.

5 For more on this, see Rachel Kerr, *The International Criminal Tribunal for the Former Yugoslavia: Law, Diplomacy and Politics* (Oxford: Oxford University Press, 2004).

6 In spite of financial and practical difficulties, the Commission managed in just 16 months to compile more than 65,000 pages of documents, 300 hours of videotape and 3,300 pages of analysis. In its first interim report on 9 February 1993, the Commission stated that the establishment of an ad hoc international criminal tribunal would be 'consistent with the direction of its work'. M. Cherif Bassiouni and P. Manikas, *The Law of the International Criminal Tribunal for the Former Yugoslavia* (New York: Transnational Publishers, 1996), p. 204.

7 Scheffer, 'International Judicial Intervention', p. 51.

8 The legal basis for the establishment of the tribunal was challenged in the first case to come before the court, that of Duško Tadić. In a motion filed on 23 June 1995 the defence challenged the jurisdiction of the tribunal on three grounds: first, that the tribunal was unlawfully established by the Security Council; second, that it was improperly given primacy over national courts; and third, that it lacked subject matter jurisdiction under Articles 2, 3 and 5 of the Statute to try the accused. After some deliberation about whether or not the tribunal was competent to rule on the legality of its establishment, the Appeals Chamber decided that it met the requirements of having been 'established by law'. Although the matter of a determination of a threat to the peace was essentially political, the choice of mechanism used to address such a threat was a legal question, to which the answer was that establishment of a tribunal fell squarely within the powers of the Security Council under Article 41 of the UN Charter. Decision on the Defence Motion for Interlocutory Appeal on Jurisdiction, *Prosecutor v. Tadić*, IT-94–1, 2 October 1995.

9 David Forsythe, 'Politics and the International Tribunal for the Former Yugoslavia', in R. Clark and M. Sann, *The Prosecution of International Crimes: A Critical Study of the International Tribunal for the Former Yugoslavia* (New Brunswick: Transaction Publishers, 1996), pp. 402–22; Michael P. Scharf, *Balkan Justice* (Durham, NC: Carolina Academic Press 1997), p. 37.

10 See, for example, A. D'Amato, 'Peace vs. Accountability in Bosnia', *American Journal of International Law* 88 (1994).

11 Some of these are discussed in Mark B. Harmon and Fergal Gaynor, 'Prosecuting Massive Crimes with Primitive Tools: Three Difficulties Encountered by Prosecutors in International Criminal Proceedings';

Minna Schrag, 'Lessons Learned from ICTY Experience'; Grant
Niemann, 'The Life and Times of a Senior Trial Attorney at the ICTY
from 1994 to 2000': all in *Journal of International Criminal Justice* 2
(2004): 403–26, 427–34, 435–45, respectively. Also see Kerr, *The
International Criminal Tribunal for the Former Yugoslavia*.

12 The process of appointing a prosecutor was fraught with difficulties
owing to the fact that it was recognized to be a crucial role with political
implications. The South African Judge, Richard Goldstone, was eventually appointed and took up office in July 1994.

13 Erik Mose, 'Main Achievements of the ICTR', *Journal of International
Criminal Justice* 3/4 (2005): 927.

14 The decision to appoint a separate prosecutor for the ICTR is commonly
attributed to problems with the current Prosecutor, Carla Del Ponte, and
her relations with the government of Rwanda. The official reason,
however, was that separate prosecutors would be better able to navigate
each tribunal through the crucial period of implementing their completion
strategy. See Mose, 'Main Achievements of the ICR', p. 929.

15 In February 1994, the judges issued a statement publicly criticizing
prosecutorial strategy, in particular the perceived lack of urgency. The
declaration was drawn up by the judges and shown to the Prosecutor
before it was released. Goldstone apparently said he could live with it.
Antonio Cassese, 'International Criminal Justice Mechanism: Are They
Really so Needed in the Present World Community?': lecture organized
by the Centre for the Study of Human Rights, London School of
Economics, 13 November 2000.

16 Dragan Nikolić was charged with 'grave breaches', violations of the laws
and customs of war and crimes against humanity for acts allegedly committed at the Susica Camp in eastern Bosnia.

17 Some of these early indictments were later withdrawn.

18 *De Telegraaf*, 27 April 1995.

19 A committee was established to look into allegations of war crimes committed by NATO forces during Operation Allied Force, but it was not
pursued because of a lack of evidence. While some took this to be an indi-
cator of the dangers of politically motivated charges being brought to the
attention of the ICC, others took it to demonstrate the importance of
having a robust and independent prosecutor to ensure that decisions on
what, how and whom to prosecute were taken independently of political
considerations. US objections, in particular, centred on misgivings about
the possibility of politically motivated prosecutions of US citizens, particularly US military forces undertaking peacekeeping operations. *UN
Law Reports*, 1 February 2000.

20 In order to deal with the large number of cases, involving somewhere
between 80,000 and 100,000 accused, the Rwandan government established a system of *gacaca* courts in 2001. These courts have evolved
from traditional communal law enforcement procedures, but they
have been criticized for not providing sufficient protection for victims.

See Rachel Rinaldo, 'Can the Gacaca Courts Deliver Justice?', available at <http://www.globalpolicy.org/intljustice/tribunals/rwanda/2004/0408justice.htm>. For further discussion, see chapter 7, box 7.2.

21 Luc Reydams, 'The ICTR Ten Years On: Back to the Nuremberg Paradigm', *Journal of International Criminal Justice* 3/4 (2005): 977–88.

22 'Foreword by the former President of the International Criminal Tribunal for the former Yugoslavia', *International Review of the Red Cross* 321 (1997): 602.

23 Separate Opinion of Judge Shahabuddeen, Decision Stating Reasons for Appeals Chamber's Order of 29 May 1998, *Prosecutor v. Aleksovski*, IT-95-14/1, 2 July 1998, p. 4.

24 Jules Dechênes, 'Towards International Criminal Justice', in Roger S. Clark and Madeleine Sann (eds), *A Critical Study of the International Tribunal for the Former Yugoslavia, Criminal Law Forum*, 5/2–3 (1994): 269.

25 The Secretary-General recognized the importance of ensuring that the tribunal apply only rules of international humanitarian law that are 'beyond any doubt part of customary law so that the problem of adherence of some but not all States to specific conventions does not arise'. Report of the Secretary-General pursuant to paragraph 2 of Security Council Resolution 808, S/25704 (1993), 3 May 1993, at 34.

26 For details, see Mose, 'Main Achievements of the ICTR', pp. 929–32.

27 Address of Antonio Cassese, President of the ICTY to the General Assembly of the United Nations, 7 November 1995.

28 Report of the International Tribunal, 23 August 1995, at 182.

29 Cited in 'Avenging Angel', *Observer*, 4 March 2001. On 30 January 2007, Del Ponte announced she will retire from her position as Chief Prosecutor in September 2007 to return to 'normal life'. See 'I'm A Frustrated Prosecutor', RFE/RL, 1 February 2007; available at <http://www.rferl.org/featuresarticle/2007/02/2fda764f-e963-4911-b6c4-417b2b1246ae.html> [16/03/07].

30 The General Framework Agreement for Peace in Bosnia and Herzegovina, also known as the Dayton Agreement or Dayton Accords, is the peace agreement ending three and a half years of war in Bosnia and Herzegovina, reached at the Wright-Patterson Air Force Base near Dayton, Ohio in November 1995, and formally signed in Paris on 14 December 1995.

31 This contention was wrong from a legal point of view, since the transfer of accused to the custody of the tribunal should not have been understood as extradition, but as surrender.

32 Sixth Annual Report of the International Tribunal for the Prosecution of Persons Responsible for Serious Violations of International Humanitarian Law Committed in the Territory of the former Yugoslavia since 1991, UN Doc. S/1999/846, 25 August 1999, p. 97.

33 'Yugoslav Rails Against UN Prosecutor', *The Boston Globe*, 25 May 2000.

34 'Bosnian Serbs Near to Handing Over Fugitives', *Guardian*, 5 July 2001; 'Croats Accused of War Crimes', *Observer*, 8 July 2001.

35 CC/PIO/030-E, 6 February 1996.
36 'Croat President Invites Serb Return', BBC News Online, 10 February 2000.
37 See Victor Peskin and Mieczyslaw P. Boduszynski, 'International Justice and Domestic Politics: Post-Tudjman Croatia and the International Criminal Tribunal for the Former Yugoslavia', *Europe-Asia Studies* 55/7 (2003): 1117–42; and Amadeo Watkins, 'Croatia at a Crossroads: The EU–ICTY Debate', Conflict Studies Research Centre Occasional Paper 05/15 (March 2005).
38 There are a number of reports detailing the crimes allegedly committed by the RPF. Among the first was Amnesty International, *Rwanda: Reports of Killings and Abductions by the Rwandese Patriotic Army, April-August 1994*, AI Index 47/016/1994, 20 October 1994.
39 For more on this, see Luc Reydams, 'The ICTR Ten Years On: Back to the Nuremberg Paradigm', *Journal of International Criminal Justice* 3/4 (2005): 977–88; and an interview with Carla Del Ponte in *Hirondelle* on 16 September 2003; available at <http://www.hirondelle.org/arusha.nsf> [27/07/06].
40 'Bringing Justice to the Former Yugoslavia: The Tribunal's Five Core Achievements'; available at <http://www.un.org/icty/glance-e/index.htm> [15/03/07]. On the record of the ICTY, see the contributions in a special symposium issue of the *Journal of International Criminal Justice* 2/2 (June 2004).
41 'Achievements of the ICTR', available at <http://69.94.11.53/ENGLISH/factsheets/achievements.htm> [27/07/06].
42 ICTR Newsletter, June/July 2006, available at <http://69.94.11.53/ENGLISH/newsletter/jun-jul06/june-july06.pdf> [27/07/06].
43 'Hague Deals Reduce Impact', IWPR Tribunal Update, 24 July 2003, available at <http://www.iwpr.net/index.pl?archive/tri/tri_321_3_eng.txt> [4/05/05].
44 Initially convicted of conspiracy to commit genocide and sentenced to 46 years, he had his sentence reduced on appeal to 35 years to reflect the finding that he was not guilty of conspiracy, but of 'aiding and abetting' genocide.
45 Discussion with Defence Counsel, ICTY, 7 February 2005.
46 For discussion of the Milošević trial, see James Gow and Ivan Zvershanovski, 'The Milosevic Trial: Purpose and Performance', *Nationalities Papers* 32/4 (December 2004). For background, see M. Scharf and P. Williams, *Slobodan Milošević on Trial: A Companion* (New York: Continuum, 2002).
47 For full discussion of the jurisprudential impact of the tribunals, see the collection of articles commemorating ten years of the ICTY in the *Journal of International Criminal Justice* 2/2 (2004); also see Human Rights Watch, *Genocide, War Crimes and Crimes Against Humanity: Topical Digests of the Case Law of the International Criminal Tribunal for Rwanda and the International Criminal Tribunal for the Former Yugoslavia* (February 2004) at <http://hrw.org/reports/2004/ij/>.

48 The trial concerned three individuals. First, Ferdinand Nahimana, Director of Radio Television Libre de Milles Collines (RTLM), and a former professor of history. RTLM was set up as the first private radio station in Rwanda when Nahimana was Director of the Rwandan National Information Office. At the trial, he was alleged to have authored essays, books and a PhD thesis promoting ideological basis for the genocide. Second, Hassan Ngeze, Kangura newspaper Editor-in-Chief, who was also a member of leadership of Interahamwe, and was charged with publishing material that incited genocide, including lists of names targeted for assassination. Third, Jean Bosco Barayagwiza, Director of the Ministry of Foreign Affairs, who was also a high-ranking board member of RTLM.

49 Mose, 'Main Achievements of the ICTR', p. 935.

50 See Theodor Meron, 'Procedural Evolution in the ICTY', *Journal of International Criminal Justice* 2 (2004): 520–5

51 See François-Xavier Nsanzuwera, 'The ICTR Contribution to National Reconciliation', *Journal of International Criminal Justice* 3/4 (2005): 944–9.

52 Lilian A. Barria and Steven D. Roper, 'How Effective are International Criminal Tribunals? An Analysis of the ICTY and the ICTR', *The International Journal of Human Rights* 9/3 (2005): 364.

53 Laurel E. Fletcher and Harvey M. Weinstein, 'A World unto Itself? The Application of International Justice in the Former Yugoslavia', in Eric Stover and Harvey M. Weinstein (eds), *My Neighbour, My Enemy: Justice and Community in the Aftermath of Mass Atrocity* (Cambridge: Cambridge University Press, 2004), p. 30.

54 James Meernik, 'Justice and Peace? How the International Criminal Tribunal Affects Societal Peace in Bosnia', *Journal of Peace Research* 42/3 (2005): 271–89.

55 The Commission was established by the RS National Assembly on 25 December 2003 following the Human Rights Chamber ruling on Srebrenica, which lambasted the failure of the RS authorities to inform people about the fate and whereabouts of their missing loved ones and called on the RS to conduct meaningful and effective investigations into the events at Srebrenica between 10 and 19 July 1995. In its final report, handed to the RS government on 14 October 2004, the Commission acknowledged that at least 7,000 were killed by Bosnian Serb forces in Srebrenica, citing a provisional figure of 7,800: 'Bosnian Serbs admit 7,000 killed in Srebrenica massacre', RFE/RL Newsline 8/196, 15 October 2004, available at <http://www.rferl.org/newsline/2004/10/151004.asp> [06/04/05].

56 International Crisis Group, 'War Criminals in Bosnia's Republika Srpska: Who Are the People in Your Neighbourhood?', ICG Balkans Report 103, 2 November 2003.

57 P. Akhavan, 'Beyond Impunity: Can International Criminal Justice Prevent Future Atrocities?', *American Journal of International Law* 95 (July 2001): 23.

58 Nsanzuwera, 'The ICTR Contribution to National Reconciliation', p. 948.

59 In light of US opposition to the ICC and pressure on the countries of the region to sign Article 98 agreements, this is seen by some as deeply hypocritical behaviour and reinforces the impression among some that the ICTY is no more than a political tool. Rachel Kerr, 'The Road from Dayton to Brussels? The International Criminal Tribunal for the Former Yugoslavia and the Politics of War Crimes in Bosnia', *European Security* 14/3 (September 2005): 319–37.

60 Robert McMahon, 'Bosnia-Herzegovina: Ashdown Cites Progress, Appeals For Help On War Crimes', United Nations, 9 October 2003, available at <http://www.globalsecurity.org/military/library/news/2003/10/mil-031009-rferl-172915.htm> [28/09/04].

61 On the ICTY outreach programme, see L. Vohrah and J. Cina, 'The Outreach Programme' in R. May et al., *Essays on ICTY Procedure and Evidence in Honour of Gabrielle Kirk McDonald* (The Hague: Kluwer, 2001), pp. 547–57; and Ralph Zacklin, 'The Failings of Ad Hoc International Tribunals', *Journal of International Criminal Justice* 2 (2004): 541–5. On the ICTR, see Victor Peskin, 'Courting Rwanda: The Promises and Pitfalls of the ICTR Outreach Programme', *Journal of International Criminal Justice* 3/4 (2005): 950–61.

62 Peskin, 'Courting Rwanda', p. 951.

63 See ibid., pp. 950–61.

64 Alison Des Forges and T. Longman, 'Legal Responses to the Genocide in Rwanda', in Stover and Weinstein (eds), *My Neighbour, My Enemy*, p. 56.

65 Eric Stover and Harvey Weinstein, 'Conclusion', in Stover and Weinstein (eds), *My Neighbour, My Enemy*.

66 Ibid.

67 Ibid, p. 953.

68 Mirko Klarin, 'The Tribunal's Four Battles', *Journal of International Criminal Justice* 2 (2004): 554.

69 See chapters 3 and 4.

70 Cited in Klarin, 'The Tribunal's Four Battles', p. 557.

### Chapter 3   The International Criminal Court

1 A permanent international criminal court was envisaged in the 1937 Draft Terrorism Treaty, which never came into force.

2 David P. Forsythe, *Human Rights in International Relations* (Cambridge: Cambridge University Press, 2000), p. 211.

3 David Scheffer, 'International Judicial Intervention', *Foreign Policy* (1996).

4 See James Crawford, 'The ILC's Draft Statute for an International Criminal Tribunal', *American Journal of International Law* 89 (1994): 140–52.

5 Philippe Kirsch and John T. Holmes, 'The Birth of the International Criminal Court: The 1998 Rome Conference', in Olympia Bekou and Robert Cryer (eds), *The International Criminal Court* (Plymouth: Ashgate, 2004), p. 6.

6  Ibid., p. 9. Others (Barbados, the Dominican Republic, Trinidad and Tobago), pushed for the inclusion of the crime of drug-trafficking and/or terrorism (India, Sri Lanka, Algeria, Turkey). A small, but vocal, minority argued forcefully for the inclusion of the death penalty.

7  Marlies Glasius, *The International Criminal Court: A Global Civil Society Achievement* (London: Routledge, 2006).

8  Kirsch and Holmes, 'The Birth of the International Criminal Court', pp. 36–7.

9  Gerry Simpson, 'Throwing a Little Remembrance on the Past: The International Court and the Politics of Sovereignty', *University of California, Davis, Journal of International Law and Politics* 5 (1999): 133–46.

10 Antonio Cassese, 'The Statute of the International Criminal Court: Some Preliminary Reflections', in Bekou and Cryer (eds), *The International Criminal Court*, p. 47.

11 Statement made at the ceremony for the solemn undertaking of the Chief Prosecutor of the ICC, Luis Moreno Ocampo, Peace Palace, The Hague, 16 June 2003; available at <http://www.icc-cpi.int/library/organs/otp/030616_moreno_ocampo_english_final.pdf> [07/12/05].

12 Bekou and Cryer (eds), *The International Criminal Court*, p. xix.

13 William A. Schabas, 'The International Criminal Court: The Secret of its Success', in ibid., p. 79.

14 Rachel Kerr, *The International Criminal Tribunal for the Former Yugoslavia: Law, Diplomacy and Politics* (Oxford: Oxford University Press, 2004).

15 Michael P. Scharf, 'Perspectives on the Future: The Amnesty Exception to the Jurisdiction of the International Criminal Court', in Bekou and Cryer (eds), *The International Criminal Court*, pp. 438–57.

16 On this precise dilemma in Haiti, see Eirin Mobekk, 'The Missing Ingredient: Justice in the International Intervention in Haiti', *International Relations* 15/1 (2000): 30–40.

17 Morten Bergsmo, 'Occasional Remarks on Certain State Concerns About the Jurisdictional Reach of the International Criminal Court and their Possible Implications for the Relationship Between the Court and the Security Council', in Bekou and Cryer (eds), *The International Criminal Court*, p. 378.

18 *UN Law Reports*, 1 February 2000.

19 Frank Berman, cited in Bergsmo, 'Occasional Remarks', p. 385.

20 Olympia Bekou and Robert Cryer, 'Introduction', in Bekou and Cryer (eds), *The International Criminal Court*, p. xxiii.

21 John Bolton, 'The Risks and the Weaknesses of the International Criminal Court from America's Perspective', *Virginia Journal of International Law* 41 (2000–1): 186–203. For full discussion of US opposition to the ICC, see Jason Ralph, *America and the International Criminal Court: An International Society Perspective* (Cambridge: Cambridge University Press, 2006).

22 *International Justice Tribune*, 21 November 2005.

23 Bergsmo, 'Occasional Remarks', p. 385, citing Frank Berman.

24 By January 2007, the Fund had received voluntary donations totalling €2.370.000,00. See International Criminal Court Victims' Trust Fund, available at <http://www.icc-cpi.int/vtf.html> [16/03/07].

25 See Tim Allen, 'War and Justice in Northern Uganda: An Assessment of the International Criminal Court's Intervention', February 2005 [Draft Report on file with author].

26 Ibid., p. iv.

27 See chapter 7.

28 Allen, 'War and Justice in Northern Uganda'.

29 Statement by Luis Moreno-Ocampo, Prosecutor of the International Criminal Court on the Uganda Arrest Warrants, The Hague, 14 October 2005; available at <http://www.icc-cpi.int/library/organs/otp/speeches/LMO_20051014_English.pdf> [24/08/06].

30 Statement of the Prosecutor of the International Criminal Court Luis Moreno-Ocampo to the Security Council, 29 June 2005, pursuant to UNSCR 1593 (2005); available at <http://www.icc-cpi.int/library/cases/LMO_UNSC_On_DARFUR-EN.pdf> [24/08/06].

31 Paper on some policy issues before the Office of the Prosecutor, September 2003; available at <http://www.icc-cpi.int/otp/otp_policy.html> [07/12/05].

32 Allen, 'War and Justice in Northern Uganda', p. iv.

33 The Prosecutor continues to monitor situations in other countries, including Côte d'Ivoire, a non-State Party, which declared its acceptance of jurisdiction over crimes on its territory.

34 Allen, 'War and Justice in Northern Uganda', p. iv.

35 'President of Uganda Refers Situation Concerning the Lord's Resistance Army (LRA) to the ICC', The Hague, 29 January 2004; available at <http://www.icc-cpi.int/pressrelease_details&id=16&l=en.html> [24/08/06].

36 'Prosecutor of the International Criminal Court Opens an Investigation into Nothern Uganda', The Hague, 29 July 2004; available at <http://www.icc-cpi.int/pressrelease_details&id=33&l=en.html> [24/08/06].

37 Joseph Kony is the leader, chairman and commander of the LRA. Kony's second in command and most trusted adviser is Vincent Otti, who is accused of personally leading attacks on civilians in Northern Uganda. Raska Lukwiya has been Army Commander of the LRA and was responsible for some of the worst attacks committed by the LRA during the investigated period. Okot Odhiambo commanded the most violent of the four brigades of the LRA and Dominic Ongwen was an LRA Brigade Commander. Statement by Moreno-Ocampo, 14 October 2005.

38 See Allen, 'War and Justice in Northern Uganda'.

39 Statement by Moreno-Ocampo, 14 October 2005.

40 ICC, 'The Office of the Prosecutor of the ICC Opens its First Investigations', The Hague, 23 June 2004.

41 'Prosecutor Receives Referral of the Situation in the Democratic Republic of Congo', The Hague, 19 April 2004; available at <http://www.icc-cpi.int/pressrelease_details&id=19&l=en.html> [24/08/06].

42  Interviews by Eirin Mobekk with Congolese NGO representatives and lawyers in the DRC, May/June 2005.
43  Interviews by Eirin Mobekk with Congolese NGO representatives in the DRC, May/June 2005.
44  'Report condemns Sudan over Darfur', BBC News online at <http://news.bbc.co.uk/1/hi/world/africa/6440719.stm> [16/03/07].
45  Report of the International Commission of Inquiry on Darfur to the United Nations Secretary-General, Pursuant to Security Council Resolution 1564 of 18 September 2004, Geneva, 25 January 2005; available at <http://www.icc-cpi.int/library/cases/Report_to_UN_on_Darfur.pdf> [24/08/06].
46  Statement of the Prosecutor of the International Criminal Court Luis Moreno Ocampo to the Security Council, 29 June.
47  On universal jurisdiction and the Alien Tort Claims Act, see Chandra Lekha Sriram, *Globalizing Justice for Mass Atrocities: A Revolution in Accountability* (London: Routledge, 2005); and Luc Reydams, *Universal Jurisdiction* (Oxford: Oxford University Press, 2003).
48  Reydams, *Universal Jurisdiction*, p. 1.
49  The Commission of Inquiry into Nazi War Criminals in Canada, established in 1985, resulted in five cases. See Jules Deschênes, 'Toward International Criminal Justice', in R. Clark and M. Sann (eds), *The Prosecution of International Crimes: A Critical Study of the International Tribunal for the Former Yugoslavia* (New Brunswick: Transaction Publishers, 1996), pp. 254–67. A similar initiative in Australia resulted in three prosecutions, and was dissolved in 1994, which freed Graham Blewitt to take up the post of Deputy Prosecutor in The Hague. Interview with Graham Blewitt, 28 March 2000.
50  The case resulted in a landmark House of Lords ruling that he could be extradited for crimes of torture committed after the 1984 Torture Convention entered into force. See M. Weller, 'On the Hazards of Foreign Travel for Dictators and Other International Criminals', *International Affairs* 75/3 (1999): 599–617; G. Hawthorn, 'Pinochet: The Politics', *International Affairs* 75/2 (1999): 253–8.
51  Talić, former commander of the 1st Krajina Corps of the Bosnian Serb Army and member of the Autonomous Region of Krajina (ARK) Crisis Staff, was arrested in Austria on 25 August 1999 on the basis of a warrant delivered to the Austrian authorities the day before. Talić was called out of the meeting and came face to face with Austrian police armed with a warrant for his arrest. Kerr, *The International Criminal Tribunal*, p. 149.
52  Richard Goldstone, *For Humanity: Reflections of a War Crimes Investigator* (New Haven: Yale University Press, 2000), p. 136.
53  Ibid.
54  Frederic L. Kirgis, 'The Indictment in Senegal of the Former Chad Head of State', *ASIL Insights* (February 2000); available at <http://www.asil.org/insights/insigh41.htm>; and Frederic L. Kirgis, 'Request for Extradition of Miguel Cavallo from Mexico to Spain for Alleged

Torture in Argentina,' *ASIL Insights* (September 2000); available at <http://www.asil.org/insights/insigh49.htm>.

55 Anne-Marie Slaughter and David L. Bosco, 'Alternative Justice Facilitated by Little-Known 18th Century Law', *The Tribunals* (Crimes of War Project) (May 2001); available at <http://www.crimesofwar.org/ tribun-mag/relate_alternative_print.html>.

56 Ibid.

57 See Henry Kissinger, 'The Pitfalls of Universal Jurisdiction: Risking Judicial Tyranny', *Foreign Affairs* 80 (2001): 2.

58 Sriram, *Globalizing Justice*.

59 Reydams, *Universal Jurisdiction*, p. 226.

60 Ibid.

## 4  'Internationalized' Courts

1 See chapters 6 and 7.

2 Beth K. Dougherty, 'Right-sizing International Criminal Justice: The Hybrid Experiment at the Special Court for Sierra Leone', *International Affairs* 80 (2004): 311–28. For discussion, see also Chandra Lekha Sriram, 'Wrong-sizing International Justice? The Hybrid Tribunal in Sierra Leone', *Fordham International Law Journal* 29 (2006): 472–506; and James Cockayne, 'The Fraying Shoestring: Rethinking Hybrid War Crimes Tribunals', *Fordham International Law Journal* 28 (2005): 616–80.

3 See box 4.1.

4 See box 4.2.

5 See box 4.3. A similar model was adopted for Bosnia, with the establishment of the Sarajevo War Crimes Chamber, in March 2005.

6 See box 4.4.

7 However, the first Chief Prosecutor, David Crane, pledged not to make use of this provision and to focus instead on those who recruited child soldiers. Sriram, 'Wrong-sizing International Justice?', p. 483.

8 There was an early dispute about the applicable law in the province, which was still officially part of Serbia. UNMIK initially ruled that the applicable laws would be those in effect in March 1999, but this caused a large degree of consternation as these laws were viewed as part of the overall policy of repression and discrimination perpetrated by the largely Serb administration. UNMIK back-pedalled and instituted instead the laws applicable in March 1989, before the autonomy of the province was revoked by Milošević.

9 Michael Hartmann, 'International Judges and Prosecutors in Kosovo: A New Model for Post-Conflict Peacekeeping', *USIP Special Report* 112 (October 2003).

10 Sylvia de Bertodano, 'Problems Arising from the Mixed Composition and Structure of the Cambodian Extraordinary Chambers', *Journal of International Criminal Justice* 4 (2006): 285–93.

11 Human Rights Watch, 'Serious Flaws: Why the UN General Assembly Should Require Changes to the Draft Khmer Rouge Tribunal Agreement', *Human Rights Watch Briefing Paper* (April 2003); available at <http://hrw.org/backgrounder/asia/cambodia040303-bck.htm> [13/01/06]; Amnesty International, 'Kingdom of Cambodia: Amnesty International's Position and Concerns Regarding the Proposed "Khmer Rouge" Tribunal', AI Index: ASA 23/005/2003 (25 April 2003); available at <http://web.amnesty.org/library/index/engasa230052003> [13/01/06]. For a critique of Amnesty's position, see Gregory H. Stanton, 'Perfection is the Enemy of Justice: A Response to Amnesty International and Human Rights Watch's Criticisms of the Agreement Between the Cambodian Government and the UN to Establish the Khmer Rouge Tribunal', available at Genocide Watch, <http://www.genocidewatch.org/aboutgenocide/stantonperfectionjustice.htm> [16/03/07].
12 Sylvia de Bertodano, 'Problems Arising from the Mixed Composition and Structure of the Cambodian Extraordinary Chambers', *Journal of International Criminal Justice* 4 (2006): 285–93.
13 Human Rights Watch, 'Serious Flaws', p. 6.
14 Ibid., p. 1.
15 Ibid.
16 Ben Kiernan, 'The Cambodian Genocide and Imperial Culture', published in *90 Years of Denial*, a special publication of *Aztag Daily* (Beirut) and the *Armenian Weekly* (Boston) in April 2005 to commemorate the 90th anniversary of the 1915 genocide of Armenians (pp. 20–1), available at the Yale University Cambodian Genocide Program, <http://www.yale.edu/cgp/us.html> [16/03/07].
17 For 2006 and 2007, the ICTY's budget is $276,474,100 and the ICTR's is $269,758,400. See <http://www.un.org/icty/glance-e/index.htm> [16/03/07] and <http://69.94.11.53/default.htm> [16/03/07].
18 Dougherty, 'Right-sizing International Criminal Justice', 326.
19 Cited in Thordis Ingadottir, 'Financial Challenges and their Possible Effects on Proceedings', *Journal of International Criminal Justice* 4 (2006): 296.
20 In early June, the sealed indictment was transmitted to the government of Ghana so that Taylor could be arrested when he arrived to attend peace talks in Accra. He was not arrested, but was sent back to Monrovia in a Ghanaian government plane. He was offered asylum by Nigeria, where he remained until March 2006 when the new President of Liberia, Ellen Johnson-Sirleaf, requested his handover and he was duly transferred to the custody of the Special Court.
21 Chandra Lekha, Sriram, *Globalizing Justice for Mass Atrocities: A Revolution in Accountability* (London: Routledge, 2005), p. 84. See also chapter 5, 'Domestic Trials'.
22 Ibid., p. 88. For discussion of Timor-Leste and Indonesia, see chapter 5, 'Domestic Trials'.

23 Susannah Linton, 'New Approaches to International Justice in Cambodia and East Timor', *International Review of the Red Cross* (2003): 114.

24 On the rebuilding of the judicial system in Kosovo and Timor-Leste, see Hans Strohmeyer, 'Building a New Judiciary for East Timor: Challenges of a Fledgling Nation', *Criminal Law Forum* 11/3 (2000); and Strohmeyer, 'Collapse and Reconstruction of a Judicial System: The United Nations Missions in Kosovo and East Timor', *American Journal of International Law* 95 (2001).

25 Sriram, 'Wrong-sizing International Justice?', p. 42.

26 Since its establishment in March 2003, the Criminal Division dealt with 305 cases, ranging from pre-judicial investigation to final verdict. These cases include war crimes (38), terrorism (22), organized crime (13), corruption (20), weapons (20), murder (33), trafficking of drugs, weapons, women or minors (18), the March 2004 riots (52) and other serious crimes (11). As of March 2003, there was a 90 per cent conviction rate. Figures taken from *UNMIK Pillar 1: Police and Justice Presentation Paper*, June 2004. Copy on file with author.

27 Jean-Christian Cady and Nicholas Booth, 'Internationalized Courts in Kosovo: An UNMIK Perspective', in Cesare P. Romano et al. (eds), *Internationalized Criminal Courts: Sierra Leone, East Timor, Kosovo and Cambodia* (Oxford: Oxford University Press, 2004), p. 74.

28 Ibid.

29 J. Cerone and C. Baldwin, 'Explaining and Evaluating the UNMIK Court System', in Romano et al. (eds), *Internationalized Criminal Courts?*, p. 56.

30 Cady and Booth, 'Internationalized Courts in Kosovo', p. 76. For forceful criticism of this, and other aspects, see Hartmann, 'International Judges and Prosecutors in Kosovo'.

31 Hartmann, 'International Judges and Prosecutors in Kosovo', p. 1. By June 2004, there were 12 judges and 12 prosecutors, an improvement on the situation in August 2001, when there were only 11 IJPs. *UNMIK Pillar 1: Police and Justice Presentation Paper*, June 2004. Copy on file with author.

32 Sylvia de Bertodano, 'East Timor: Trials and Tribulations', in Romano et al. (eds), *Internationalized Criminal Courts*, p. 79.

33 Ibid., p. 92.

34 East Timor Report, 28 February 2003, CSDG, King's College London, para. 270.

35 Charles Scheiner, cited in 'East Timor Still Awaits Justice One Year After UN call for International Tribunal', East Timor Action Network, 31 January 2001; available at <http://www.etan.org/news/2001a/01tribl.htm>.

36 For more on the Indonesian HRC see box 5.2 below.

37 See Avril McDonald, 'Sierra Leone's shoestring Special Court', *International Review of the Red Cross* 84/845 (2002): 121–43.

38 *Report of the Security Council Mission to West Africa*, S/2004/525 (2 July 2004), para. 9.

39 Lansana Gberie, 'Briefing: The Special Court of Sierra Leone', *African Affairs* 102/409 (2003): 637–48; Peter Penfold, 'Will Justice Help Peace in Sierra Leone?', *Observer* (20 October 2002), available at <http://observer.guardian.co.uk/comment/story/0,,814949,00.html>.

40 Human Rights Watch, 'Serious Flaws'.

41 Suzannah Linton, 'Safeguarding the Independence and Impartiality of the Cambodian Extraordinary Chambers', *Journal of International Criminal Justice* 4 (2006): 329.

42 Ibid., p. 341.

43 Hartmann, 'International Judges and Prosecutors in Kosovo', p. 13.

44 Strohmeyer, 'Collapse and Reconstruction of a Judicial System', p. 47.

45 Daphna Shraga, 'The Second Generation UN-Based Tribunals: A Diversity of Mixed Jurisdiction', in Romano et al. (eds), *Internationalized Criminal Courts*, p. 54.

46 *Report of the Security Council Mission to West Africa*, para. 9.

47 Tom Periello and Marieke Wierda, *The Special Court for Sierra Leone Under Scrutiny*, International Center for Transitional Justice (March 2006).

48 The TRC was established to 'address impunity, break the cycle of violence [and] provide a forum for both the victims and the perpetrators of human rights violations to tell their story'. Based on the model of the South African TRC, it was intended that it would function by conducting its own investigation and research into the history and background of events, by holding closed and public sessions with testimony from individual victims, witnesses and perpetrators and taking individual statements. It had power to compel the production of reports, records, documents or any information from any source, including governmental authorities; to request information from foreign governments; to visit any establishment or place without giving prior notice; to enter any premises for the purpose of obtaining information, inspecting property or taking copies of documents; to interview any individual, group or members of organizations or institutions, including foreign persons; to compel the attendance of any person by issuing summonses and subpoenas; and finally to request and receive police assistance as necessary for the enforcement of its powers. Initially mandated for one year, it was to submit its report at the end of that period. Work was suspended by the May 2000 hostage-taking and renewal of violence. It was finally inaugurated on 5 July 2002 and wound up activities at the end of 2003. but it was another year before it produced its final report, in October 2004. See chapter 6 below.

49 Pyt Douma and Jeroen de Zeeuw, 'From Transitional to Sustainable Justice. Human Rights Assistance to Sierra Leone', in *CRU Policy Brief* (The Hague: Clingendael, 2004); available at <http://www.clingendael.nl/publications/2004/20040800_cru_policy_brief_1.pdf?> [16/03/07].

50 'Ex-Combatant Views of the Truth and Reconciliation Commission and the Special Court in Sierra Leone': a study by the Post-conflict Reintegration Initiative for Development and Empowerment (PRIDE) in partnership with the International Center for Transitional Justice, Freetown, 12 September 2002.

51 Richard Dowden, 'Justice Goes on Trial in Sierra Leone', *Guardian* (3 October 2002); available at <http://www.guardian.co.uk/international/story/0,,803280,00.html>.

52 See chapter 6.

53 Douma and de Zeeuw, 'From Transitional to Sustainable Justice'.

54 In the DRC, several civil society organizations and local lawyers were positive about the prospects of 'internationalized' domestic trials specifically because it was felt that they would considerably heighten the legitimacy of the prosecutions and limit political and military influence and involvement. At the same time they felt that this would be a locally owned process, taking place within the societies that experienced the abuse and not removed from the victims and majority of perpetrators. Interestingly, this was emphasized by both human rights lawyers and NGOs, as well as by a representative of the military courts and a member of the Ministry of Justice. It was stressed in particular that it would reinforce rule of law because it was taking place within local society and have a positive impact upon domestic judicial reform. In June 2005, a seminar was organized in Kinshasa by a coalition of Congolese organizations, with the support of the ICTJ and the UN Mission in Congo (MONUC), where the objective was to discuss the positive and negative sides of establishing a hybrid court in the DRC. The seminar concluded with the unanimous adoption of the 'Declaration of Nganda', which stated that the participants supported the idea of the creation of a special mixed chamber for the DRC. Interviews conducted by Eirin Mobekk in Kinshasa, DRC, May/June 2005; Coalition Congolaise pour la Justice Transitionnelle, *Rapport Final du Seminaire sur les Chambres Specialisées Mixtes au sein des Juridictions Congolaises*, Centre Caholic Nganda, Kinshasa, juin 2005.

55 Jane Alexander, *A Scoping Study of Transitional Justice and Poverty Reduction* (London: Department for International Development, January 2003), p. 23.

56 A. Pellet, 'Internationalized Courts: Better Than Nothing', in Romano et al. (eds), *Internationalized Criminal Courts*, p. 444.

57 David J. Scheffer, 'Justice for Cambodia', *New York Times* (21 December 2002).

58 R. Fanthorpe, 'Neither Citizen Nor Subject? Lumpen Agency and the Legacy of Native Administration in Sierra Leone', *African Affairs* 100 (2001): 362–86.

59 Gberie, 'Briefing: The Special Court of Sierra Leone'.

60 The Conflict Security and Development Group, *A Review of Peace Operations: A Case for Change* (London: King's College London, 2003).

61 'Agreement Between the United Nations and the Government of Sierra Leone on the Establishment of a Special Court for Sierra Leone, Done at Freetown' (16 January 2002); available at <http://www.specialcourt.org/documents/Agreement.htm>.

62 Publicity brochure of the Special Court for Sierra Leone on the outreach programme, March 2003, p. 14.

63 Strohmeyer, 'Collapse and Reconstruction of a Judicial System', p. 48.

64 The Conflict Security and Development Group, *A Review of Peace Operations*, p. 165.

65 It was estimated that in just two weeks there was a backlog of more than 200 detainees, many of them held for serious criminal offences such as arson, violent assault and murder. Strohmeyer, 'Collapse and Reconstruction of a Judicial System', p. 49. See also *Report of the Secretary-General on the United Nations Interim Administration Mission in Kosovo*, S/1999/779 (12 July 1999).

66 *Report of the Secretary-General on the United Nations Interim Administration Mission in Kosovo*, S/1999/779 (12 July 1999).

67 Strohmeyer, 'Collapse and Reconstruction of a Judicial System', p. 53.

68 Ibid.

69 *Report of the Secretary-General on the United Nations Interim Administration Mission in Kosovo*, S/2000/538 (6 June 2000).

70 William O'Neill, UNMIK Senior Adviser on Human Rights from August 1999 to February 2000, said that 'instances of bias against Serbs and other minorities among the Albanian judiciary surfaced early [on] . . . Albanians arrested on serious charges, often caught red-handed by KFOR or UNMIK police, were frequently released immediately or were not indicted and were subsequently released. Meanwhile, Serbs, Roma and other minorities arrested on even minor charges with flimsy evidence were almost always detained': see O'Neill, *Kosovo: An Unfinished Peace* (Boulder, CO: Lynne Rienner, 2002). See also Hartmann, 'International Judges and Prosecutors in Kosovo'.

71 Hartmann, 'International Judges and Prosecutors in Kosovo'.

72 The immediate cause was the outbreak of inter-ethnic violence and riots in the city following a rocket attack on a UNHCR bus transporting 49 Serbs into Mitrovica. IJPs were inserted to help deal with the highly sensitive and politically inflammatory cases that resulted once order had been re-established. The decision was formalized in UNMIK Regulation 2000/6 (15 February 2000) in view of a need to 'curb bias and enhance professionalism'. See ICG, 'Finding the Balance: The Scales of Justice in Kosovo', in *International Crisis Group Balkans Report* (Brussels: International Crisis Group, 2002). Following a hunger strike by Serb detainees in Mitrovica about the length of their pre-trial detention and judicial bias, the role of international judges and prosecutors was further extended in UNMIK Regulation 2000/34 (27 May 2000), which extended the capacity of international legal personnel to work throughout Kosovo. See O'Neill, *Kosovo: An Unfinished Peace*, p. 90.

73 UNMIK Regulation 2000/64, 15 December 2000, provided that the prosecutor, accused or defence counsel may submit a petition to the Department for Judicial Affairs (DJA) at any stage of a case for international legal personnel to be assigned by the SRSG on the recommendation of the DJA.

74 The Conflict Security and Development Group, *A Review of Peace Operations*, p. 166.

75 See, for example, Nicholas J. Wheeler and Tim Dunne, 'East Timor and the New Humanitarian Interventionism,' *International Affairs* 77/4 (2001): 807.

76 For an excellent account of the state-building effort, see Jarat Chopra, 'Building State Failure in East Timor,' *Development and Change* 33/5 (2002).

77 The Conflict Security and Development Group, *A Review of Peace Operations*, p. 216.

78 Chopra, 'Building State Failure', p. 984.

79 UN A/64/654, 13 December 1999, para. 42.

80 The Conflict Security and Development Group, *A Review of Peace Operations*, p. 266. See *Resolution of the Commission on Human Rights*, UN/E/CN.4/RES/1999/S-4/1 (27 September 1999), para. 4.

81 Strohmeyer, 'Collapse and Reconstruction of a Judicial System', p. 50. See also Strohmeyer, 'Building a New Judiciary for East Timor'.

82 Strohmeyer, 'Collapse and Reconstruction of a Judicial System', p. 180.

83 Cambodian Genocide Program, Yale University; available at <http://www.yale.edu/cgp/> [13/01/06].

84 UN Doc A/51/930-S/1997/488.

85 A/53/850-S/1999/231.

86 Human Rights Watch, 'Serious Flaws'.

87 $43 million of the $56 million estimated budget had been secured, with the Cambodian government pledged to provide the rest. Anthony Dworkin, 'Cambodian War Crimes Tribunal Given Go-Ahead', *Crimes of War Project*, 5 May 2005; available at <http:www.crimesofwar.org/onnews/news-cambodia2.html> [15/06/05].

### Chapter 5    Domestic Trials

1 See, e.g., J. Snyder and L. Vinjamuri, 'Trials and Errors: Principle and Pragmatism in Strategies of International Justice', *International Security* 28/3 (Winter 2003/4): 5, 25

2 K. Sikkink and C. Booth Walling, 'Errors about Trials: The Political Reality of the Justice Cascade and Its Impact': paper presented at the annual meeting of the APSA, 2005, p. 8.

3 Although, in Iraq, it should be noted that the establishment of the Iraqi Special Tribunal was with significant involvement from the then occupying powers: the United States and the United Kingdom.

4 Sikkink and Walling, 'Errors about Trials', p. 10.

5 Ibid.

6 For example, in South Africa, Timor-Leste, Haiti, Rwanda and Sierra Leone.

7 For in-depth discussion on the development of international law see chapter 1.

8 See for example, Convention on the Prevention and Punishment of the Crime of Genocide, 1948; The Geneva Conventions (I–IV), 1949; International Covenant on Civil and Political Rights, 1966; International Covenant on Economic, Social and Cultural Rights, 1966; Convention against Torture and Other Cruel, Inhuman or Degrading Treatment or Punishment, 1984.

9 Rome Statute to the International Criminal Court, Article 19. See discussion of complementarity regime in chapter 1. Also see Diane Orentlicher, *Independent Study on Best Practices, Including Recommendations, to Assist States in Strengthening their Domestic Capacity to Combat all Aspects of Impunity*, E/CN.4/2004/88, 27 February 2004, p. 11.

10 See, e.g., Universal Declaration of Human Rights, 1948, Article 8, ICCPR, article 9.

11 See, e.g., Jane Alexander, *A Scoping Study of Transitional Justice and Poverty Reduction* (London: Department for International Development, January 2003), p. 13.

12 Universal Declaration of Human Rights, Article 10.

13 Office for the High Commissioner of Human Rights, Resolution 2004/72, Article 13.

14 Christiane Wilke, *Domestic Prosecutions for Massive Human Rights Violations: Lessons from Argentina and Germany*, Memorandum for the International Center for Transitional Justice, 18 November 2004, p. 11.

15 Rama Mani, *Beyond Retribution: Seeking Justice in the Shadows of War* (Cambridge: Polity, 2002), p. 73.

16 'Prosecuting Genocide in Rwanda: A Human Rights First Report on the ICTR and National Trials', Human Rights First Publications, July 1997.

17 Due to limitations of space, police and penal reform and their link to the judicial system cannot be discussed at any length here.

18 UNDP, *Access to Justice*, Practice Note, 09/03/2003, p. 15.

19 See also Catalina Smulovitz, quoted in ibid., p. 29.

20 Sikkink and Walling, 'Errors about Trials', p. 11.

21 However, it is acknowledged that both these regions are different in terms of the ability to hold trials, their resources and the conflicts they faced compared to, for example, post-conflict societies in Africa and Asia, where many fewer trials have been held.

22 Gunnar Theissen, *Supporting Justice, Co-existence and Reconciliation after Armed Conflict: Strategies for Dealing with the Past*, Berghof Research Centre; available at <http://www.berghof-handbook.net/uploads/download/theissen_handbook.pdf> p. 12.

23 Judy Barsalou, *Trauma and Transitional Justice in Divided Societies*, United States Institute of Peace Special Report 135, April 2005, p. 5

24 See box 5.1.

25 For *gacaca* courts, see box 7.2.

26 See chapter 4.

27 D. Pion-Berlin, 'To Prosecute or to Pardon? Human Rights Decisions in the Latin American Southern Cone', *Human Rights Quarterly* 15 (1994): 117.

28 Ibid., pp. 106 and 121.

29 Ibid., p. 108. In Uruguay a much larger number of people were imprisoned than in Argentina, hence affecting a larger proportion of the general population.

30 This can be seen in Latin America: see ibid., pp. 115–18; and in Timor-Leste: see above.

31 Luc Huyse, 'Justice', in David Bloomfield et al. (eds), *Reconciliation After Violent Conflict. A Handbook* (Stockholm: International IDEA, 2003), p. 97.

32 Interview by Eirin Mobekk with Ministry of Justice official, Kinshasa, May/June 2005.

33 Ibid.

34 'Xanana Gusmao's Views on Justice'; available at <http://www.easttimor-reconciliation.org/Gusmao_Justice-E.htm>.

35 Snyder and Vinjamuri, 'Trials and Errors', p. 16.

36 Ibid., p. 6.

37 Ibid.

38 Alexander, *Scoping Study of Transitional Justice*, p. 45.

39 For more on Sierra Leone, see chapter 4.

40 See, e.g., Eirin Mobekk, 'DDR in Haiti: Past Negligence, Present Problems, Future Possibilities', in Ann Fitz-Gerald (ed.), *From Conflict to Community: A Combatant's Return to Citizenship*, GFN-SSR (2005).

41 Snyder and Vinjamuri, 'Trials and Errors', p. 14.

42 Sikkink and Walling, 'Errors about Trials', p. 29.

43 Amnesty International, 'Algeria: President Calls Referendum to Obliterate Crimes of the Past', AI Index Mde 28/010/2005 (28 August 2005); available at <http://web.amnesty.org/library/Index/ENGMDE280102005>.

44 Ibid. Human Rights Watch, 'Algeria: Amnesty Law Risks Legalizing Impunity for Crimes Against Humanity', 14 April 2005; available at <http://hrw.org/english/docs/2005/04/14/algeri10485.htm>. International Center for Transitional Justice, 'Algerian Charter Risks Reinforcing Impunity and Undermining Reconciliation', 26 September 2005; available at <http://www.ictj.org/en/news/press/release/257.html>.

45 Daikha Dridi, 'Victims Groups Question Algeria Amnesty', Algeria-Watch (28 August 2005). Middle East Online, 'Algeria to vote on controversial peace charter', 9 September 2005.

46 Daho Djerbal, 'Algeria: Amnesty and Oligarchy', Carnegie Endowment for International Peace, 30 September 2005.
47 Foreign Report – Janes.com, 'Algeria: Amnesty or Amnesia?', 26 October 2005.
48 World Tribune.com, 'Salafists Again Ignore Amnesty Offer in Algeria', 10 November 2005.
49 For more on Mozambique, see J. Hanlon, 'Bringing It All Together: A Case Study of Mozambique', in Gerd Junne and Willemijn Verkoren, *Post-Conflict Development* (Boulder, CO: Lynne Rienner, 2005).
50 Mani, *Beyond Retribution*, p. 96.
51 Eirin Mobekk, 'The Missing Ingredient: Justice in the International Intervention in Haiti', *International Relations* 15/1 (April 2000). See also chapter 6 on the truth commission in Haiti.
52 During a press conference held in Kigali in June 2006, Rwandan President Paul Kagame denounced the court for costing up to $1.5 billion and for delivering less than 40 verdicts in almost 11 years. 'Rwanda: Cost of the ICTR to Reach $1 Billion by the End of 2007', *Hirondelle News Agency*; available at <http//www.hirondelle.org>.
53 Ayreh Neier, in Juan Mendez, 'Accountability for Past Abuses', *Human Rights Quarterly* 19 (1997): 276 n64.
54 Martha Minow, *Between Vengeance and Forgiveness: Facing History after Genocide and Mass Violence* (Boston: Beacon Press, 1998), p. 26.
55 See, e.g., ibid., p. 45; L. Huyse, 'Justice', p. 105; Alexander, *Scoping Study of Transitional Justice*, p. 16, para. 4.1.4
56 Mendez, 'Accountability for Past Abuses', p. 274. Depending upon the mandate of the TC, both victims and perpetrators are self-selected as to whether or not they wish to contribute and give statements to the commissions.
57 Paul van Zyl, 'Promoting Transitional Justice in Post-Conflict Societies', in Alan Bryden and Heiner Hanggi (eds), *Security Governance in Post-Conflict Peacebuilding* (Geneva: DCAF, 2005), p. 211.
58 See box 7.2 for more details.
59 See box 5.1
60 Wilke, *Domestic Prosecutions*, p. 16.
61 Stephan Landsman, 'Alternative Responses to Serious Human Rights Abuses: Of Prosecution and Truth Commissions', *Law and Contemporary Problems* 59/4 (Autumn 1996), p. 85.
62 Ibid.
63 See also Zyl, 'Promoting Transitional Justice', p. 211.
64 Mani, *Beyond Retribution*, p. 100.
65 Huyse, 'Justice', pp. 104–5; Theissen, *Supporting Justice*, p. 3.
66 Minow, *Between Vengeance and Forgiveness*, p. 26.
67 Mendez, 'Accountability for Past Abuses', p. 277.
68 Mani, *Beyond Retribution*, p. 97.
69 Ibid., pp. 96–7.

70 Interview by Eirin Mobekk with Congolese lawyer in Kinshasa, May/June 2005.
71 Interview by Eirin Mobekk with UN lawyer in Kinshasa, May/June 2005.
72 Ibid.
73 For this same problem in 'internationalized' domestic trials, see chapter 4.
74 Interview by Eirin Mobekk with Congolese lawyer in Kinshasa, May/June 2005.
75 See also Wilke, *Domestic Prosecutions*, p. 5.
76 See also Alexander, *Scoping Study of Transitional Justice*, p. 23.
77 Wilke, *Domestic Prosecutions*, p. 1.
78 Zyl, 'Promoting Transitional Justice', p. 211.
79 Justice Robert Jackson, opening statement to Nuremberg tribunal, 'The Trial of German Major War Criminals, the International Military Tribunal at Nuremberg, 1945', in Minow, *Between Vengeance and Forgiveness*, p. 25.
80 For more on deterrence, see also chapter 6.
81 Mendez, 'Accountability for Past Abuses', p. 266.
82 For example, the military commander of the region which included Timor-Leste, General Adam Damiri, missed several appearances in the Human Rights Court because he was taking part in the military assault on Aceh. 'Indonesian Court's Final East Timor Sentence "a Joke" ', ETAN (5 August 2003); available at <http://www.etan.org/news>. For information/overview on Aceh, see, e.g., Eva-Lotta Hedman, *Aceh under Martial Law: Conflict, Violence and Displacement*, RCS Working Paper Series no. 24, Oxford (2004); Stephen Sherlock, 'Conflict in Aceh: A Military Solution?', Information, Analysis and Advice for the Parliament, Current Issues Brief, No. 32 2002–3 (23 June 2003).
83 Huyse, 'Justice', p. 106.
84 Ibid., p. 4.
85 Mendez, 'Accountability for Past Abuses', p. 273.
86 Steven Ratner and Jason Abrams, quoted in Alexander, *Scoping Study of Transitional Justice*, p. 17.
87 Alexander, *Scoping Study of Transitional Justice*, p. 18.
88 Jeremy Sarakin, 'The Tension Between Justice and Reconciliation in Rwanda: Politics, Human Rights, Due Process and the Role of the *Gacaca* Courts in Dealing with the Genocide', *Journal of African Law* 45/2 (2001): 158.
89 International Crisis Group, in Alexander, *Scoping Study of Transitional Justice*, p. 19.
90 The Government of Rwanda, *Genocide and Justice*; available at: <http://www.gov.rw/government/genocidef.html> [15/11/05].
91 For more on *gacaca* courts, see box 7.2.
92 Sarakin, 'Tension Between Justice and Reconciliation in Rwanda', p. 157.

93 See chapter 2, detailing the ICTR.
94 'Indonesia delays East Timor Atrocities trials', *East Timor Observatory*, ref: JUS05-2002-01-25eg; available at < http://www.tip.net.au>.
95 Ibid.
96 Amnesty International, 'Indonesia and Timor-Leste: International Responsibility for Justice', 14 April 2003, p. 3; available at <http://web.amnesty.org/library/Index/ENGASA030012003>.
97 Royal Netherlands Institute of Southeast Asian and Caribbean Studies, 'Indonesian ad hoc Human Rights Court Proven Not Able to Fulfill International Demands', 17 August 2002.
98 JSMP and Amnesty International, 'East Timor Trials Deliver Neither Truth Nor Justice': press release, 15 August 2002.
99 ICTJ Briefing Paper, 'Creation and First Trials of the Supreme Iraqi Criminal Tribunal', October 2005, p. 2.
100 Ibid., pp. 8–9.
101 Ibid., p. 9.
102 Associated Press, 'Judge Chastises Defendants in Saddam Trial, Says Their Hands "soaked with blood" ', 24 July 2006.
103 BBC, 'Iraq trial resumes without Saddam', 24 July 2006.

## 6 Truth Commissions

1 For details of the Latin American commissions see, e.g., USIP, *Truth Commissions Digital Collection*, available at <http://www.usip.org/library/truth.html>; P. Hayner, *Unspeakable Truths. Facing the Challenges of Truth Commissions* (London: Routledge, 2002).
2 See, e.g., R. Rotberg and D. Thompson (eds), *Truth v. Justice: The Morality of Truth Commissions* (Princeton: Princeton University Press, 2000), D. Shea, *The South African Truth Commission: The Politics of Reconciliation* (Washington, DC: USIP Press, 2000); P. Hayner, 'Fifteen Truth Commissions: 1974 to 1994: A Comparative Study', *Human Rights Quarterly* 16 (1994); N. Kritz, *Transitional Justice: How Emerging Democracies Reckon with Former Regimes*, vols 1–3 (Washington, DC: USIP Press, 1995); M. Popkin and N. Bhuta, 'Latin American Amnesties in Comparative Perspective: Can the Past Be Buried', *Ethics and International Affairs* 13 (1999); P. Ball and A. R Chapman, *The Truth of Truth Commissions: Comparative Lessons from Haiti, South Africa, and Guatemala*, The Urban Morgan Institute (Baltimore: Johns Hopkins University Press, 2001); J. L. Gibson, 'Truth, Justice, and Reconciliation: Judging the Fairness of Amnesty in South Africa', *American Journal of Political Science* 46/3 (2002); D. Gairdner, *Truth in Transition: The Role of Truth Commissions in Political Transition in Chile and El Salvador* (Bergen: Chr. Michelsen Institute, 1999).
3 For creation and design of truth commissions see, e.g., <http://www.truthcommission.org>, which details setting up such commissions.

4 J. D. Tepperman, 'Truth and Consequences', *Foreign Affairs* (March/ April 2002), p. 1.

5 For example, Congressional Commissions in the United States and the Bloody Sunday Inquiry in Northern Ireland.

6 M. Freeman and P. Hayner, 'Truth-Telling', in David Bloomfield et al. (eds), *Reconciliation after Violent Conflict. A Handbook* (Stockholm: IDEA, 2003), p. 124.

7 We cannot give an exhaustive account of all the truth commissions that have been established, but shall simply use some as examples.

8 For example, the Truth and Reconciliation Commission in Sierra Leone made extensive and wide-ranging recommendations, most of which have yet to be implemented by the government of Sierra Leone. This is often cited as a measure of the TRC's failure to have a real impact, but it should be noted that whether or not its recommendations are implemented falls outside of the powers of the TRC.

9 For definitions, see also, e.g., USIP, 'Background', in *Truth Commissions Digital Collection*; and P. Hayner, 'Commissioning the Truth: Further Research Questions', *Third World Quarterly* 17/1 (1996): 20–1.

10 See also P. Hayner, 'International Guidelines for the Creation and Operation of Truth Commissions: A Preliminary Proposal', *Law and Contemporary Problems* 59/173 (Autumn 1996): 176; USIP, *Truth Commissions Digital Collection*; Margareth Popkin and Naomi Roth-Arriaza, quoted in Eric Brahm, *Truth Commissions*, June 2004, available at <www.beyondintractability.org/m/truth_commissions.jsp>.

11 Hayner, 'International Guidelines', p. 174.

12 Freeman and Hayner, 'Truth-Telling', p. 129. Moreover, in Chad and Uganda the commissions were structured so as to legitimize the new regime and discredit the former regime. See Brahm, *Truth Commissions*, pp. 2–3.

13 The CNRT is an umbrella organization which brought together all political organizations and movements that were pro-independence.

14 The Truth and Reconciliation Act 2000, Schedule, Subsection 1 of section 3, a, ii.

15 See boxes 6.1 and 6.2 for DRC and South Africa.

16 The National Reconciliation Act, Ghana, 2002, paras 10 and 11.

17 The Truth and Reconciliation Act 2000, 8, 2, a–h.

18 Agreement on the Establishment of the Commission to Clarify Past Human Rights Violations and Acts of Violence that have Caused the Guatemalan Population to Suffer.

19 See Statuts de L'Instance Equité et Réconciliation, 10 April 2004; also Eric Goldstein, 'A New Moroccan Commission, but How Much Truth?', Human Rights Watch, June 2003.

20 See also Freeman and Hayner, 'Truth-Telling', pp. 131–2.

21 Mark Freeman and Priscilla Hayner, 'The Truth Commissions of South Africa and Guatemala', in Bloomfield et al. (eds), *Reconciliation After Violent Conflict*, p. 142.

22  See, e.g., Joanna Quinn, 'Dealing with a Legacy of Mass Atrocity: Truth Commissions in Uganda and Chile', *Netherlands Quarterly of Human Rights* 19/4 (2001): 387–8.

23  K. Avruch and B. Vejarano, 'Truth and Reconciliation Commissions: A Review Essay and Annotated Bibliography', *The Online Journal of Peace and Conflict Resolution* 4/2 (Spring 2002): 3.

24  Tepperman, 'Truth and Consequences', p. 6.

25  Avruch and Vejarano, 'Truth and Reconciliation Commissions', p. 3.

26  *Ubuntu* is a concept which encompasses and emphasizes healing, restorative justice and nurture of social relationships – not vengeance.

27  See also Freeman and Hayner, 'Truth-Telling', p. 122.

28  Mike Kaye, 'The Role of Truth Commissions in the Search for Justice, Reconciliation and Democratization: the Salvadorean and Honduran Cases', *Journal of Latin American Studies* 29 (1997): 707.

29  Principle 1, Annex II, 'Set of Principles for the Protection and Promotion of Human Rights Through Action to Combat Impunity', *The Administration of Justice and The Human Rights of Detainees*, Commission on Human Rights, Sub-Commission on Prevention of Discrimination and Protection of Minorities, E/CH.4/Sub.2/1997/20/Rev.1.

30  For details on each case, see Hayner, *Unspeakable Truths*: Mozambique, pp. 186–95 and Cambodia, pp. 195–200.

31  See also Hayner, 'International Guidelines', p. 177.

32  See chapter 5 for further details on Mozambique and the use of amnesties and TIJM.

33  See, e.g., Bloomfield et al. (eds), *Reconciliation After Violent Conflict*.

34  See chapter 7 for traditional informal justice mechanisms.

35  See, e.g., Brahm, *Truth Commissions*, p. 1.

36  Stephan Landsman, 'Alternative Responses to Serious Human Rights Abuses: Of Prosecution and Truth Commissions', *Law and Contemporary Problems* 59/4 (Autumn 1996): 88.

37  See, e.g., Ingrid Agger and Soren Jensen, in Martha Minow, *Between Vengeance and Forgiveness. Facing History after Genocide and Mass Violence* (Boston: Beacon Press, 1998), pp. 65–6.

38  Minow, *Between Vengeance and Forgiveness*, p. 73.

39  Ibid., p. 70.

40  Ibid., p. 66.

41  This has been found to be particularly so in relation to women and rape: see Josi Salem-Pickartz, 'Psychosocial Interventions in Post-War Situations', in M. Vlachova and L. Biason (eds), *Women in an Insecure World: Facts and Analysis on Violence Against Women* (DCAF, 2005), pp. 279–80.

42  Susan Slyomovics, 'Morocco's Justice and Reconciliation Commission', *Middle East Report Online* (4 April 2005), p. 6.

43  See also chapters 4 and 5.

44  Interview by Eirin Mobekk with adviser to CAVR, December 2005.

45  Landsman, 'Alternative Responses', p. 88.

46 Freeman and Hayner, 'Truth-Telling', p. 129.
47 Freeman and Hayner in Bloomfield et al. (eds), *Reconciliation After Violent Conflict*, p. 137.
48 See also Timothy Garton Ash, in Minow, *Between Vengeance and Forgiveness*, p. 61.
49 R. Mosier, 'Impunity, Truth Commissions: Peddling Impunity?', Human Rights Features, *Voice of the Asia Pacific Human Rights Network*, Special Weekly Edition for the Duration of the 59th Session of the Commission on Human Rights, vol. 6, no. 5 (14–20 April 2003), p. 2.
50 See box 6.2.
51 Pricilla Hayner, 'Truth Commissions: Exhuming the Past', *North American Congress on Latin America* 32/2 (Sept/Oct 1998): 31.
52 See chapter 5.
53 See also Freeman and Hayner, 'Truth-Telling', p. 136.
54 Jose Zalaquett, quoted in Kaye, 'The Role of Truth Commissions', p. 701.
55 Minow, *Between Vengeance and Forgiveness*, p. 86. For more on El Salvador, see also Kaye, 'The Role of Truth Commissions'.
56 Hayner, *Unspeakable Truths*, p. 40.
57 Brahm, *Truth Commissions*, p. 4.
58 Slyomovics, 'Morocco's Justice and Reconciliation Commission', p. 4.
59 Christian Tomuschatof, quoted in Tepperman, 'Truth and Consequences', p. 5. The Guatemalan commission published the report 'Memory of Silence' in February 1999, in which the military was blamed for nearly all violations.
60 Amnesty International, *Haiti: Still Crying Out for Justice*, July 1998, p. 8.
61 Eirin Mobekk, 'DDR in Haiti: Past Negligence, Present Problems, Future Possibilities', in Ann Fitz-Gerald (ed.), *From Conflict to Community: A Combatant's Return to Citizenship*, GFN-SSR (2005).
62 Landsman, 'Alternative Responses', p. 83.
63 Avruch and Vejarano, 'Truth and Reconciliation Commissions', p. 3.
64 Elin Skar, 'Truth Commissions, Trials – or Nothing? Policy Options in Democratic Transitions', *Third World Quarterly* 20/6 (1999): 1111.
65 Landsman, 'Alternative Responses', p. 82.
66 Priscilla Hayner, 'Justice in Transition: Challenges and Opportunities', Presentation to 55th Annual DPI/NGO Conference, *Rebuilding Societies Emerging from Conflict: A Shared Responsibility*, United Nations (9 September 2002), p. 6.
67 Tepperman, 'Truth and Consequences', p. 5.
68 USIP, Truth Commissions Digital Collection, Bolivia and Ecuador; Bolivia: National Commission of Inquiry into Disappearances; Ecuador: Truth and Justice Commission.
69 Kaye, 'The Role of Truth Commissions', p. 697. Rettig was the chair of the commission.
70 Andrew North, 'Afghans Adopt Justice Action Plan', BBC News (13 December 2005).

71 Meredith Wain, 'Ghana's National Reconciliation Commission', *Peace Magazine* (April–June 2003), p. 3.
72 Slyomovics, 'Morocco's Justice and Reconciliation Commission', p. 3.
73 *Si M Pa Rele* (If I Don't Cry Out), Preface, Mot du Ministre la Justice, March 1997. Moreover, until the end of 1998 it was only published in French – a language inaccessible to the vast majority of the population.
74 Interviews conducted in Haiti by Eirin Mobekk, 1997–8.
75 Interview with former adviser to the CAVR, December 2005.
76 Report of Secretary-General, *A/51/935* (26 June 1997).
77 Amnesty International, *Haiti*, p. 7 This committee forwarded a resolution demanding the return of the Front for the Advancement and Progress of Haiti (FRAPH) documents, and suggesting the creation of a special tribunal to facilitate the judgment of the accused of crimes during the coup era. 'Le Ministère de la Justice déclare soutenir une résolution des victimes du coup d'état', *Le Matin* (15 May 1998), p. 1.
78 Interviews by Eirin Mobekk with representatives from civil society in Haiti, 1998.
79 See also Hayner, 'Truth Commissions', p. 2.
80 Kaye, 'The Role of Truth Commissions', p. 697.
81 Tepperman, 'Truth and Consequences', p. 9.
82 See also Hayner, 'Truth Commissions', p. 3.
83 See also Roberta Bacic, 'Truth Commissions: One option when Dealing with the Recent Past in Countries that have Endured War or Dictatorships', *Committee for Conflict Transformation Support*, Newsletter 18; available at <http://www.c-r.org/ccts/ccts18/trucomm.htm>.
84 See also Hayner, 'International Guidelines', pp. 177–8.
85 Interviews conducted by Eirin Mobekk in Kinshasa, DRC, June 2005.
86 Fredrico Borello, *A First Few Steps. The Long Road to a Just Peace in DRC*, Occasional Paper, ICTJ (October 2004), p. 40.
87 Interviews conducted by Eirin Mobekk in Kinshasa, DRC, June 2005.
88 Ibid.
89 Borello, *A First Few Steps*, p. 43.
90 For further reading and facts on the TRC, see USIP, *Truth Commissions Digital Collection*; Hayner, *Unspeakable Truths*, pp. 40–5; and <http://www.truthcommission.org>.
91 Hayner, *Unspeakable Truths*, p. 41.
92 For more regarding amnesties, see chapter 5.
93 Tepperman, 'Truth and Consequences', p. 4.
94 Ibid.
95 Ibid., p. 9.
96 'Tutu Urges Apartheid Prosecutions', BBC News (16 December 2005).
97 USIP Digital Collection, 'From Madness to Hope: The 12-year War in El Salvador'; available at <http://www.usip.org/library/tc/doc/reports/el_salvador/tc_es_03151993_mandate.html>.

98 Hayner, *Unspeakable Truths*, p. 39.
99 Ibid.
100 Ibid., p. 118.
101 USIP Digital Collection, 'From Madness to Hope', Recommendations V.

## 7   Traditional Informal Justice Mechanisms

1 For example, the UN Secretary-General mentioned traditional mechanisms in the Secretary-General's *Report on Rule of Law and Transitional Justice in Conflict and Post-Conflict Societies*, S/2004/616 (23 August 2004).
2 Ibid, p. 12.
3 See box 7.1.
4 Rwanda's *gacaca* courts have frequently been cited as an example of a traditional mechanism, although in reality they are a hybrid of domestic formal and informal justice. See box 7.2.
5 This was also emphasized in interviews by Eirin Mobekk with UN staff, conducted in New York and DRC, May and June 2005.
6 Interviews by Eirin Mobekk with UN staff in New York, May 2005.
7 Dfid Briefing, 'Non-State Justice and Security Systems', Policy Division (May 2004), p. 1.
8 UNDP, *Access to Justice*, Practice Note (9 March 2003), p. 9. Yet importantly, 80 per cent of development assistance goes to formal systems.
9 See, e.g., International Crisis Group, *Peacebuilding in Afghanistan*, Asia Report 64 (29 September 2003).
10 See, e.g., Julio Faundez, 'Non-State Justice Systems in Latin America, Case Studies: Peru and Columbia', Working Paper (January 2003), III A2C.
11 Dfid Briefing, 'Non-State Justice and Security Systems', p. 1.
12 For a discussion on definitions regarding customs, see, e.g., Leon Sheleff, *The Future of Tradition. Customary Law, Common Law and Legal Pluralism* (London: Frank Cass, 2000), p. 12.
13 For further discussion regarding tradition, see, e.g., Patrick Glenn, *Legal Traditions of the World. Sustainable Diversity in Law* (Oxford: Oxford University Press, 2004).
14 Max Gluckmann (ed.), *Ideas and Procedures in African Customary Law*, Studies Presented at the 8th International African Seminar at the Haile Sellassie I University, Addis Ababa, January 1966 (Oxford: Oxford University Press, 1969), p. 9.
15 Interview by Eirin Mobekk with UN staff in Timor-Leste, April 2001.
16 USIP, *Afghanistan – Special Report*, no. 117 (March 2004).
17 For more discussion on problems of definitional clarity, see Faundez, 'Non-State Justice Systems'.
18 See Stephen Golub, 'Non-State Justice Systems in Bangladesh and the Philippines', Working Paper (January 2003); Celestine Nyamu-Musembi, 'Review of Experience in Engaging with Non-State Justice Systems in East Africa', Working Paper (January 2003).

19 Marianne Nielsen, 'Criminal Justice and Native Self-Government in Canada: Is the Incorporation of Traditional Justice Practices Feasible?', *Law and Anthropology, Internationales Jahrbuch fur Rechtsanthropolgie* 6 (1991): 8–9.
20 Ibid., p. 9.
21 See, e.g., Alcinda Honwana, 'Sealing the Past, Facing the Future: Trauma Healing in Rural Mozambique', *Conciliation Resources* (1998), available at <http://www.c-r.org/our-work/accord/mozambique/past-future.php>; J. Chissano, 'Healing Wounds of Past Conflicts: Mozambique Opts for a culture of Peace', *UN Chronicle* (Winter 1998).
22 Sheleff, *The Future of Tradition*, p. 4.
23 *African Conference on Local Courts and Customary Law*, Record of the Proceedings of the Conference held in Dar es Salaam, Tanganyika (September 1963), p. 11.
24 See chapter 5.
25 Marco Toscano-Rivalta, Drury Allen, UNAMA, Rule of Law Unit, *Securing Afghanistan's Future, Considerations on Criteria and Actions for Strengthening the Justice System, Proposals for a Long-Term Strategic Framework*, 4.2.10 Traditional Systems (February 2004).
26 *African Conference on Local Courts and Customary Law*, p. 11.
27 Ibid., pp. 16–17.
28 Ibid., p. 17.
29 L. P. Vorster, 'Indigenous Knowledge and Customary Law in South Africa', *South African Journal of Ethnology* 24/2 (2001): 52–3.
30 Lee Van Cott, in Dfid Briefing, 'Non-State Justice and Security Systems', p. 5.
31 Jean G. Zorn, 'Making Law in Papua New Guinea: The Influence of Customary Law on Common Law', *Pacific Studies* 14/4 (December 1991): 5.
32 Faundez, 'Non-State Justice Systems', III A1.
33 Gluckmann (ed.), *Ideas and Procedures*, p. 32.
34 Dfid Briefing, 'Non-State Justice and Security Systems', p. 14.
35 See, e.g., Glenn, *Legal Traditions*; Gluckmann (ed.), *Ideas and Procedures*; Leon Sheleff, *The Future of Tradition*; Zorn, 'Making Law in Papua New Guinea'; Vorster, 'Indigenous Knowledge'.
36 See, e.g., UNDP, *Access to Justice*; Dfid Briefing, 'Non-State Justice and Security Systems'; Faundez, 'Non-State Justice Systems'; Golub, 'Non-State Justice Systems'; Nyamu-Musembi, 'Review of Experience'.
37 For example, the UN Secretary-General mentioned traditional mechanisms in the Introductory Statement at the Security Council meeting on the Rule of Law and Transitional Justice in Conflict and Post-Conflict Societies, 6 October 2004. In practice, in, for example, Timor-Leste, the international civilian police were encouraged to support it.
38 Dfid Briefing, 'Non-State Justice and Security Systems', p. 3.

39 Nyamu-Musembi, 'Review of Experience', p. 18.
40 Sumaiya Khair et al., in Golub, 'Non-State Justice Systems', II A.
41 Ibid.
42 See, e.g., Nyamu-Musembi, 'Review of Experience', p. 22.
43 Luc Huyse, 'Justice', in David Bloomfield et al. (eds), *Reconciliation After Violent Conflict. A Handbook* (Stockholm: International IDEA, 2003), p. 113.
44 Sheleff, *The Future of Tradition*, p. 18.
45 Honour killings are particularly rife in Arabic countries.
46 Interview by Eirin Mobekk with the police officer in Timor-Leste who found the man, 2001.
47 Penal Reform International, *Access to Justice in Sub-Saharan Africa: The Role of Traditional and Informal Justice Systems* (November 2000), p. 3.
48 Khair et al., in Golub, 'Non-State Justice Systems', II A.
49 Mona Elthaway and Adam Jones, 'Rooted in Tradition: Community-Based Violence against Women', in Marie Vlachova and Lea Biason (eds), *Women in an Insecure World. Violence against Women: Facts, Figures, Analysis* (Geneva: DCAF, 2005), pp. 27–30.
50 Wilfried Scharf, 'Non-State Justice Systems in Southern Africa: How Should Governments Respond?', Working Paper (January 2003), pp. 17–18.
51 Faundez, 'Non-State Justice Systems', III A2e.
52 Interviews by Eirin Mobekk with Congolese in DRC, May/June 2005.
53 Interview by Eirin Mobekk with NGO representative in DRC, May/June 2005.
54 See, e.g., Dfid Briefing, 'Non-State Justice and Security Systems', p. 6.
55 See also ibid. Interviews by Eirin Mobekk with members of the formal judicial system in DRC, May/June 2005.
56 Interviews by Eirin Mobekk with lawyers in DRC, May 2005.
57 Ibid.
58 *African Conference on Local Courts and Customary Law*, p. 20.
59 Golub, 'Non-State Justice Systems', III B.
60 Ibid.
61 Rosalind Shaw, *Forgive and Forget: Rethinking Memory in Sierra Leone's Truth and Reconciliation Commission*, Fellow Project Report, USIP (April 2004).
62 Emily Wax, 'In Exploring a Solution for Darfur, Sudan Opts for Local Justice', *Washington Post* Foreign Service (2 April 2005), p. A16.
63 Ibid.
64 See chapter 6.
65 See chapter 5.
66 For more on Mozambique and the use of traditional methods, see, e.g., Honwana, 'Sealing the Past'; Chissano, 'Healing Wounds of Past Conflicts'; C. Thompson, 'Beyond Civil Society: Child Soldiers as Citizens in Mozambique', *Review of African Political Economy* 26/80 (June 1999).

67 Interview by Eirin Mobekk with UN representative who had been working in Mozambique, November 2004.
68 Interviews by Eirin Mobekk with Timorese civil society and international civilian police in Timor-Leste, 2001.
69 Thompson, 'Beyond Civil Society', p. 192.
70 Golub, 'Non-State Justice Systems', III B.
71 For more on Timor-Leste and justice, see, e.g., 'A Review of Peace Operations. A Case for Change', King's College London (March 2003), pp. 265–72; Tanja Hohe and Rod Nixon, *Reconciling Justice: Traditional Law and State Judiciary in East Timor*, USIP (January 2003).
72 Interviews by Eirin Mobekk with UN CIVPOL officers in Dili and districts, Timor-Leste, 2001.
73 *Crime Reports*, UNTAET.
74 Interviews by Eirin Mobekk with civil society and UNPOL officers in Timor-Leste, 2001.
75 The CIVPOL officers in one particular rape case did not view it as endorsing the process, but emphasized that the community wanted it solved in this way and therefore they complied.
76 There are numerous problems with the *gacaca* courts; for futher discussion, see, e.g., Radha Webley, *Gacaca Courts in Post-Genocide Rwanda*, Report for UC Berkeley War Crimes Studies Center, 2003; P. Uvin, *The Introduction of a Modernized Gacaca for Judging Suspects of Participation in the Genocide and the Massacres of 1994 in Rwanda*, discussion paper prepared for the Belgian Secretary of State for Development Cooperation, 2000.
77 See box 5.1.
78 Webley, *Gacaca Courts*. Note that estimates on the number of courts, judges and alleged perpetrators vary according to different sources.
79 IRIN, 'Gacaca Courts Get under Way', 21 June 2002.
80 Ibid.
81 Webley, *Gacaca Courts*, p. 3.

### Conclusion

1 Report of the Secretary-General, *The Rule of Law and Transitional Justice in Conflict and Post-conflict Societies*, S/2004/616, United Nations Security Council (23 August 2004).

# Selected Bibliography

Afghanistan Independent Human Rights Commission. *A Call for Justice: A National Consultation on Past Human Rights Violations in Afghanistan*, 2005.

African Conference on Local Courts and Customary Law. Record of the Proceedings of the Conference held in Dar es Salaam, Tanganyika, September 1963.

Akhavan, P. 'Beyond Impunity: Can International Criminal Justice Prevent Future Atrocities?', *American Journal of International Law* 95 (July 2001): 7–31.

Akhavan, P. 'The International Criminal Tribunal for Rwanda: The Politics and Pragmatics of Punishment', *American Journal of International Law* 90 (1996): 501–9.

Akhavan, P. 'Punishing War Crimes in the Former Yugoslavia: A Critical Juncture for the New World Order', *Human Rights Quarterly* 15 (1993): 262–89.

Aldrich, G. H. 'Jurisdiction of the International Criminal Tribunal for the Former Yugoslavia', *American Journal of International Law* 90 (1996): 64–8

Alexander, Jane. *A Scoping Study of Transitional Justice and Poverty Reduction* (London: Department for International Development, January 2003).

Allen, Tim. *War and Justice in Northern Uganda: An Assessment of the International Criminal Court's Intervention*, February 2005 (Draft).

Alvarez, Jose. 'Crimes of States/Crimes of Hate: Lessons from Rwanda', *Yale Journal of International Law* 24 (1999): 365–83.

Amnesty International. Algeria: President Calls Referendum to Obliterate Crimes of the Past, AI Index Mde 28/010/2005 (28 August 2005).

Amnesty International. *East Timor Police* (2003).

Amnesty International. *Haiti: Still Crying Out for Justice* (July 1998).

Amnesty International. *Indonesia and Timor-Leste: International Responsibility for Justice* (2003).

Amnesty International. 'Kingdom of Cambodia: Amnesty International's Position and Concerns Regarding the Proposed "Khmer Rouge" Tribunal', AI Index: ASA 23/005/2003 (25 April 2003); available at <http://web.amnesty.org/library/index/engasa230052003> [13/01/06].

Anonymous. 'Human Rights in Peace Negotiations', *Human Rights Quarterly* 18 (1996): 249–58.

Avruch, K. and B. Vejarano. 'Truth and Reconciliation Commissions: A Review Essay and Annotated Bibliography', *Online Journal of Peace and Conflict Resolution* 4/2 (Spring 2002).

Bacic, R. 'Truth Commissions: One Option When Dealing with the Recent Past in Countries that have Endured War or Dictatorships', Committee for Conflict Transformation Support, Newsletter 18; available at <http://www.c-r.org/ccts/ccts 18/trucomm.htm>.

Bailey, Sydney D. *The UN Security Council and Human Rights* (London: St Martin's Press, 1994).

Ball, P. and A. R. Chapman, *The Truth of Truth Commissions: Comparative Lessons from Haiti, South Africa, and Guatemala*. The Urban Morgan Institute (Baltimore: Johns Hopkins University Press, 2001).

Barria, Lilian A. and Steven D. Roper, 'How Effective are International Criminal Tribunals? An Analysis of the ICTY and the ICTR', *The International Journal of Human Rights* 9/3 (2005): 364.

Barsalou, Judy. *Trauma and Transitional Justice in Divided Societies*. United States Institute of Peace Special Report 135 (April 2005).

Bass, G. J. *Stay the Hand of Vengeance: The Politics of War Crimes Tribunals* (Princeton: Princeton University Press, 2000).

Bassiouni, M. Cherif. *A Draft International Criminal Code and Draft Statute for an International Criminal Tribunal* (London: Martinus Nijhoff Publishers, 1987), p. 2.

Bassiouni, M. Cherif. 'Former Yugoslavia: Investigating Violations of IHL and Establishing an ICT', in *Security Dialogue* 25/4 (December 1994).

Bassiouni, M. Cherif and P. Manikas. *The Law of the International Criminal Tribunal for the Former Yugoslavia* (New York: Transnational Publishers, 1996).

Beigbeder, Y. *Judging War Criminals: The Politics of International Justice* (London: Macmillan, 1999).

Bekou, Olympia and Robert Cryer (eds). *The International Criminal Court* (Plymouth: Ashgate, 2004).

Best, G. *War and Law Since 1945* (Oxford: Clarendon Press, 1994).

Bloomfield, David, Teresa Barnes and Luc Huyse (eds). *Reconciliation After Violent Conflict. A Handbook* (Stockholm: International IDEA, 2003).

Bloxham, Donald. *Genocide on Trial: War Crimes Trials and the Formation of Holocaust History and Memory* (Oxford: Oxford University Press, 2001).

Bolton, John. 'The Risks and the Weaknesses of the International Criminal Court from America's Perspective', *Virginia Journal of International Law* 41 (2000–1): 186–203.

Boraine, Alex. *A Country Unmasked: Inside South Africa's Truth and Reconciliation Commission* (Oxford: Oxford University Press, 2000).

Boraine, Alex, Janet Levy and Ronel Scheffer (eds). *Dealing with the Past: Truth and Reconciliation in South Africa* (Cape Town: IDASA, 1994).

Borello, Fredrico. *A First Few Steps. The Long Road To a Just Peace in DRC.* Occasional Paper, ICTJ.

Broomhall, Bruce. *International Justice and the International Criminal Court: Between Sovereignty and the Rule of Law* (Oxford: Oxford University Press, 2003).

Bryden, Alan and Heiner Hanggi (eds). *Security Governance in Post-Conflict Peacebuilding* (Geneva: DCAF, 2005).

Calvocoressi, P. *Nuremberg: The Facts, the Law and the Consequences* (London: Chatto & Windus, 1947).

Carothers, Thomas. *The Rule of Law Revival, Promoting Rule of Law Abroad: In Search of Knowledge* (Washington DC: Carnegie Endowment for International Peace, 2006).

Cassese, A. *International Criminal Law* (Oxford: Oxford University Press, 2003).

Cassese, A. 'Reflections on International Criminal Justice', *The Modern Law Review* 61/1 (January 1998): 1–10.

Cassese, A. *The Rome Statute of the International Criminal Court: A Commentary* (Oxford: Oxford University Press, 2002).

Chesterman, Simon. *Civilians in War* (London: Lynne Rienner, 2001).

Chesterman, Simon. *Justice Under International Administration: Kosovo, East Timor and Afghanistan* (New York: International Peace Academy, 2002).

Chissano, J. 'Healing Wounds of Past Conflicts: Mozambique Opts for a Culture of Peace', *UN Chronicle* (Winter 1998).

Chopra, Jarat. 'Building State Failure in East Timor', *Development & Change* 33/5 (2002).

Chuter, David. *War Crimes: Confronting Atrocity in the Modern World* (London: Lynne Rienner, 2003).

Cisse, C. 'The International Tribunals for the Former Yugoslavia and Rwanda: Some Elements of Comparison', *Transnational Law and Contemporary Problems* 7 (1997): 103–18.

Clark, R. and M. Sann. *The Prosecution of International Crimes: A Critical Study of the International Tribunal for the Former Yugoslavia* (New Brunswick: Transaction Publishers, 1996).

Coalition Congolaise pour la Justice Transitionnelle. *Rapport Final du Seminaire sur les Chambres Specialisées Mixtes au sein des Juridictions Congolaises*, Centre Catholique Nganda, Kinshasa (Juin 2005).

Coates, A. J. *The Ethics of War* (Manchester: Manchester University Press, 1997).

Cockayne, James. 'The Fraying Shoestring: Rethinking Hybrid War Crimes Tribunals', *Fordham International Law Journal* 28 (2005).

Cohen, Stanley. *States of Denial: Knowing About Atrocities and Suffering* (Cambridge: Polity, 2001).

Colson, Aurelien. 'The Logic of Peace and the Logic of Justice', *International Relations* 15/1 (April 2000): 51–62.

Conflict Security and Development Group. *A Review of Peace Operations: A Case for Change* (2003).

Corey, A. and S. F. Joireman. 'Retributive Justice: The *Gacaca* Courts in Rwanda', *African Affairs* 103/410 (2004): 73–89.

Crane, David. 'Dancing with the Devil. Prosecuting War. West Africa's Warlords: Current Lessons Learnt and Challenges'. Georgetown University Law Center lecture (2004).

Crawford, James. 'The ILC's Draft Statue for an International Criminal Court', *American Journal of International Law* 88 (1994): 141.

D'Amato, A. 'Peace vs. Accountability in Bosnia', *American Journal of International Law* 88 (1994).

De Bertodano, Sylvia. 'Problems Arising from the Mixed Composition and Structure of the Cambodian Extraordinary Chambers', *Journal of International Criminal Justice* 4 (2006): 285–93.

Dfid Briefing. 'Non-State Justice and Security Systems', Policy Division (May 2004).

Dinstein, Y. and M. Tabory (eds). *War Crimes in International Law* (Boston: Martinus Nijhoff, 1996).

Djerbal, Daho. 'Algeria: Amnesty and Oligarchy', Carnegie Endowment for International Peace (30 September 2005).

Dougherty, Beth K. 'Right-Sizing International Criminal Justice: The Hybrid Experiment at the Special Court for Sierra Leone', *International Affairs* 80/2 (2004): 311–28.

Douma, Pyt and Jeroen de Zeeuw. 'From Transitional to Sustainable Justice. Human Rights Assistance to Sierra Leone', *CRU Policy Brief* (The Hague: Clingendael, 2004).

Drumbl, Mark A. 'Punishment, Postgenocide: From Guilt to Shame to "Civis" in Rwanda', *New York University Law Review* 75/5 (November 2000): 1221–326.

Fanthorpe, R. 'Neither Citizen Nor Subject? Lumpen Agency and the Legacy of Native Administration in Sierra Leone', *African Affairs* 100 (2001): 362–86.

Farer, T. J. 'Restraining the Barbarians: Can International Criminal Law Help?', *Human Rights Quarterly* 22/1 (2000): 90–117.

Faundez, Julio. 'Non-State Justice Systems in Latin America, Case Studies: Peru and Columbia', Dfid Working Paper (January 2003).

Fenrick, W. J. 'The Application of the Geneva Conventions by the International Criminal Tribunal for the Former Yugoslavia', *International Review of the Red Cross* 81 (1999): 317–29.

Fitz-Gerald, Ann (ed.). *From Conflict to Community: A Combatant's Return to Citizenship*, GFN-SSR (2005).

Fletcher, Laurel E. and Harvey Weinstein. 'Violence and Social Repair: Rethinking the Contribution of Justice to Reconciliation', *Human Rights Quarterly* 24/3 (2002): 573–639.

Foreign Report – Janes.com. 'Algeria: Amnesty or Amnesia?' (26 October 2005).

Forsythe, David P. *Human Rights in International Relations* (Cambridge: Cambridge University Press, 2000).

Fox, Hazel. 'An International Tribunal for War Crimes: Will the UN Succeed Where the Nuremberg Failed?', *The World Today* 49/10 (October 1993): 194–7.

Freeman, Mark and Veerle Opgenhaffen. *Transitional Justice in Morocco: A Progress Report*, ICTJ (November 2005).

Fritz, Nicole and Alison Smith. 'Current Apathy for Coming Anarchy: Building the Special Court for Sierra Leone', *Fordham International Law Journal* 25/2 (2001): 391.

Frulli, M. 'The Special Court for Sierra Leone: Some Preliminary Comments', *European Journal of International Law* 11/4 (2000): 857–69.

Gaeta, Paola. 'Is NATO Authorized or Obliged to Arrest Persons Indicted by the International Criminal Tribunal for the Former Yugoslavia', *European Journal of International Law* 9 (1998): 174–81.

Gairdner, D. *Truth in Transition: The Role of Truth Commissions in Political Transition in Chile and El Salvador* (Bergen: Chr. Michelsen Institute, 1999).

Gberie, Lansana. 'Briefing: The Special Court of Sierra Leone', *African Affairs* 102/409 (2003): 637–48.

Gibson, J. L. 'Truth, Justice, and Reconciliation: Judging the Fairness of Amnesty in South Africa', *American Journal of Political Science* 46/3 (2002).

Ginsburgs, G. and V. N. Kudriavstev (eds). *The Nuremberg Trial and International Law* (London: Martinus Nijhoff, 1990).

Glasius, Marlies. *The International Criminal Court: A Global Civil Society Achievement* (London: Routledge, 2006).

Glenn, Patrick. *Legal Traditions of the World. Sustainable Diversity in Law* (Oxford: Oxford University Press, 2004).

Gluckmann, Max (ed.). *Ideas and Procedures in African Customary Law*, Studies Presented at the 8th International African Seminar at the Haile Sellassie I University Addis Ababa, January 1966 (Oxford: Oxford University Press, 1969).

Goldstein, Eric. 'A New Moroccan Commission, But How Much Truth?', Human Rights Watch (June 2003).

Goldstone, R. *For Humanity: Reflections of a War Crimes Investigator* (New Haven: Yale University Press, 2000).

Golub, Stephen. 'Non-State Justice Systems in Bangladesh and the Philippines', Dfid Working Paper (January 2003).

Gow, James. 'Law, War and Kosovo: Further Loosening the Bands of Wickedness', *Human Rights Review* 1/2 (January–March 2000): 94–102.

Gow, James. 'A Revolution in International Affairs: Governance, Justice and War', *International Relations* 15/1 (2000): 1–10.

Gow, James. *The Serbian Project and Its Adversaries: A Strategy of War Crimes* (London: Hurst & Co., 2003).

Greenwood, Christopher. 'International Humanitarian Law and the Tadic Case', *European Journal of International Law* 7 (1996): 265–83.

Gutman, R. and D. Rieff. *Crimes of War: What the Public Should Know* (London: W. W. Norton & Co., 1999).

Hamber, Brandon. 'Past Imperfect: Dealing With the Past in Northern Ireland and Societies in Transition', paper presented at 'Moving Towards Pluralism', 4th International Conference of the Ethnic Studies Network, 8–11 June 1999, Institute of Ethnology and Anthropology, Russian Academy of Science, Leninsky Prospeckt, Moscow. See <http://www.brandonhamber.com>.

Hampson, Francine. *Violations of Fundamental Human Rights in the Former Yugoslavia*. Part Two: *The Case for a War Crimes Tribunal* (London: David Davies Memorial Institute Occasional Paper, 1993).

Harmon, Mark B. and Fergal Gaynor. 'Prosecuting Massive Crimes with Primitive Tools: Three Difficulties Encountered by Prosecutors in International Criminal Proceedings', *Journal of International Criminal Justice* 2 (2004): 403–26.

Harris, Marshall, Bruce Hitchner and Paul Williams. *Bringing War Criminals to Justice*, Centre for International Programs, University of Dayton 1997.

Hartmann, Michael. 'International Judges and Prosecutors in Kosovo: A New Model for Post-Conflict Peacekeeping', United States Institute of Peace Special Report 112 (October 2003).

Hawthorn, Geoffrey. 'Pinochet: The Politics', *International Affairs* 75/2 (1999): 253–8.

Hayner, Priscilla. 'Commissioning the Truth: Further Research Questions', *Third World Quarterly* 17/1 (1996).

Hayner, Priscilla. 'Fifteen Truth Commissions – 1974 to 1994: A Comparative Study', *Human Rights Quarterly* 16 (1994).

Hayner, Priscilla. 'International guidelines for the Creation and Operation of Truth Commissions: A Preliminary Proposal', *Law and Contemporary Problems* 59/173 (Autumn 1996).

Hayner, Priscilla. 'Justice in Transition: Challenges and Opportunities', Presentation to 55th Annual DPI/NGO Conference, 'Rebuilding Societies Emerging from Conflict: A Shared Responsibility', United Nations (9 September 2002).

Hayner, Priscilla. 'Truth Commissions: Exhuming the Past', *North American Congress on Latin America* 32/2 (Sept. Oct. 1998).

Hayner, Priscilla. *Unspeakable Truths. Facing the Challenges of Truth Commissions* (London: Routledge, 2002).

Hesse, Carla and Robert Post (eds). *Human Rights in Political Transitions: Gettysburg to Bosnia* (Boston: MIT Press, 2000).

Hohe, Tanja. 'Justice without Judiciary in East Timor', *Conflict, Security and Development* 3/3 (2003): 335.

Hohe, Tanja and Rod Nixon. 'Traditional Law and State Judiciary in East Timor', Working Paper (January 2003).

Honig, J. W. and N. Both. *Srebrenica: Record of a War Crime* (London: Penguin, 1996).

Howard, M., G. J. Andreopoulos and M. R. Shulman (eds). *The Laws of War: Constraints on Warfare in the Western World* (New Haven: Yale University Press, 1994).

Human Rights First. 'Prosecuting Genocide in Rwanda: A Human Rights First Report on the ICTRY and National Trials' (July 1997).

Human Rights Watch. *Accessibility and Legacy* (September 2004).

Human Rights Watch. 'Algeria: Amnesty Law Risks Legalizing Impunity for Crimes Against Humanity' (14 April 2005).

Human Rights Watch. *Bringing Justice: The Special Court for Sierra Leone* (New York: Human Rights Watch, 2004).

Human Rights Watch. 'Genocide, War Crimes and Crimes Against Humanity: Topical Digests of the Case Law of the International Criminal Tribunal for Rwanda and the International Criminal Tribunal for the Former Yugoslavia' (February 2004); available at <http://hrw.org/reports/2004/ij/>.

Human Rights Watch. 'Justice Denied for East Timor' (2002).

Human Rights Watch. 'Serious Flaws: Why the U.N. General Assembly Should Require Changes to the Draft Khmer Rouge Tribunal Agreement', Human Rights Watch Briefing Paper (April 2003); available at <http://hrw.org/backgrounder/asia/cambodia040303-bck.htm> [13/01/06].

Huntington, Samuel P. *The Third Wave: Democratization in the Late Twentieth Century* (Norman: University of Oklahoma Press, 1991).

Hurwitz, Agnes and Kaysie Studdard. 'Rule of Law Programs in Peace Operations', International Peace Academy, Policy Paper (August 2005).

Huyse, Luc. 'Justice after Transition: On the Choices Successor Elites Make in Dealing with the Past', *Law and Social Inquiry* 20/1 (Winter 1995).

Ignatieff, M. *The Warrior's Honour: Ethnic War and the Modern Conscience* (London: Chatto & Windus, 1998).

Ingadottir, Thordis. 'Financial Challenges and their Possible Effects on Proceedings', *Journal of International Criminal Justice* 4 (2006): 296.

International Center for Transitional Justice. 'Algerian Charter risks reinforcing impunity and undermining reconciliation' (26 September 2005).

International Center for Transitional Justice. 'Creation and the First Trials of the Supreme Iraqi Criminal Tribunal', Briefing Paper (October 2005).

International Center for Transitional Justice. 'Iraqi Voices Attitudes towards Transitional Justice and Social Reconstruction', Occasional Paper Series (May 2004).

International Center for Transitional Justice. 'The Special Court for Sierra Leone: The First 18 Months' (March 2004).

International Crisis Group. 'Peacebuilding in Afghanistan', Asia Report 64 (29 September 2003).

International Crisis Group. 'The Special Court for Sierra Leone: Promises and Pitfalls of a "New Model"', Africa Briefing. Freetown/Brussels: International Crisis Group (2003).

International Crisis Group. 'War Criminals in Bosnia's Republika Srpska: Who Are the People in Your Neighbourhood?', ICG Balkans Report 103 (2 November 2003).

Jarvis, Helen. 'Trials and Tribulations: The Latest Twists in the Long Quest for Justice for the Cambodian Genocide', *Critical Asian Studies* (special edition) 34/4 (2002): 607–10.

Jenkins C. 'A Truth Commission for East Timor: Lessons from South Africa?', *Journal of Conflict and Security Law* 7/2 (2002): 233–52.

Jones, Seth, Jeremy Wilson, Andrew Rathmell and Jack Riley. *Establishing Law and Order after Conflict* (RAND, 2005).

Junne, Gerd and Willemijn Verkoren. *Post-Conflict Development* (Boulder: Lynne Rienner, 2005).

Katzenstein, S. 'Hybrid Tribunals: Searching for Justice in East Timor', *Harvard Human Rights Journal* 16 (2003): 245.

Kaye, Mike. 'The Role of Truth Commissions in the Search for Justice, Reconciliation and Democratisation: the Salvadorean and Honduran Cases', *Journal of Latin American Studies* 29/3 (1997): 693–717.

Keegan, M. J. 'The Preparation of Cases for the ICTY', *Transnational Law and Contemporary Problems* 7 (1997): 119–27.

Kerr, Rachel. *The International Criminal Tribunal for the Former Yugoslavia: An Exercise in Law, Politics and Diplomacy* (Oxford University Press, 2004).

Kerr, Rachel. 'International Judicial Intervention: The International Criminal Tribunal for the Former Yugoslavia', *International Relations* 15/2 (August 2000): 17–26.

Kerr, Rachel. 'Operational Justice: The Reality of War Crimes Prosecutions in the International Criminal Tribunal for the Former Yugoslavia', *International Journal of Human Rights* 5/4 (2001): 110–22.

Kerr, Rachel. 'Prosecuting War Crimes: Trials and Tribulations', *International Journal of Human Rights* 10/1 (March 2006): 79–87.

Kerr, Rachel. 'The Road from Dayton to Brussels? The International Criminal Tribunal for the former Yugoslavia and the Politics of War Crimes in Bosnia', *European Security* 14/3 (September 2005): 319–37.

Kiernan, Ben. *The Pol Pot Regime: Race, Power and Genocide Under the Khmer Rouge, 1975–79*, 2nd edn. (New Haven: Yale University Press, 2002).

Kirsch, P. and J. T. Holmes. 'The Birth of the International Criminal Court: The 1998 Rome Conference', *Canadian Yearbook of International Law* 36 (1998): 3–40.

Kissinger, Henry. 'The Pitfalls of Universal Jurisdiction: Risking Judicial Tyranny', *Foreign Affairs* 80 (2001).

Klarin, Mirko. 'The Tribunal's Four Battles', *Journal of International Criminal Justice* 2/2 (2004): 554.

Kritz, Neil. *Transitional Justice: How Emerging Democracies Reckon with Former Regimes*, vols 1–3 (Washington DC: United States Institute of Peace Press, 1995).

Lamin, A. R. 'Building Peace through Accountability in Sierra Leone: The Truth and Reconciliation Commission and the Special Court', *Journal of Asian and African Studies* 38/2–3 (2003): 295–320.

Landsman, Stephan. 'Alternative Responses to Serious Human Rights Abuses: Of Prosecution and Truth Commissions', *Law and Contemporary Problems* 59/4 (Autumn 1996).

Linton, Suzannah. 'Cambodia, East Timor and Sierra Leone: Experiments in International Justice', *Criminal Law Forum* 12 (2001).

Linton, Suzannah. 'New Approaches to International Justice in Cambodia and East Timor', *International Review of the Red Cross* 84/845 (2002): 93–119.

Linton, Suzannah. 'Safeguarding the Independence and Impartiality of the Cambodian Extraordinary Chambers', *Journal of International Criminal Justice* 4 (2006): 329.

Magnarella, Paul J. *Justice in Africa: Rwanda's Genocide, Its Courts, and the UN Criminal Tribunal* (Aldershot: Ashgate, 2000).

Malamud-Goti, Jaime. 'Transitional Governments in the Breach: Why Punish State Criminals?', *Human Rights Quarterly* 12/1 (1990).

Mani, Rama. 'Balancing Peace with Justice in the Aftermath of Violent Conflict', *Development* 48/3 (2005).

Mani, Rama. *Beyond Retribution: Seeking Justice in the Shadows of War* (Cambridge: Polity, 2002).

Maogoto, Jackson Nyamuya. *War Crimes and Realpolitik: International Justice from World War I to the 21st Century* (Boulder, CO: Lynne Rienner, 2004).

McCoubrey, Hilaire. 'The Concept and Treatment of War Crimes', *Journal of Armed Conflict Law* 1 (1996): 121–40.

McDonald, Avril. 'Sierra Leone's shoestring Special Court', *International Review of the Red Cross* 84/845 (2002): 121–43.

McKay, Fiona. 'Universal Jurisdiction in Europe: Criminal Prosecutions in Europe Since 1990 for War Crimes, Crimes against Humanity, Torture and Genocide' (Redress, 1999); available at <http://redress.org/documents/unijeur.html>.

Meernik, James. 'Justice and Peace? How the International Criminal Tribunal Affects Societal Peace in Bosnia', *Journal of Peace Research* 42/3 (2005): 271–89.

Memory of Silence. *Report of the Historical Clarification Commission* (Guatemala, 1999).

Mendez, Juan. 'Accountability for Past Abuses', *Human Rights Quarterly* 19 (1997).

Meron, Theodor. 'Procedural Evolution in the ICTY', *Journal of International Criminal Justice* 2 (2004): 520–5.

Meron, Theodor. *War Crimes Law Comes of Age: Essays* (Oxford: Clarendon Press, 1998).

Minear, R. H. *Victor's Justice: The Tokyo War Crimes Trial* (Princeton: Princeton University Press, 1971).

Minow, Martha. *Between Vengeance and Forgiveness: Facing History after Genocide and Mass Violence* (Boston: Beacon Press, 1998).

Mobekk, Eirin. 'International Involvement in Restructing and Creating Security Forces: The Case of Haiti', *Small Wars and Insurgencies* 12/3 (Autumn 2001).

Mobekk, Eirin. 'The Missing Ingredient: Justice in the International Intervention in Haiti', *International Relations* 15/1 (2000): 30–40.

Morris, Virginia and Michael P. Scharf. *An Insider's Guide to the International Criminal Tribunal for the Former Yugoslavia*, vols I and II (New York: Transnational Publishers, 1995).

Mose, Erik. 'Main Achievements of the ICTR', *Journal of International Criminal Justice* 3/4 (2005).

Mosier, R. 'Impunity, Truth Commissions: Peddling Impunity?', Human Rights Features, Voice of the Asia Pacific Human Rights Network, Special Weekly Edition for the Duration of the 59th Session of the Commission on Human Rights 6/5 (14–20 April 2003).

Murphy, S. D. 'Progress and Jurisprudence of the International Criminal Tribunal for the Former Yugoslavia', *American Journal of International Law* 93/1 (1999): 57–97.

Neier, A. *War Crimes: Brutality, Genocide, Terror, and the Struggle for Justice* (New York: Random House, 1998).

Niarchos, C. N. 'Women, War and Rape: Challenges Facing the International Tribunal for the Former Yugoslavia', *Human Rights Quarterly* 17 (1995): 649–90.

Nielsen, Marianne. 'Criminal Justice and Native Self-Government in Canada: Is the Incorporation of Traditional Justice Practices Feasible?', *Law and Anthropology, Internationales Jahrbuch fur Rechtsanthropolgie* 6 (1991).

Niemann, Grant. 'The Life and Times of a Senior Trial Attorney at the ICTY from 1994 to 2000', *Journal of International Criminal Justice* 2 (2004): 435–45.

Nsanzuwera, François-Xavier. 'The ICTR Contribution to National Reconciliation', *Journal of International Criminal Justice* 3/4 (2005).

Nyamu-Musembi, Celestine. 'Review of Experience in Engaging with Non-State Justice Systems in East Africa', Dfid Working Paper (January 2003).

O'Brien, Kevin. 'Truth and Reconciliation in South Africa: Confronting the Past, Building the Future?' *International Relations* 15/2 (August 2000).

Odendaal, A. 'For All Its Flaws. The TRC as a Peacebuilding Tool', *CCR* 6/3–4 (December 1997).

Off, C. *The Lion, the Fox and the Eagle: A Story of Generals and Justice in Yugoslavia and Rwanda* (Toronto: Random House, 2000).

Olonisakin, Funmi. 'Peace and Justice in Africa: Post-Cold War Issues', *International Relations* 15/1 (2000): 41–50.

O'Neill, William G. *Kosovo: An Unfinished Peace* (Boulder, CO: Lynne Rienner, 2002).

Orentlicher, Diane. 'Independent Study on Best Practices, Including Recommendations, to Assist States in Strengthening their Domestic Capacity to Combat all Aspects of Impunity', E/CN.4/2004/88 (27 February 2004).

Orentlicher, Diane. 'Settling Accounts: The Duty to Prosecute Human Rights Violations of a Prior Regime', *Yale Law Journal* 100 (1991): 2537–615.

Osiel, Mark. *Mass Atrocity, Collective Memory and the Law* (New Brunswick: Transaction Publishers, 1997).

Osiel, Mark. 'Why Prosecute? Critics of Punishment for Mass Atrocity', *Human Rights Quarterly* 22 (2000): 125.

Paskins, Barrie and James Gow. 'The Creation of the International Tribunals from the Perspectives of Pragmatism, Realism and Liberalism', *International Relations* 15/3 (December 2000).

Penal Reform International. *Access to Justice in Sub-Saharan Africa: The Role of Traditional and Informal Justice System* (November 2000).

Periello, Tom and Marieke Wierda. *The Special Court for Sierra Leone Under Scrutiny*, International Center for Transitional Justice (March 2006).

Peskin, Victor. 'Courting Rwanda: The Promises and Pitfalls of the ICTR Outreach Programme', *Journal of International Criminal Justice* 3/4 (2005): 950–61.

Peskin, Victor and Mieczyslaw P. Boduszynski. 'International Justice and Domestic Politics: Post-Tudjman Croatia and the International Criminal Tribunal for the Former Yugoslavia', *Europe–Asia Studies* 55/7 (2003): 1117–42.

Pictet, Jean. *Development and Principles of International Humanitarian Law* (Dordrecht: Martinus Nijhoff Publishers, 1985).

Pigou, Piers. *Crying without Tears: In Pursuit of Justice and Reconciliation in Timor-Leste – Community Perspectives and Expectations*, ICTJ (August 2003).

Pion-Berlin, D. 'To Prosecute or to Pardon? Human Rights Decisions in the Latin American Southern Cone', *Human Rights Quarterly* 15 (1994).

Popkin, M. and N. Bhuta. 'Latin American Amnesties in Comparative Perspective: Can the Past Be Buried', *Ethics & International Affairs* 13 (1999).

Popovski, Vesselin. 'The International Criminal Court: A Synthesis of Retributive and Restorative Justice', *International Relations* 15/3 (December 2000).

PRIDE. 'Ex-Combatatant Views of the Truth and Reconciliation Commission and the Special Court in Sierra Leone', a study by the Post-conflict Reintegration Initiative for Development and Empowerment (PRIDE) in partnership with the International Center for Transitional Justice, Freetown (12 September 2002).

Quinn, Joanna. 'Dealing with a Legacy of Mass Atrocity: Truth Commissions in Uganda and Chile', *Netherlands Quarterly of Human Rights* 19/4 (2001).

Ralph, Jason. *America and the International Criminal Court: An International Society Perspective* (Cambridge: Cambridge University Press, 2006).

Ratner, Steven R. and Jason S. Abrams. *Accountability for Human Rights Atrocities in International Law: Beyond the Nuremberg Legacy* (Oxford: Oxford University Press, 2001).

Reydams, Luc. 'The ICTR Ten Years On: Back to the Nuremberg Paradigm', *Journal of International Criminal Justice* 3/4 (2005): 977–88.

Reydams, Luc. *Universal Jurisdiction: International and Muncipal Legal Perspectives*, Oxford Monographs in International Law (Oxford: Oxford University Press, 2003).

Roberts, A. and R. Guelff. *Documents on the Laws of War*, 3rd edn. (Oxford: Clarendon Press, 2003).

Roberts, Adam and Benedict Kingsbury (eds). *United Nations, Divided World: The UN's Roles in International Relations* (Oxford: Clarendon Press, 1993).

Robertson, G. *Crimes against Humanity: The Struggle for Global Justice* (London: Penguin, 1999).

Rodley, Nigel (ed.). *To Loose the Bands of Wickedness* (London: Brassey's, 1992).

Rogers, A. P. V. *Law on the Battlefield*, 2nd edn. (Manchester: Manchester University Press, 2004).

Roht Arriaza, N. 'The Developing Jurisprudence on Amnesty', *Human Rights Quarterly* 20 (1998): 843–85.

Roling, B. V. A. and Antonio Cassese. *The Tokyo Trial and Beyond: Reflections of a Peacemonger* (Cambridge: Polity, 1993).

Romano, Cesare P., Andrew Nollkaemper and Jann K. Kleffner. *Internationalized Criminal Courts: Sierra Leone, East Timor, Kosovo and Cambodia* (Oxford: Oxford University Press, 2004).

Rotberg, R. and D. Thompson (eds). *Truth v. Justice: The Morality of Truth Commissions* (Princeton: Princeton University Press, 2000).

Roth, Kenneth. 'The Case For Universal Jurisdiction', *Foreign Affairs* (September–October 2001).

Sarakin, Jeremy. 'The Tension Between Justice and Reconciliation in Rwanda: Politics, Human Rights, Due Process and the Role of the *Gacaca* Courts in Dealing with the Genocide', *Journal of African Law* 45/2 (2001).

Schabas, William. 'The Relationship between Truth Commissions and International Courts: The Case of Sierra Leone', *Human Rights Quarterly* 25/4 (2003): 1035–66.

Scharf, Michael P. *Balkan Justice: The Story Behind the First International War Crimes Trial Since Nuremberg* (Durham, NC: North Carolina Academic Press, 1997).

Scharf, Michael P. and William A. Schabas. *Slobodan Milosevic on Trial: A Companion* (New York and London: Continuum, 2002).

Scharf, Michael P. and P. Williams. *Peace with Justice? War Crimes and Accountability in the Former Yugoslavia. New International Relations of Europe* (Lanham, MD: Rowman & Littlefield, 2002).

Scharf, Wilfried. 'Non-State Justice Systems in Southern Africa: How Should Governments Respond?', Dfid Working Paper (January 2003).

Scheffer, David J. 'International Judicial Intervention', *Foreign Policy* (1996): 34–51.

Scheffer, David J. 'The United States and the International Criminal Court', *American Journal of International Law* 93/1 (1999): 12–22.

Schrag, Minna. 'Lessons Learned from ICTY Experience', *Journal of International Criminal Justice* 2 (2004): 427–34.

Shaw, Martin. *War and Genocide* (Cambridge: Polity, 2002).

Shea, D. *The South African Truth Commission: The Politics of Reconciliation* (Washington, DC: United States Institute of Peace Press, 2000).

Sheleff, Leon. *The Future of Tradition. Customary Law, Common Law and Legal Pluralism* (London: Frank Cass, 2000).

Shklar, Judith N. *Legalism: Law, Morals and Political Trials* (Cambridge: Harvard University Press, 1964).

*Si M Pa Rele* ('If I Don't Cry Out'). Report of the Haitian National Truth and Justice Commission (March 1997).

Sieff, M. 'Prosecuting War Crimes in Sierra Leone: War Criminals, Watch Out', *World Today* 57/2 (2001): 18–20.

Sikkink, K. and C. Booth Walling. 'Errors about Trials: The Political Reality of the Justice Cascade and Its Impact', paper presented at the annual meeting of the APSA (2005).

Simpson, Gerry. 'Throwing a Little Remembrance on the Past: The International Court and the Politics of Sovereignty', *University of California, Davis, Journal of International Law and Politics* 5 (1999): 133–46.

Snyder, Jack and Leslie Vinjamuri. 'Trials and Errors: Principle and Pragmatism in Strategies of International Justice', *International Security* 28/3 (Winter 2003/4).

Sriram, Chandra Lekha. *Globalizing Justice for Mass Atrocities: A Revolution in Accountability* (London: Routledge, 2005).

Sriram, Chandra Lekha. *Justice vs Peace in Times of Transition* (London: Frank Cass, 2004).

Sriram, Chandra Lekha. 'Revolutions in Accountability: New Approaches to Past Abuses', *American University International Law Review* 19 (2003): 301–429.

Sriram, Chandra Lekha. 'Truth Commissions and the Quest for Justice: Stability and Accountability after Internal Strife', in A. Adebajo and C. L. Sriram (eds), *Managing Armed Conflicts in the 21st Century* (London: Frank Cass, 2001).

Sriram, Chandra Lekha. 'Wrong-Sizing International Justice? The Hybrid Tribunal in Sierra Leone', *Fordham International Law Journal* 29 (2006).

Staub, Ervin. 'Preventing Violence and Generating Humane Values: Healing and Reconciliation in Rwanda', *International Review of the Red Cross* 85/852 (2003): 791–806.

Stedman, S. 'Spoiler Problems in Peace Processes', *International Security* 22/2 (1997): 5–53.

Stone, Christopher, Joel Miller, Monica Thornton and Jennifer Miller. *Supporting Security, Justice and Development: Lessons for a New Era*, Vera Institute of Justice (June 2005).

Stover, Eric and Harvey M. Weinstein (eds). *My Neighbour, My Enemy: Justice and Community in the Aftermath of Mass Atrocity* (Cambridge: Cambridge University Press, 2004).

Strohmeyer, Hans. 'Building a New Judiciary for East Timor: Challenges of a Fledgling Nation', *Criminal Law Forum* 11/3 (2000): 259–85.

Strohmeyer, Hans. 'Collapse and Reconstruction of a Judicial System: The United Nations Missions in Kosovo and East Timor', *American Journal of International Law* 95 (2001).

Sunga, Lyal. *Individual Responsibility in International Law for Serious Human Rights Violations* (Dordrecht: M. Nijhoff, 1992).

Taylor, Telford. *The Anatomy of the Nuremberg Trials* (London: Bloomsbury, 1993).

Teitel, Ruti G. *Transitional Justice* (Oxford: Oxford University Press, 2002).

Tepperman, J. D. 'Truth and Consequences', *Foreign Affairs* (March/April 2002).

Theissen, Gunnar. *Supporting Justice, Co-existence and Reconciliation after Armed Conflict: Strategies for Dealing with the Past*, Berghof Research Centre; available at <http://www.berghof-handbook.net>.

Thompson, C. 'Beyond Civil Society: Child Soldiers as Citizens in Mozambique', *Review of African Political Economy* 26/80 (June 1999).

Toscano-Rivalta, Marco. Drury Allen, UNAMA, Rule of Law Unit, 'Securing Afghanistan's Future, Considerations on Criteria and Actions for Strengthening the Justice System, Proposals for a Long-Term Strategic Framework' (February 2004).

Tusa, A. and J. Tusa. *The Nuremberg Trial* (London: Macmillan, 1983).

Tutu, Desmond. *No Future Without Forgiveness* (London: Rider, 1999).

UNA-USA, DPKO. 'Program on Peace Building and Rule of Law, Partnership Program on Peace Building and Rule of Law' (2003).

UNDP. 'Access to Justice', Practice Note (9 March 2003).

UNDP. 'Justice and SSR, BPCR's Programmic Approach' (November 2002).

United Nations. 'Set of Principles for the Protection and Promotion of Human Rights Through Action to Combat Impunity', The Administration of Justice and The Human Rights of Detainees, Commission on Human Rights, Sub-Commission on Prevention of Discrimination and Protection of Minorities, E/CH.4/Sub.2/1997/20/Rev.1 (2 October 1997).

United Nations. 'Civil and Political Rights, Including the Questions of: Independence of the Judiciary, Administration of Justice, Impunity', ECOSOC Commission on Human Rights, E/CN.4/2000/62 (18 January 2000).

United Nations. 'Impunity, Office for the High Commissioner of Human Rights', Resolution 2004/72 (21 April 2004).

United Nations. 'In Larger Freedom, Towards Development, Security and Human Rights for All', S/59/2005 (21 March 2005).

United Nations. *Report of the International Commission of Inquiry on Darfur to the United Nations Secretary-General, Pursuant to Security Council Resolution 1564 of 18 September 2004*, Geneva (25 January 2005).

United Nations. *Report of the Secretary-General's High Level Panel on Threat, Challenges and Change. A More Secure World: Our Shared Responsibility*, (2004).

United Nations. *Report of the Secretary-General on The Rule of Law and Transitional Justice in Conflict and Post-conflict Societies*, S/2004/616 (23 August 2004).

United Nations. *Report of the Secretary-General on the United Nations Interim Administration Mission in Kosovo*, S/1999/779 (12 July 1999).

United Nations. *Report of the UN High Commissioner for Human Rights, Situation of Human Rights in Timor-Leste*, E/CN.4/2003/37 (4 March 2003).

United States Institute for Peace. *Afghanistan: Special Report* 117 (March 2004).

United States Institute for Peace. *Rwanda: Accountability for War Crimes and Genocide: Special Report* 13 (January 1995).

United States Institute for Peace. Truth Commissions Digital Collection; available at <http://www.usip.org/library/truth.html>.

Vera Institute of Justice. *Justice Indicators* (April 2005).

Vinjamuri, Leslie and Jack Snyder. 'Trials and Errors: Principle and Pragmatism in Strategies of International Justice', *International Security* 28/3 (Winter 2003/4): 5–44.

Vlachova, M. and L. Biason (eds). *Women in an Insecure World. Violence against Women: Facts, Figures, Analysis* (Geneva: DCAF, 2005).

Vohrah, L. and J. Cina. 'The Outreach Programme', in R. May et al., *Essays on ICTY Procedure and Evidence in Honour of Gabrielle Kirk McDonald* (The Hague: Kluwer, 2001), pp. 547–57.

Vorster, L. P. 'Indigenous Knowledge and Customary Law in South Africa', *South African Journal of Ethnology* 24/2 (2001).

Wain, Meredith. 'Ghana's National Reconciliation Commission', *Peace Magazine* (April–June 2003).

Walzer, M. *Arguing About War* (New Haven: Yale University Press, 2004).

Walzer, M. *Just and Unjust Wars: A Moral Argument with Historical Illustration*, 2nd edn. (London: Basic Books, 1992).

Watkins, Amadeo. 'Croatia at a Crossroads: The EU–ICTY Debate', Conflict Studies Research Centre Occasional Paper 05/15 (March 2005).

Wedgwood, R. 'Fiddling in Rome', *Foreign Affairs* (1998).

Wedgwood, R. 'The ICC: An American View', *European Journal of International Law* 93 (1999).

Weller, M. 'On the Hazards of Foreign Travel for Dictators and Other International Criminals', *International Affairs* 75/3 (1999): 599–617.

Wembou, D. 'The International Criminal Tribunal for Rwanda. Its Role in the African Context', *International review of the Red Cross* 37 (1997): 685–93.

Wheeler, Nicholas J. and Tim Dunne. 'East Timor and the New Humanitarian Interventionism', *International Affairs* 77/4 (2001): 805–27.

White, N. D. *Keeping the Peace: The United Nations and International Peace and Security* (Manchester: Manchester University Press, 1993).

Wilke, Christiane. 'Domestic Prosecutions for Massive Human Rights Violations: Lessons from Argentina and Germany', Memorandum for the International Center for Transitional Justice (18 November 2004).

Zacklin, Ralph. 'The Failings of Ad Hoc International Tribunals', *Journal of International Criminal Justice* 2 (2004): 541–5.

Zehr, H. 'South Africa's Truth and Reconciliation Commission is an Unprecedented Experiment of Breathtaking Stakes', Mennonite Central Committee, News Service (7 March 1997).

Zorn, Jean G. 'Making Law in Papua New Guinea: The Influence of Customary Law on Common Law', *Pacific Studies* 14/4 (December 1991).

# Index